W9-CCO-247

12.99

California
KOSHER

Contemporary and Traditional
Jewish Cuisine

A
collection of recipes
from the
Women's League of
Adat Ari El Synagogue
North Hollywood, California

California Kosher

These recipes were contributed by members and friends of Adat Ari El, a Conservative Jewish Congregation in North Hollywood, California. All the recipes have been triple tested; all are great looking and great tasting, and most are easy to prepare.

All recipes and complete holiday menu suggestions comply with the laws of *kashrut* regarding prohibited foods, restrictions on permitted foods, the preparation of meat, and the separation of meat and milk. Each recipe title carries a "Meat," "Dairy" or "Pareve" (neutral) designation to help the reader plan menus that comply with these laws.

We wish to express our sincere appreciation to all those members, their families and friends who contributed their favorite recipes and the more than 100 testers (see p. 6) who helped us select the best ones. Without their enthusiastic support, this book could not have been accomplished. A special thank you to our spouses for their patience and help.

—The Cookbook Editors, Staff and Committee

Copyright © 1991
Women's League
of
Adat Ari El
North Hollywood, California

ISBN 0-9630953-0-7
Library of Congress Catalog Card Number 91-066106
First Printing – November, 1991
Second Printing – May, 1992
Third Printing – March, 1993

Printed in the USA by
WIMMER BROTHERS
A Wimmer Company
Memphis • Dallas

Introduction

California Kosher reflects a merging of cuisines from everywhere in the world that Jews have lived, combined with the dazzling variety of fresh foods available in California — while still observing the traditional Jewish dietary laws.

Food has always played an important role in Jewish culture, for it is at the center of the Sabbath observance in the home each week and is equally important in celebrating the Jewish holidays.

California is a cook's paradise, with its trend-setting cooking styles and rainbow of cultures and peoples. The state's culinary diversity encourages Californians to break from tradition, to experiment — and the Jewish population is no exception.

Thus, you will find that innovation and tradition are the twin themes of this cookbook. Our collection includes many contemporary, creative recipes — recipes that represent the growing interest in lighter and healthier fare, and California's mild weather and "outdoorsy" lifestyle. Many of these recipes make use of such time savers as microwaves and food processors; many are simple, family fare for those "everyday" meals.

Yet here also are many traditional recipes, because when we celebrate the Jewish holidays, most of us return to the foods that tie us to our Jewish roots. We may alter traditional recipes to suit our modern tastes; we may create traditions of our own; we may follow traditions that vary from culture to culture and from family to family. But the specialness, the separateness that comes from setting aside certain well-loved dishes for the holidays, helps link one year's celebration to the next and one generation to the next.

Additionally, many of our customs concerning food are rooted in the traditional *mitzvot* (commandments) of visiting the homes of the sick or the bereaved with comforting gifts of food, such as chicken soup, a one-pot meal or baked goods. Our recipes will help you give a most appreciated gift.

Here, then, are the Jewish "culinary classics" — recipes so delicious, so permanently woven into our collective culture, that they have been handed down from generation to generation, like the love of food itself. Whether you are beginning your odyssey into the rich heritage of Jewish cooking or have mastered the classics and would like to branch out, we hope this cookbook will serve as inspiration and guide.

3

Who We Are...

Adat Ari El, the oldest Jewish Congregation in California's San Fernando Valley, was founded in 1939 as the Valley Jewish Community Center. A ladies' auxiliary was organized the following year. Over the years, as other Jewish congregations and centers emerged, our congregation changed its name to Adat Ari El, and we evolved into the Women's League of Adat Ari El.

In 1948, we affiliated with the Women's League for Conservative Judaism. We thus became part of an international organization (which today has more than 200,000 members throughout the United States, Canada, Mexico and Israel) dedicated to the preservation of Jewish ideals and traditions. Important beneficiaries of our efforts include the state of Israel, the Jewish Theological Seminary in New York and the University of Judaism here in Los Angeles.

Our primary concern is the welfare of our synagogue, its religious functions and other programs. In addition, we create fund-raising activities to support youth and adult education programs, and for more than 30 years have continuously provided a weekly adult education program offering a selection of classes to approximately 250 people. We also co-sponsor the North Hollywood Food Pantry, are involved with aid to the homeless, support a local shelter for battered women and help to settle new immigrants in our area. Our community and national organizations continue to look to us for creative leadership.

California Kosher is the fourth cookbook we have published; it follows *Food for Goodness' Sake* (1955), *V.J.C.C. Cooks Tour* (1959) and *Flavored with Love* (1973, 1977, 1980, 1987).

Cookbook Committee

Project Director and Editor: Pearl Elias Roseman

Associate Editors: Marcia Abelson, Juli Kinrich

Art Director and Cover Design: Nedra Klein

Graphic Designer: Caryl Liberman Bass

Photography: Mark Silverstein

Testing Coordinator: Idele Deutsch

Computer Editor: Pam Kaizer

Computer Consultant: Jackie Yaacobi

Cookbook Committee: Cirel Blitz, Paddi Bregman, Barbara Bresler, Elaine Brown, Rose Engel, Marcia Fink, Claire Gering, Miriam Goldfarb, Sylvia Levine, Ida Liberman, Walter Richemer, Judy & Marty Rosenbaum, Marilyn Smith, Rosalie Weiner, Janis & J.D. Weiss, Miriam Wise, Claudia Wolff, Jackie Yaacobi

Section Editors: Marcia Abelson, Beverly Barak, Alice Barnett, Eunice Berman, Eleanor Botney, Elaine Brown, Idele Deutsch, Miriam Freedman, Claire Gering, Ruth Giden, Pearl Leonard, Eve Marcus, Emma Schlesinger, Diane Tapper, Marian Wail, Rosalie Weiner, Miriam Wise

Special Thanks to: Irv Abelson, Patricia Elias, Marty Lasker, Ed Roseman, Judy Unger, Miriam Wise, Claudia Wolff, Julie Wynn

Advisors: Rabbi Leslie J. Alexander, Rabbi Yitz Et-Shalom, Rabbi Moshe J. Rothblum, Rabbi Emeritus Aaron M. and Miriam Wise

Recipe Testers

Marcia Abelson
Hedy Asher
Janet Arzt
Shirley Azaren

Freda Balsham
Beverly Barak
Mary Barbas
Alice Barnett
Eunice Berman
Annette Biatch
Cirel Blitz
Ingrid Blumenstein
Leona Board
Eleanor Botney
Susan Brandes
Paddi Bregman
Barbara Bresler
Elaine Brown

Jan Chernoff
Augusta Cutter

Millie Davis
Idele Deutsch

Elinor Einy
Carole Enowitz

Janet Farber
Eleanor Fisher
Miriam Freedman
Helyn Friedman

Lynda Gentilcore
Claire Gering
Ruth Giden
Kala Ginsburg
Lillian Goff

Miriam Goldfarb
Doris Goodman
Ruth Grover
Greta Grunwald°

Eleanor Gold Hirsch
Frances Hoffnung

Shirley Izenstark

Lela Jacoby

Pam Kaizer
Julie Kantrowitz
Muriel Kaplan
Anita Kast
Ruth King
Juli Kinrich
Nedra Klein
Mary Kovshoff
Linda Krasnoff
Helen Krevitz

Trana Labowe
Riva Lager
Jill Lasker
Pearl Leonard
Sylvia Levine
Ida Liberman
Ivy Liebross
Celia Littenberg

Eve Marcus
Marilyn Mars
Amy Masor
Shelley Maxwell
Adria Metson
Shirley Moore
Paula Moskowitz

Sylvia Newman

Jo-Carole Oberstein

Rae Polland
Sylvia Price

Bea Reynolds
Walter Richeimer
Pearl Roseman
Sylvia Rosenberg
Wendy Rosenthal

Phyllis Sarto
Elaine Schermer
Emma Schlesinger
Marcia Schlesinger
Ray Shapero
Thanya Shulkin
Dotty Simmons
Bebe Simon
Marilyn Smith
Theja Sommer
Vickie Sonnenberg
Linda Spivack
Adelaide Suplin

Diane Tapper
Pearl Taylor
Norman Tyre

Marian Wail
Merryl Weber
Lillian Weinberg
Rosalie Weiner
Lucille Weisel
Tami Weiser
Janis Weiss
Vivian Glucksman-Weiss
Miriam Wise
Julie Wynn

Jackie Yaacobi

6   °Of blessed memory

Table of Contents

Holidays We Celebrate

⮞⮜

Shabbat
Rosh Hashanah
Yom Kippur
Sukkot
Thanksgiving
Hanukkah
Tu B'Shvat
Purim
Pesach
Yom Ha' Atzma'ut, Fourth of July
Shavuot
Tisha B'Av

(With Suggested Menus)

Shabbat

The Sabbath

"It is a sign between me and the children of Israel forever; for in six days the Lord made heaven and earth, and on the seventh day He ceased from work and rested." — Exodus 31:17

Shabbat (the Sabbath) is a day so special and central to Judaism that it is impossible to convey its importance in this brief introduction.

Shabbat may be one of Judaism's most important gifts to the world, for before the Torah proclaimed this concept, most people the world over toiled long hours, seven days a week. The notion of "a day of rest" ultimately changed the quality of life for much of the world. Small wonder that the Sabbath was adopted by those religions that sprang from Judaism — Christianity and Islam.

For thousands of years, observant Jews have celebrated *Shabbat* as they do today, with rest, prayer, study and the enjoyment of the three traditional *Shabbat* meals. Each meal is endowed with a specialness reserved for *Shabbat*, which begins before sundown on Friday night with the lighting of the *Shabbat* candles. For this most important meal of the week, everyone wears fresh clothing, and the table is set more festively than on weekdays, with fresh flowers, wine and the beautiful loaves of *challah* bread. In a very real sense, the table becomes an altar around which family and friends gather to recite or sing the blessings over the candles, wine and challah. In this way, everyone present joins the rhythm of Jewish life that has linked Jews from generation to generation through the centuries and around the Jewish world.

Because tradition forbids kindling or extinguishing a fire during the *Shabbat*, Jewish cooks have used their ingenuity to create recipes that can be served unheated, or that are prepared by slow cooking for many hours, such as beans or *cholent*, for the midday meal on *Shabbat*. The third and last *Shabbat* meal traditionally is something delicious that requires no heating.

On Saturday evening we say farewell to *Shabbat* with the lovely *Havdalah* ceremony, using a braided, multi-wick candle, a brimming cup of wine and a special box of sweet spices, such as cinnamon or nutmeg, for a final whiff of the "sweetness" of the Sabbath day.

Suggested Menus
for
Shabbat

Challah, wine and the most festive meal of the week are the only requirements for Erev Shabbat dinner. European Jews have traditionally served fish, chicken noodle soup and a roast chicken dish. A pareve noodle or potato kugel and a vegetable in season is also typical. Jews from other cultures may have other preferences. Any holiday menu is also appropriate.

Menu #1
Kosher wine
Challah (p. 108)
Chicken Soup (p. 72)
Balsamic Chicken (p. 156) or Roast Chicken
Apricot or Cherry Noodle Kugel (p. 124)
Walnut Carrots (p. 199) or Steamed Green Beans
Fresh Fruit with Pecan Squares (p. 257)

Menu #2
Mushroom/Zucchini Salad (p. 95)
Brown Sugar Baked Salmon (p. 154)
Carrots and Potatoes Caraway (p. 197)
Steamed Broccoli
Fruit Platter
Gateau au Citron (p. 229)

Entree Alternatives
Pineapple Duckling (p. 168)
Stuffed Veal Breast (p. 178)
Spicy Lamb Shanks (p. 180)
Chicken Artichoke Casserole (p. 156)

Rosh Hashanah

Jewish New Year

"May it be your will, Lord our God and God of our ancestors, to grant us a good and sweet New Year." — *High Holy Day Prayer Book*

Rosh Hashanah marks the beginning of the Jewish High Holy Days, and it serves as the Jewish New Year. Prayer, contemplation, the blasts of the *shofar* (ram's horn), and inner soul-searching are "on the menu." But so are round loaves of *challah*, dotted through with golden raisins, and crisp apples dipped in honey — to symbolize the hope expressed in the above quotation; that the New Year be sweet, and that good health, good fortune and happiness be our blessing. It is customary for family and friends to come together to observe this most sacred and significant religious season of the year.

On the second (and last) day of *Rosh Hashanah*, it is also customary that a fruit not tasted since last season be dipped in honey and eaten before dinner, and the appropriate blessing recited. Many families enjoy the traditional Jewish dishes at this time — such as chicken soup with *kreplach* (similar to ravioli), *kasha and varnishkes* (buckwheat groats with bow tie noodles) and roast chicken — but on the second day of Rosh Hashanah often serve more contemporary dishes.

For this holiday, no bitter or sour foods are served, lest the sweetness of the New Year be diminished.

Suggested Menus
for
Rosh Hashanah

Apple, honey, wine and challah (p. 110)
are served with all menus.

Erev Rosh Hashanah
Gefilte Fish (p. 144)
Chicken Soup (p. 72) with Matzo Balls (p. 73)
Roast Chicken
Carrot Tzimmes (p. 198)
California Kugel (p. 125)
Fresh Fruit Platter
Honey Cake (p. 236)

Rosh Hashanah Dinner
Mock Chopped Liver (p. 62)
Chicken Soup (p. 72) with
Kreplach (p. 75)
Brisket (p. 174)
Broccoli with Ginger (p. 201)
Kasha Varnishkes (p. 210)
Taiglach (p. 249)
Apfelkuchen (Apple Cake) (p. 234)

Rosh Hashanah Lunch #1
Chinese Chicken Salad (p. 102)
Curried Rice (p. 208)
Mandarin Orange Mold (p. 100)
Sorbet
Judith's Deluxe Mandelbrot (p. 250)
Chocolate Cherry Cake (p. 222)

Rosh Hashanah Lunch #2
Foil-Poached Salmon (p. 147)
Cold Vegetable Platter and Sauce Verte (p. 194)
Aunt Rollie's Noodle Kugel (p.126)
Apple Honey Cake (p. 235)
Chocolate Mint Brownies (p. 262)

Yom Kippur
The Day of Atonement

"On Rosh Hashanah the decree is signed and on Yom Kippur it is sealed...but Repentance, Prayer and Good Deeds can annul a harsh decree."
— *High Holy Day Prayer Book*

Yom Kippur is the holiest day of the Jewish religious calendar — the "Sabbath of Sabbaths," as it is called. To feel and absorb the real meaning of the prayers and introspection, *Yom Kippur* requires 25 hours of fasting. The evening meal, served before sunset on the eve of the holiday (*Erev Yom Kippur*), is usually kept simple and not spicy. There are conflicting theories on how to prepare for the Fast, from "eat enough to last all day" to "eat lightly to accomplish the Fast most comfortably." A common greeting is to wish one's friends "an easy Fast."

In either case, the Break-the-Fast meal served at the end of *Yom Kippur* is an important one. It marks the end of the High Holy Days and is the first meal eaten after our spiritual "cleansing" during the synagogue service.

For some, the meal at the end of *Yom Kippur* is a simple one, with just family attending. For many others, it is a time for friends and relatives to come together for a festive gathering. But simple or lavish, dairy or meat, the Break-the-Fast meal features dishes that can be completely prepared ahead, requiring only a quick warm up. On the opposite page we offer some menus for dairy meals that are frequently served in California. (If you prefer a full, "dinner"-type meal, any holiday dinner menu or the leftovers from *Erev Yom Kippur* work well.)

To further celebrate the end of the Fast and of *Yom Kippur*, many Jews joyfully observe the *mitzvah* (commandment) of beginning preparations for the next holiday, *Sukkot*, by putting up at least the first post of the family's *sukkah* [see **p. 16**].

Suggested Menus

for

Yom Kippur

Erev Yom Kippur
Challah (p. 109)
Chicken Soup (p. 72)
Sesame Chicken (p. 161)
Baked Potatoes
Italian Vegetables (p. 207)
Hot Fruit Compote (p. 273)
Melon
Kamishbroit (p. 248)

Break-the-Fast #1
Gravlax (p. 149) and Smoked Fish
Cream Cheese and Bagels
Chopped Herring (p. 59)
Marinated Tomatoes (p. 101)
Blintz Casserole (p. 135)
Fresh Fruit Platter
Strudel (p. 247)
Baklava (p. 274)
Peanut Butter Balls (p. 268)
Chocolate Cream Cheese
Swirl Cake (p. 218)

Break-the-Fast #2
Corn Rye Bread (p. 111)
Pumpernickel Bread (p. 112)
Egg/Caviar Appetizer (p. 63)
Sliced Tomatoes with Cucumber
"Anbeissen" Herring Salad (p. 59)
Knishes (p. 69)
Rugelach (p. 248)
Plum Cake (p. 231)
Magic Cookie Bars (p. 261)

Sukkot

The Festival of Booths

"That your generations may know that I placed the children of Israel in tabernacles when I took them out of the Land of Egypt. I am the Lord your God." — Leviticus 23:43

Sukkot occurs two weeks after *Rosh Hashanah* and lasts nine days (eight in Israel). *Shemini Atzeret* is observed on the eighth day. On the ninth day, the Fall Festival which began with *Rosh Hashanah*, is concluded with the joyous celebration of Simhat Torah in the Synagogue.

Sukkot has two origins. It is an ancient harvest festival of thanksgiving celebrating the gathering-in of crops. It is also an historical reminder of the years following the Exodus from Egypt, during which the Israelites wandered in the desert and lived in frail little huts, referred to as "tabernacles" in the Bible. It is this ancient harvest festival that inspired the Pilgrims in the Massachusetts Bay Colony to likewise express their Thanksgiving for God's bountiful gift of food. [see "Thanksgiving," p. 18].

The festival is celebrated both in the synagogue and the home, where it centers around the *sukkah* — an outdoor, temporary structure decorated with colorful fall fruits and vegetables, with a roof of branches through which the sky can be seen.

The entire week of *Sukkot* is one of great festivity, celebrated with many joyous meals and much visiting back and forth among the homes of family, friends and neighbors. Today we observe the ancient tradition by eating our meals, featuring fruits and vegetables, in the *sukkah*, and we frequently invite guests to join us.

In Southern California, with our mild climate and strong emphasis on outdoor entertaining, this is an especially pleasant time to celebrate with family and friends as we give thanks for the abundance of nature and for our many other blessings.

One-pot meals and casseroles, easily carried from kitchen to patio or garden, are perfect for this holiday. Fresh fruit and other desserts of choice add the final, sweet finish to this season of joy and thanksgiving.

Suggested Menus
for
Sukkot

Menu #1
Mixed Green Salad with Onion Salad Dressing (p. 96)
Anadama Bread (p. 115)
Stuffed Cabbage (p. 185)
Roasted Potatoes
Fresh Fruit   Apple Cake (p. 235)

Menu #2
Sliced Tomatoes and Avocado
with Onion Salad Dressing (p. 96)
Stuffed Vegetables (p. 211)
Swedish Limpa Bread (p. 114)
Fresh Fruit Pie (p. 239)

Menu #3
Hot Spinach Salad (p. 98)
Raisin Chicken Santa Fe (p. 158)
Steamed Rice   Broccoli
Chocolate Halo Cake (p. 221)

Menu #4
Sweet Bouquet of Vegetable Soup (p. 80)
Tuna Pasta Salad (p. 98)
Sliced Tomatoes   Asparagus   Olives
Hot Rolls
Chocolate Chip Date Cake (p. 225)

Entree Alternatives
Eggplant Parmesan (p. 197)
Mushroom Tetrazzini (p. 128)
Vegetarian Lasagna (p. 129)
Harrira Soup (p. 79)
Hy's North-of-the-Border Turkey Chili (p. 167)
Mediterranean Meat Salad (p. 90)

Thanksgiving

"Sing unto the Lord in thanksgiving. Acclaim Him with joy, all the earth."
— Psalm 100

What is a chapter on an American holiday doing in a Jewish cookbook? The answer is a fascinating example of the extent to which Judaism has influenced the Western world. The holiday has been embraced by Jews as our own, as indeed it has been, ever since Biblical times.

The first Thanksgiving Day was celebrated by the Plymouth colony Puritans in 1621, after they endured a year of great privation and struggle in their newly adopted land. The celebration included all religious groups, colonists and Indians as well. The Puritans, who built their community on the principles of the Bible, modeled their Thanksgiving celebration after the ancient Jewish harvest festival *Sukkot* [see *"Sukkot,"* **p. 16**]. They likened themselves to the ancient Hebrews, for they, too, had fled from oppression and crossed "the Red Sea," and they had come to an unknown land in search of freedom. The Thanksgiving custom spread rapidly with the growth of the republic and is now a legal holiday in the United States and Canada.

Thanksgiving, as it is observed in the United States, is an ecumenical, nonsectarian holiday celebrated by people from many faiths and ethnic backgrounds. Unlike some other holidays, it does not conflict with Jewish beliefs or ethics. The holiday is customarily celebrated with a family dinner featuring turkey, to remind us of the four wild turkeys served at the Pilgrims' first Thanksgiving feast. Thanksgiving is another expression of the recurring Jewish theme, with its emphasis on family, home, wonderful food and gratitude for our blessings.

At Thanksgiving many families and groups plan co-op dinners. Here we suggest recipes that can travel well and that taste even better if made ahead, as well as delicious, "nonturkey" ideas for a glamorous meal.

However you choose to do yours, have a joyous and kosher Thanksgiving!

$\mathcal{S}$uggested $\mathcal{M}$enus
for
Thanksgiving

Menu #1
Chopped Liver (p. 61)
with Rye Rounds and Eggplant "Caviar" (p. 63)
Turkey with Stuffing
Glazed Yams with
Duchess Potatoes (p. 212)
Spinach/Pear Puree (p. 204)
Cranberry Sauce
Fresh Fruit Platter
Pumpkin Pie (p. 243) or Apple Pie
Pumpkin Chiffon Spice Cake (p. 234)
Fresh Fruit Pies (p. 239)

Menu #2
Mock Chopped Liver (p. 62) with
Rye Rounds
Mushroom Appetizer (p. 56)
Gazpacho (p. 84)
Hearts of Palm Salad (p. 90)
Salmon en Croute (p. 146)
Cauliflower/Broccoli Beehive (p. 202)
Brown Rice with Peas (p. 209)
Molded Cranberry-Apple (p. 272)
Pumpkin-Pecan Pie (p. 243)
Bourbon Apple Pie with Ice Cream (p. 240)

Hanukkah

The Festival of Lights

"Hanukkah, O Hanukkah, come light the menorah/Let's have a party, we'll all dance the hora/Gather 'round the table, we'll give you a treat/Draydels to play with and latkes to eat."   —Traditional song

Hanukkah, an eight-day festival, commemorates the 2nd Century B.C.E. victory of the Jewish Maccabees over the Greek-Syrian forces that occupied and desecrated the Temple in Jerusalem. It was probably the first battle fought for religious freedom.

Hanukkah is also called "the Festival of Lights," for when Judah Maccabee and his followers recaptured the Temple, they found insufficient oil for the Eternal Light—the very first "oil shortage" in history. The small vial that was found was enough for only one day. Tradition says that, miraculously, the oil burned for eight days until additional oil could arrive.

Candles are lit every evening during the eight days of *Hanukkah*. A special eight-branch candle holder, called a *menorah*, is used. One special candle, which sits higher on the menorah, serves as the *shamash* (helper) and is used to light the candles each night. One candle is lit the first night, and an additional candle is lit each night, until all eight are shining brightly. Some families collect menorahs so that each family member has his or hers to light each night. Blessings of thanksgiving are offered, and a prayer is recited to celebrate the release of our people from oppression and the miracle of the oil that lasted for eight days. The evenings are spent in a joyous manner, with holiday songs and games. We spin the *draydel* (a special top), play cards, share stories and exchange small gifts.

This happy holiday gives us additional opportunities for much celebrating and entertaining with potluck suppers, or wine and cheese or dessert parties. It is the season for family gatherings, children's parties, and special get-togethers with friends and neighbors.

The *Hanukkah* table usually includes special dishes. Different cultures have different traditions, and each family has its own, but most include certain deep-fried foods, to commemorate the "miracle of the oil." Ashkenazic Jews (usually of Eastern or Central European descent) eat *latkes* (potato pancakes) with applesauce and sour cream. Sephardic Jews (those whose ancestors lived in Spain) serve *bimuelos* (round doughnuts rolled in cinnamon honey). Israelis serve *sufganiyot* (jelly-filled doughnuts). Dairy dishes, such as kugels, blintzes and cheesecake, are also traditional for this festival.

Suggested Menus
for
Hanukkah

Menu #1
Challah (p. 108)
Sweet-and-Sour Cucumber Salad (p. 95)
Brisket (p. 174)
Potato Latkes (p. 190) with Applesauce
Italian Vegetables (p. 207)
Doughnuts
Lemon Mousse Pie (p. 244)

Menu #2
Egg/Caviar Appetizer (p. 63)
Falafel in Pita or
Tabouli Salad (p. 91)
Frozen Fruit Delight (p. 272)
Sufganiyot

Menu #3
Marinated Tomato Salad (p. 101)
Natural Bread (p. 115)
Harold's Southwestern Barbecued Salmon (p. 154)
Zucchini Latkes (p. 190)
Wild Rice
Dark Chocolate Cheesecake (p. 215)

Menu #4
Creamy Zucchini Soup (p. 82)
Garlic Coleslaw (p. 93)
Mexican Cheese Strata (p. 138)
Steamed Broccoli
Strawberry Yogurt Pie (p. 245)

Suggested Fried Entrees
Blintzes (p. 134)
Fish Croquettes or Patties
Pan-Fried Fish Fillets

Tu B'Shvat
Arbor Day or New Year of the Trees

"And they shall sit every man under his vine and under his fig-tree, and none shall make them afraid." — Micah 4:4

After 40 years of wandering, the children of Israel returned to the land of their ancestors. God instructed them to plant trees, as well as all manner of growing things — fruits, vegetables and grains. Some families reenact the custom of ancient times, when the birth of a newborn is commemorated by planting a cedar for a boy and a cypress or pine for a girl. On their wedding day, a *huppa* (bower of branches) is constructed from branches cut from the trees, now full grown like the children.

Planting a tree on Tu B'Shvat is a *mitzvah* (commandment) observed by all Israelis today. School is suspended, and hundreds of thousands of youths gather in the yet unforested areas of Israel to plant the barren countryside. Jewish children do likewise wherever they may live, planting trees and enjoying snacks of honey, almonds and carob.

Weather permitting, it can be a lovely time of year to enjoy a picnic. Decorate a table with flowers and fruit, and enjoy a luscious fruit or wine soup, fresh vegetable dishes, and honey cakes or cookies in honor of nature's bounty and the Lord's blessing.

The holiday falls in the late winter, an ideal time to plant trees in California and Israel. Should the weather be cold or wet, a hot soup carried in a thermos can warm the celebrants.

Suggested Menus
for
Tu B'Shvat

For a "tree planting" picnic on a cold winter day!

Challah (p. 109) and/or
Pumpernickel Bread (p. 112) or
Natural Bread (p. 115)
Cabbage Soup (p. 80) or
Bean Barley Soup (p. 78)
Fresh Apples or Dried Fruit
Macadamia Mandelbrot (p. 251) or
Oatmeal Chocolate Chip Cookies (p. 266)

Any "Take-Along" item
from "California Kosher"

Purim

The Feast of Esther

"Oh, once there was a wicked, wicked man, and Haman was his name, sir./He lied and lied about the Jews, but they were not to blame, sir./Oh, today we'll merry, merry be and 'nosh' some hamantaschen."
— *Children's song*

Purim, an early spring festival, is celebrated with great rejoicing and merrymaking, both in the synagogue and at home. In the synagogue, the *Megillah* (the Book of Esther) is read, recounting how beautiful Queen Esther and her wise uncle, Mordecai, saved the Jewish people from destruction by the wicked Haman. He was defeated and destroyed; and good prevailed over evil.

It has become customary to celebrate *Purim* with parties (for the children and grownups as well), costumes, masquerades, feasting and drinking, singing and dancing. All kinds of pastries are prepared and consumed (to help use up any flour in the house before the onset of Passover). Honey cakes, strudels, cookies and especially *hamantaschen* (three-cornered, filled pastries supposed to resemble Haman's hat), are traditional for Ashkenazi Jews, while Sephardic Jews serve *foulares* (hard-cooked eggs in pastry, said to represent Haman in jail or on the gallows).

On this holiday, gifts of food (cookies, foulares, dried fruits, etc.) — called *"Shalach Manot"* or *"Mishloah Manot"* — are exchanged among friends, neighbors and relatives. Sweets and money are distributed to the poor.

Suggested Menus
for
Purim

Suggestions for Shalach Manot or Mishloah Manot gift baskets for family and friends. Any one or a combination of these recipes makes very delicious gifts. Baking with family or friends can multiply the fun..."Hag Sameach!"

East European Hamantaschen (p. 252)
Low-Cholesterol Hamantaschen (p. 253)
Easy Hamantaschen (p. 254)
Classic Hamantaschen (p. 254)
Assorted Filling for Hamantaschen (p. 255 and 256)
Strudel (p. 247)
Edy's Strudel (p. 247)
Rugelach (p. 248)
Raisin Cheesecake Cookies (p. 265)
Dried Fruits and Nuts
Zucchini Bread (p. 113)
Date and Nut Bread (p. 119)
Apple Honey Cake (p. 235)

Pesach

Passover

"And thou shalt speak to thy child on that day, saying, 'This is what the Lord did for ME when I went forth from Egypt." — *Passover Haggadah*

This great holiday of freedom, rooted in the Bible, rejoices in the liberation of the Hebrews from bondage in Egypt and calls on modern Jews to deepen their commitment to human liberty today in our world.

Passover is the family experience most celebrated by Jews the world over. It is not uncommon for nonreligious Jews, along with non-Jews, members of extended or blended families, neighbors, and interfaith groups to join together around the Passover *Seder* table to share in this special ceremonial meal, which takes the form of a sociodrama.

"Seder" literally means "order of the service." It refers to the prescribed sequence of the ritual that takes place as we tell the story of the Hebrew Exodus from Egypt.

During the reading of the *Haggadah*, or narration, which precedes the dinner, the youngest member at the table recites the traditional Four Questions. The *afikoman* (a special piece of matzo) is hidden and redeemed later, and the front door is opened to welcome the prophet Elijah. The evening passes as the ritual unfolds in the warmth of ancient remembrances, modern interpretations, special food, storytelling and song.

Immediately after *Purim*, preparation for Passover properly begins with a thorough spring cleaning of the entire house. Several days before the first *Seder*, the kitchen is thoroughly cleaned, with every crumb of *hametz* (leavened food) removed. The kitchen is carefully prepared for the eight days when special plates and utensils are used. Those items used the rest of the year are put away. Only unleavened food that is *kosher l'Pesach* ("kosher for Passover") is served, since the laws of Passover prohibit the use of leavening agents in cooking and baking. Because *hametz* is forbidden, Jewish cooks were challenged to create special recipes as part of the Passover observance for their home-centered rituals and cuisine. This custom continues today, as creative cooks adapt favorite recipes and cuisines to Passover guidelines. The results today, as our recipes demonstrate, are dishes everyone looks forward to eating.

For most of us, the special foods served at the *Seder* table conjure up warm memories of *Sedarim* past. On the first two nights of the festival (only one night in Israel), the *Seder* table is set with candles, wine, a covered plate of *matzot* and — most important — the *Seder* plate, with its six symbolic foods (roasted egg, roasted shank bone, charoset, parsley, horseradish and romaine lettuce) functioning as a sort of "show and tell" to help recount the Passover story.

Because Passover lasts for eight days (seven in Israel, where the entire week is a national holiday), it is an ideal time to entertain and visit. Since observant Jews eat only at home or in another strictly kosher-for-Passover home during this time, many meals are home-cooked throughout the festival week. (Because Passover cooking differs from that of the rest of the year, we have included a selection of recipes special to this holiday, beginning on **p. 35**.) This offers the creative cook a wonderful opportunity to entertain with the great variety of foods that represent the many regions where Jews have lived in the 30 centuries since the Exodus.

Sephardic Jewish dishes for this time of year abound in vegetables such as eggplant, artichokes, celery root, fava beans and okra. (Unlike Ashkenazim, Sephardim allow the use of corn, rice, peas and beans during Passover.) Yemenite, Iranian and Iraqi Jews use highly spiced dishes. Ashkenazi cuisine differs greatly from all of these, featuring gefilte fish, chicken soup with matzo balls, matzo kugels and tzimmes. Each of these cuisines features its own delicious desserts.

Suggested menus for Passover appear on page 34.

Independence Days

"Proclaim Liberty throughout the land, unto all the inhabitants thereof."
— *Leviticus 25:10*

Yom Ha'Atzma'ut in Israel

The joy of independence bursts upon Israel at the end of its Memorial Day (*Yom Ha Zikaron*), when all Israelis remember those who have fallen in the struggle to create and maintain our Jewish homeland, which was established in 1948. After sunset, there follows a night of fireworks and dancing, and the streets are filled with happy celebrants, greeting one another with *"Hag Sameach!"* ("Happy Holiday!"). The following day, youth organizations, soldiers in uniform and tourists are seen everywhere. Diplomats and tourists are greeted at official receptions on this holiday.

On a more casual note, city folk pack their picnic baskets and flock to the beaches and parks to enjoy the national holiday. The standard picnic for the day is similar to American picnic fare: barbecued meats, salads and fresh fruit.

Fourth of July in the United States

The fourth of July holiday, which commemorates America's independence from England, is also celebrated with barbecues, parades, picnics and family gatherings. Since the holiday often means a three- or four-day weekend, many people plan mini-vacations, trips or family reunions, or celebrate with a gala, all-day picnic, ending with community fireworks.

It is an ideal time to recite the *Shehechiyanu* (the special prayer of thanksgiving) as we recall those who came to America seeking religious freedom and those who have worked and died to protect that freedom for us to enjoy. It should also be remembered that many Jews made notable contributions to that effort.

Suggested Menus

for
Yom Ha'Atzma'ut

Picnic to go....

Barbecued Steak
Tabouli Salad (p. 91)
Pita Bread and Corn Rye Bread (p. 111)
Eggplant/Caviar Appetizer (p. 63)
Raw Vegetables - Sliced Tomatoes
Fresh Fruit
Mandelbrot (p. 250)
Wine
Soft Drinks
Coffee & Tea

for
Fourth of July

Picnic at home!

Raw Vegetables
Barbecued Lemon Chicken (p. 160)
Tangy Potato Salad (p. 99)
Chinese Coleslaw (p. 100)
Year-Round Fresh Fruit Pie (p. 239)
Chocolate Mint Brownies (p. 262)
Watermelon
Lemonade
Soft Drinks
Coffee & Tea

Shavuot
Spring Harvest of Thanksgiving

"You shall celebrate three pilgrimages in the year: The festival of Matzot....the ingathering of the first fruits [of the spring harvest] which you planted and the festival of the harvest [in the fall]." — Exodus 23:16

Forty-nine days following the beginning of Passover, the first spring harvest is celebrated on *Shavuot* with song and thanksgiving. *Shavuot* is the twofold celebration of the spring harvest and of the giving of the Torah to Moses, after the Exodus from Egypt.

In modern Israel's early years, agricultural settlements used to load their trucks high with farm products, bringing them to the cities for festive parades and "selling" their wares for the benefit of the Jewish National Fund — the agency that redeems and reforests the soil of the Land of Israel.

For *Shavuot*, the synagogue is decorated with fruits and grains. Included in the service is the reading of The Book of Ruth, a convert who pledged "thy people shall be my people." Confirmation ceremonies are held for teenagers, who repeat Ruth's words as they confirm their allegiance to Judaism. Torah scholars and *havurot* (study groups) traditionally study through the night of *Erev Shavuot* to celebrate receiving the Torah on that day, returning home after the sunrise.

After the morning synagogue service, celebrants return home to a meal that traditionally includes dairy foods because the Torah is often compared with "milk and honey." Some of these dishes include cheese blintzes, *borscht* (beet soup) with sour cream, honey cakes, and sour cream or cheese cakes.

Suggested Menus
for
Shavuot

Menu #1
Wine
Challah (p. 110)
Sweet Bouquet of Vegetable Soup (p. 80)
Fillet of Sole Veronique (p. 153)
Sweet and Sour Cucumber Salad (p. 95)
Lemon Noodle Kugel (p. 123)
Pistachio Pineapple Mold (p. 271)
Nel de Groot Ice Box Cookies (p. 266)
Fresh Fruit

Menu #2
Wine
Challah (p. 108)
Beet Borscht (p. 83)
Salmon Salad Molds (p. 148)
Sliced Tomatoes
Blintzes (p. 134) or Blintz Casserole (p. 135)
Fresh Strawberries with Whipped Cream
Magic Cookie Bars (p. 261)

Tisha B'Av

Ninth Day of Av

"By the rivers of Babylon we sat and wept when we remembered Zion."
— Psalms 137:1

During the summer of the year 586 B.C.E., the kingdom of Judah, home to Jerusalem and the Temple, found itself in the midst of a political struggle between Egypt and Babylonia. Judah's kings sided with Egypt, but the Babylonians won the war. The Jews, their numbers decimated, were taken into captivity in Babylonia. Jerusalem and the Temple, which had been built by King Solomon, were laid waste.

Seventy years later, after Babylonia was defeated by the Persians, the captives returned, and the Temple was rebuilt. It was again the center for Jewish worship. But some 650 years later, in the year 70 C.E., Jerusalem again was besieged, this time by Titus and his Roman Legions. The inhabitants were starved, and the magnificent Temple was burned to the ground. Only the Western Wall of the courtyard was left standing; it remains to this day. The Temple itself was never rebuilt.

The ninth day of the month of Av — also referred to as the Black Fast — commemorates both of these national calamities. Unlike *Yom Kippur*, a time for reflection and penitence, this is a day of mourning and sadness. For Sephardic Jews, it is additionally the anniversary of their final departure from Spain in 1492, after years of torment by the Catholic Inquisition. Thus *Tisha B'Av* is filled with various customs, which commemorate several cataclysmic events in Jewish history.

One would expect that the recipes for a fast day might be sparse. Nonetheless, there are many traditions for the days preceding and concluding this holiday. Before the days of refrigeration, Jewish housewives used to bring home live fish before the first of Av to be kept in a tub of water. When the family began the period of mourning — the nine days of Av — and abstained from eating meat or fowl, they had fresh fish to eat.

Before the fast, Sephardim traditionally serve *"Huevos con Tomat"* (eggs with tomatoes) and lentils. The fast is broken with a light meal of cheeses, eggs and vegetables, while Ashkenazim might often serve fish with hard round rolls or bagels.

Suggested Menus
for
Tisha B'Av

Erev Tisha B'Av
Challah (p. 110)
Huevos con Tomat y Queso (p. 136) or
Lentil Soup (p. 78)
Fresh Fruit
Lemon Poppy Seed Bowties (p. 268)

Tisha B'Av Break-the-Fast
Challah (p. 109) or French Bread
Wine or Fruit Juice
Sole Fillets Tarragon (p. 150)
Creamed Parsnips (p. 201)
Broccoli Spinach Soufflé (p. 202)
Fresh Fruit
Fresh Peach Pie (p. 241) or
Mandelbrot (p. 250) or
Preposterous Pecan Chocolate Bars (p. 258)

$\mathscr{S}uggested\ \mathscr{M}enus$
for
Pesach
(Items required for the Seder are described on page 27)

First and Second Seder Dinners
Gefilte Fish (p. 144) or Chopped Liver (p. 61)
or Chofesh (p. 37)
Chicken Soup (p. 72) with Matzo Balls (p. 73)
Roast Chicken with Stuffing (p. 36)
or Brisket (p. 174) or Stuffed Veal Breast (p. 178)
Carrot Tzimmes (p. 198) or Carrot Ring (p. 38)
Asparagus or Spinach/Pear Puree (p. 204)
Farfel Puffs (p. 36) or Farfel Kugel (p. 40)
Apple-Plum Pudding (p. 40) or Chremsels (p. 39)
Frozen Strawberry Meringue Torte (p. 50) or
Chocolate Mousse Cake (p. 45)
Chocolate Macaroons (p. 51) or
Brownies (p. 52)   or   Date and Nut Bars (p. 49) or
Ingberlach (p. 54)   or   Kamish Bars (p. 51)

Weekday Menu #1
Tossed Salad
Halibut Ragout (p. 145)   Spinach Cheese Bake (p. 43)
Layered Vegetable Terrine (p. 192)
Walnut Torte (p. 45)   Fruit Pudding (p. 41)

Weekday Menu #2
Garlic Coleslaw (p. 93)
Meat/Mashed Potato Pie (p. 43)
Broccoli with Ginger (p. 201)
Chocolate Torte (p. 47) or
Chocolate/Nut Cake (p. 46)
Fresh Fruit

Israeli-Style Charoset (Pareve)

Made to look like mortar, charoset is a vital part of the Passover Seder and tastes better than it looks.

1	apple, peeled, cored and sliced
3	bananas, sliced
10	dates
1/2	cup raisins
	Rind of 1/2 lemon
1/2	cup nuts
1/2	cup dry red wine
	Juice of 1/2 lemon
	Matzo meal
	Pinch of salt
1	teaspoon cinnamon
	Sugar to taste

Combine the apple, bananas, dates, raisins, lemon rind and nuts in a blender. Use medium speed for desired texture. Add the wine and lemon juice.The mixture will be very watery. Transfer the mixture to a bowl and add matzo meal for desired consistency. Season with salt, cinnamon and sugar. Yields 3 1/2 cups.

Variation: Walnuts, almonds or pecans can be used.

Ruth Giden

Charoset for Passover (Pareve)

This is a traditional recipe of the Sephardic Jews from Turkey. Our children also love it as a jam on matzo.

8	ounces pitted dates
8	ounces raisins, golden or dark
2	apples, peeled, cored and grated
1/2	cup finely chopped walnuts or almonds
	Orange juice or wine

Using an old-fashioned meat grinder, grind the fruit. Moisten with juice or wine, and add nuts. Yields approximately 3 1/2 cups.

Note: Keeps for several weeks in the refrigerator.

Pearl Roseman

Passover Roast Chicken with Stuffing (Meat)

This is one of my favorite Seder dinner dishes as it can be assembled earlier in the day, roasted during the Seder and served right from the oven. It multiplies well for any number of guests.

1-2   **roasting chickens, cut in eighths**
1   **cup chopped onion**
1/2   **cup diced celery**
1/2   **cup coarsely chopped nuts**
6   **tablespoons vegetable oil**
3   **cups matzo farfel**
1/2   **teaspoon salt**
1/8   **teaspoon pepper**
  Ginger to taste
  Garlic powder to taste
2   **teaspoons paprika**
1   **egg, slightly beaten**
1   **cup chicken soup (made from 2 cubes or 2 teaspoons soup mix)**

Sauté onions, celery and nuts in oil until tender. Add farfel and stir until lightly toasted.

Combine seasonings, egg and soup. Add to matzo mixture. Spread in a 9x13-inch glass baking dish. Lay pieces of cut-up chicken that have been seasoned with ginger, garlic powder and lots of paprika very close together over the stuffing. Roast for 1 1/2 hours in a 350 degree oven or until done and golden brown. Serves 6 - 8.

Variations: Stuffing works well for cornish hens, duck or turkey. May be baked separately in a casserole if desired for approximately 30-40 minutes at 350 degrees.

Pearl Roseman

Farfel Puffs (Pareve)

A delicious, easy Passover dinner roll.

3   **cups hot water**
8   **cups farfel**
8   **eggs, beaten**
6   **tablespoons margarine**
  Salt and pepper to taste

Place farfel, margarine and seasonings in a large bowl. Pour hot water over all; mix and let cool.

Add eggs to farfel mixture and blend well. Pour into greased cupcake tins. Bake for 45 minutes in a preheated oven at 375 degrees. Yields approximately 2 dozen.

Variation: For a different flavor try onion-flavored nyafat instead of margarine.

Idele Deutsch

Chofesh (Stuffed Rhubarb) (Meat)

Chofesh in Hebrew means freedom. This traditional Passover recipe is from my mother-in-law's family in Israel. We serve it as a first course at our Seder.

1   **pound strawberry rhubarb, peeled and cut into 2 1/2- to 3-inch pieces (if rhubarb is thick, slice width as well)**

Filling:
1   **pound ground meat**
1   **egg**
1/2   **cup matzo meal**
     Salt and pepper to taste

Sauce:
1   **28-ounce can tomatoes**
1   **green bell pepper**
1/2   **onion**
     Salt and pepper, to taste
1/2   **teaspoon each, basil and/or oregano**
1/4   **cup sugar (or to taste)**

Coating:
1/2   **cup matzo meal, approximately**
1 or 2 **eggs, beaten**
1/2   **cup oil**

Filling: Mix ground meat, egg, matzo meal, salt and pepper together in bowl and set aside.

Sauce: Process tomatoes, bell pepper, onion, salt, pepper, basil and oregano. Pour half of sauce into baking dish.

To fill rhubarb: Take large spoonful of meat mixture and pack each rhubarb rib. Press 3-4 ribs together to form roll. Gently squeeze to pack tightly. (See illustration).

To coat: Dip rhubarb rolls in beaten eggs and roll in matzo meal. Brown all sides in hot oil. Turn carefully.

Place browned rolls in baking dish and add remaining sauce. Cut up any remaining pieces of rhubarb and add to sauce.

Depending on tartness desired, sprinkle sugar over sauce. Bake uncovered at 350 degrees (preheated). As sauce cooks, add sugar to taste. Yields 8 servings.

Note: Chofesh may be frozen. To serve, defrost and reheat, covered, for 20-30 minutes.

Sally Weber

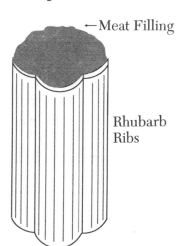

←Meat Filling

Rhubarb Ribs

Carrot Ring (Pareve)

Even people who don't care for carrots will like this!

3	tablespoons potato starch
1/2	cup red sweet wine
1/4	cup margarine
1/2	cup matzo meal
1	pound raw, grated carrots
1/4	cup raisins
1/2	cup sugar
1	teaspoon cinnamon
1	teaspoon ginger
	Juice and grated peel of 1 lemon
1	egg
1/2	teaspoon salt

In a small bowl, dissolve potato starch in the wine (it takes a bit of mixing). In a large bowl, cream the margarine and matzo meal. Add the rest of the ingredients and mix well. Pour into a well-greased ring mold or casserole and bake for 1 hour in a preheated 350 degree oven. Unmold to serve. Serves 10 - 12.

Leona Board

Orange-Carrot Soufflé (Pareve)

Carrot lovers will enjoy this special soufflé.

1 1/2	pounds frozen carrots, cooked, with liquid reserved
2-2 1/2	cups orange juice
4	eggs, separated
1/4	cup melted margarine
1	teaspoon grated orange rind
1/4	cup cake meal
2	tablespoons honey
3/4	teaspoon cinnamon
1/2	teaspoon salt, optional

Combine the liquid from the cooked carrots and the orange juice. Put carrots in blender or food processor. Pour a little orange-carrot liquid at a time into the cooked carrots and puree at high speed.

In a large bowl, combine pureed carrots with lightly beaten egg yolks, margarine, cake meal, honey, orange rind, cinnamon and salt.

In a small mixing bowl, beat the egg whites until stiff but not dry and fold into carrot mixture. Pour mixture into a well-greased 2 1/2-quart casserole. Bake for 45 minutes in a preheated 350 degree oven. Garnish with paprika and serve at once. Serves 10.

Walter Richeimer

Chremsels (Pareve)

*Equally good as a side dish at dinner or
main dish for breakfast or luncheon.*

Matzo Meal Batter:

1/3	cup honey
3/4	cup sugar
2 1/2	cups boiling water
3	tablespoons vegetable shortening
1	pound matzo meal
1	teaspoon salt
8	eggs
	Oil for frying

Filling:

1	pound cooked, mashed prunes
1/2	cup chopped nuts
1	lemon rind, grated, optional
1/2	teaspoon cinnamon, or to taste

In a saucepan, bring honey, sugar, water, shortening and salt to a boil.

Place matzo meal in a large mixing bowl. Pour honey mixture into matzo meal and stir. Cover the bowl and let cool for five minutes.

Beat one egg at a time into cooled matzo meal mixture. (It should be the consistency of a meat loaf. If it's too stiff, add a little water.) Form into 1 1/2-inch balls with moistened hands.

Filling: Mix prunes, nuts, lemon rind and cinnamon. Press 1/2 teaspoon of the prune filling into each ball and reshape to cover the filling. Flatten into pancake. Drop into hot oil and fry lightly on both sides. Remove from pan and place on a brown paper bag or paper towels to drain.

At this point chremsels can be frozen. When ready to use, place on a greased baking dish. Drizzle with honey and bake in a preheated oven at 350 degrees for 5-10 minutes or until golden brown. Yields 50 pancakes.

Variation: *Chremsels can be made without the filling.*

Adelaide Suplin

Farfel Kugel (Pareve)

An excellent side dish.

3	large onions, chopped
1/2	cup vegetable shortening
1	green bell pepper, chopped
1	cup sliced mushrooms
7	cups matzo farfel
1/2	teaspoon pepper
2	teaspoons paprika
1	teaspoon garlic powder, optional
	Salt to taste
2	cups chicken soup (pareve mix)
2	cups water
4	eggs, beaten

In a large skillet, sauté onions in shortening until soft. Add bell pepper and mushrooms; sauté until soft. Add farfel and mix until slightly brown. Add seasonings, soup and water; mix together. Add the eggs and mix. Pour batter into a well-greased 11x14 -inch casserole. Bake for 1 hour in a preheated oven at 350 degrees or until golden brown. Yields approximately 34 - 40 pieces.

Variation: Vegetables can be varied using celery, carrots or zucchini.

Elinor Einy

Passover Apple-Plum Pudding (Pareve)

My mother-in-law, Tillie Lasker, makes this favorite every Seder.

2	cups matzo farfel
2	cups boiling water
6	eggs
6	medium tart apples, peeled, cored and coarsely grated
1	cup golden raisins
1	cup plum jam
1 1/4	cups sugar (scant)
	Juice and rind of 1 lemon
4	tablespoons sweet wine
4	tablespoons honey
1/2	teaspoon salt
1	teaspoon cinnamon
	Oil for glass baking dish

In a large bowl, mix farfel and boiling water. Cool. Beat eggs and add to farfel. In another bowl combine grated apples and raisins. Fold farfel mixture into the fruit. Add jam, salt, cinnamon and sugar.

Cover the bottom of a 3-quart glass baking dish with a little oil and heat for 3 minutes in a preheated oven at 350 degrees. Pour the combined mixture in and bake for 25 minutes more.

While this is baking, combine lemon juice and rind with wine and honey and bring to a boil. Pour over pudding and bake for another 25 minutes or until golden brown on top. Serves 12 - 16.

Variation: Can be made with 8 apples instead of plum jam.

Jill Lasker

Babanatza (Passover Pudding) (Pareve)

Delicious warm or cold.

6	whole matzos
1	cup raisins
6	eggs
1	cup chopped walnuts
2	green apples, peeled, cored and diced
1/4	cup oil
1/2	cup honey
1/4	cup sugar
2	tablespoons margarine, cut in pieces
1	teaspoon ground cinnamon
	Boiling water

Break matzos into pieces in a large mixing bowl and pour a little boiling water over to soften them. Squeeze out excess water.

Mix raisins and eggs with matzos.

In a separate bowl, mix walnuts, apples, oil, honey and sugar. Add apple mixture to the matzo mixture and blend thoroughly.

Grease a deep, 1 1/2-quart, oven-proof dish and pour in the pudding mixture. Sprinkle with cinnamon and dot with margarine pieces. Bake for 1 hour at 350 degrees in a preheated oven. Serve warm, or chill and serve with applesauce. Serves 6 - 8.

Suggestion: Deep-fry tablespoons of batter in hot oil (350 degrees), and you have a dish from Central and Eastern Europe called "Chremsel."

Maxine Russell

Fruit Pudding for Passover (Pareve)

This recipe is from my cousin, Shellie Sheanin.

8	eggs, beaten
1	cup crushed pineapple, drained, with juice reserved
2/3	cup sugar
1/2	cup oil
1/2	cup matzo meal
3	apples, peeled and sliced
1/2	pound pitted, chopped prunes
1/2	cup chopped, dried apricots
	Pinch of salt

In a large bowl, beat the eggs and add 3/4 cup of the reserved pineapple juice. Add the remaining ingredients. The mixture should be very loose.

Pour the mixture into a well-greased 9x13-inch glass baking dish. Bake in a preheated 350 degree oven until set and browned, approximately 45 minutes. Yields approximately 12 servings.

Marcia Abelson

Sweet Farfel Kugel (Pareve)

Bananas make this kugel different. Makes a nice breakfast dish.

5	cups matzo farfel
5	eggs, beaten
1/2	cup sugar
1	teaspoon salt
4	ounces margarine, melted
2	large apples, cored and grated
1/2	cup ground nuts
2	bananas, mashed

Cover farfel with cold water and drain immediately.

Add eggs, sugar, salt and margarine. Add apple, bananas and 1/4 cup of nuts. Pour into an 8x11- or 9x13-inch greased glass baking dish.

Sprinkle remaining nuts on top. Bake in a 350 degree oven for 1 hour. Yields approximately 12 servings.

Marcia Abelson

Pineapple-Cheese Pesach Kugel (Dairy)

A dairy kugel delicious with or without the topping.

6	eggs
2	cups milk
1	pint cottage cheese
3	tablespoons lemon juice
1	tablespoon lemon rind, grated
3/4	cup sugar
	Dash salt
1	8-ounce can crushed pineapple, drained
6	matzos, broken, moistened and drained
1/4	cup margarine, melted
1/4	cup cinnamon sugar

Optional Topping:

2	cups sour cream
3	tablespoons sugar
1	tablespoon lemon juice

Beat eggs with milk and cottage cheese. Add lemon juice, lemon rind, sugar, salt and pineapple. Add matzo and mix again. Grease a 9x13-inch pan; pour in mixture and drizzle melted margarine on top. Sprinkle with cinnamon sugar. Bake for one hour in a preheated 350 degree oven. (Casserole may be frozen at this time.)

If desired, just before serving, top with sour cream mixed with sugar and lemon juice. Heat at 450 for 10 minutes. Serves 12.

Alice Greenfield

Spinach Cheese Bake (Dairy)

Makes a nice luncheon side dish for Passover.

2   cups cottage cheese
     (regular or low fat)
8   ounces cheddar cheese,
     grated or crumbled
1   10-ounce package
     chopped spinach,
     thawed
6   tablespoons matzo meal
6   eggs, beaten
1/2 teaspoon garlic powder
     Pepper to taste
     Sliced mushrooms
     (optional)

In a large bowl, combine all ingredients except the eggs and mix well. Add eggs, mix thoroughly and pour into a lightly greased 8x12-inch glass pan. Bake for one hour in a preheated oven at 350 degrees or until top is golden brown. Serves 10 - 12.

Variations: *Other vegetables, such as diced green pepper or zucchini, can be added. If you add vegetables, increase the garlic powder to 1 teaspoon.*

Beverly Barak

Meat/Mashed Potato Pie (Meat)

My Bubbee made it during Pesach.

1   large onion, chopped
1 1/2 pounds ground beef
1/4   teaspoon parsley
1/2   teaspoon garlic powder
       Paprika, salt and pepper,
       to taste
1   tablespoon olive oil
1/2   cup sliced mushrooms
4   cups mashed potatoes

In a skillet, sauté onion, beef, parsley and seasonings in olive oil until lightly browned. Add mushrooms and cook 1 minute longer.

Grease a 10-inch pie plate with vegetable cooking spray. Line the bottom of the pie plate with half of the mashed potatoes. Add meat mixture. Top with remaining mashed potatoes. Bake for 45 minutes at 350 degrees. Serves 6.

Suggestions: *Can be made ahead of time and frozen. Ground veal, turkey or chicken may be substituted for ground beef.*

Elaine Dozoretz

Passover Lasagna (Meat)

Pine nuts add an unusual note to this entree.

2	pounds extra-lean ground beef
1	small onion, finely chopped
1	bell pepper, diced (green, red or gold)
6	large mushrooms, diced
1	heaping teaspoon garlic powder
	Salt to taste
1/4	teaspoon pepper
1/2 - 1	teaspoon cumin
1/3	cup pine nuts
7	matzos
6	eggs, well beaten

Brown meat in a skillet and drain excess fat. Add onion, bell pepper, mushrooms and seasonings; saute until vegetables are tender. Add pine nuts.

Grease an 11x14-inch glass dish. Line the bottom with matzos that have been slightly softened by dipping them in a bowl of hot water. Layer 1/2 of the meat mixture over the matzo. Repeat with another layer of matzo, the second half of the meat mixture and top with a final layer of matzo. Pour the beaten eggs over the top and bake for approximately 40 minutes in a 350 degree oven or until brown on top. Serves 12 - 14.

Variations: Add one 8-ounce can of tomato sauce between layers. Also, vegetables like zucchini may be used instead of bell peppers.

Beverly Barak

Walnut Torte (Dairy)

This torte is always a sensation, whenever it is served!

12	eggs, separated
1	pound Passover powdered sugar, less 4 tablespoons for whipped cream
	Pinch salt
2	tablespoons orange juice
1	pound ground nuts
4	tablespoons matzo meal
1	pint whipping cream
2	tablespoons Passover brandy

In a large bowl, beat egg yolks and add sugar, salt and juice.

In a second bowl, combine ground nuts and matzo meal; add to egg yolk mixture. Beat egg whites until stiff and shiny. Gently fold egg whites into the nut mixture. Pour the batter into a 10-inch springform pan that has been well-greased and lightly dusted with matzo meal. Bake in a preheated oven at 325 degrees for about one hour or until a toothpick comes out dry when inserted into torte.

Cool on a rack. When torte is cool, remove side of springform pan. Whip cream and blend in brandy and 4 tablespoons powdered sugar.

Cut torte into 2 layers and spread center with cream filling. Serves 8 - 10.

Variations: Any jam may be used as a filling with either fruit or whipped cream on top. Bake a single layer in a 12-inch springform pan and frost top with whipped cream or wine-flavored fruit.

Elaine Leonard

Passover Chocolate Mousse Cake (Pareve)

Delicious; may be prepared in advance and frozen.

10	ounce can macaroons (sliced, reserve any crumbs)
8	ounces semisweet chocolate
3	egg yolks
3	tablespoons sugar
3	tablespoons coffee or water
4	egg whites
1/4	cup sweet wine (optional)

Line the bottom and sides of a greased 8-inch springform pan with 24 slices of macaroons. If desired, drizzle wine over the macaroons.

Melt chocolate in a double boiler. In a large bowl, combine egg yolks, sugar and coffee. Slowly blend chocolate into yolk mixture. Beat egg whites until stiff but not dry. Fold egg whites into the cooled chocolate mixture. Pour into the macaroon-lined pan. Refrigerate 2-3 hours or until set. Unmold and garnish with macaroon crumbs on top. Serves 8.

Variations: For a less sweet taste, bittersweet chocolate can be used.

Janet Weinstein Abelson

Chocolate/Nut Cake (Pareve)

Light, flavorful and freezes well.

9	eggs, separated
2	cups sugar
6	tablespoons water
2 1/2	teaspoons grated lemon rind
1/4	cup lemon juice
3/4	cup cake meal
3/4	cup potato starch
1/2	teaspoon salt
1 1/2	cups chopped nuts
3/4-1	cup semisweet chocolate chips or grated chocolate bar

In a large mixing bowl, beat egg yolks slightly. Gradually beat in sugar until the mixture is light and fluffy. Add water, lemon rind and lemon juice. Beat thoroughly. Gradually add cake meal and potato starch.

In a separate bowl, beat egg whites with salt until stiff but not dry. Fold nuts, chocolate and beaten egg whites into the rest of the ingredients. Pour into an ungreased 10-inch tube pan.

Bake in a preheated 325 degree oven for 1 1/2 hours or until cake springs back when touched gently. Invert pan and cool thoroughly before removing cake. Serves 16.

Elaine Schermer

Pesach Compote Cake (Pareve)

Light and moist, with a subtle, fruity flavor.

9	eggs, separated
1 1/3	cups sugar
2/3	cup cake meal
1/3	cup potato starch
1	cup cooked compote (from mixed dried fruits)
1/2	cup chopped walnuts

In a large mixing bowl, beat the egg whites, adding 1/3 cup sugar.

In a second large bowl, beat yolks, and add the remaining cup of sugar. Beat well. Add the cake meal, potato starch and cooked, mashed compote. Then add the nuts and fold in the beaten egg whites. Bake in an ungreased 10-inch tube pan for one hour at 325 degrees or microwave at 375 degrees for 10 minutes. Invert to cool. Serves 8 - 10.

Arlene Purchin

Chocolate Torte (Pareve)

An outstanding dessert.

Cake:

7	eggs, separated
7	tablespoons sugar
6	ounces semisweet chocolate
4	tablespoons water
4	teaspoons instant coffee, dissolved into 3 teaspoons water
2	cups ground walnuts

Frosting:

4	ounces pareve margarine
	Scant cup powdered sugar, Kosher for Passover
3-4	squares bittersweet chocolate
1	egg

Beat egg whites until stiff but not dry.

Mix yolks and sugar. Melt chocolate and 4 tablespoons water in a double boiler and add coffee mixture. Cool slightly and add chocolate to yolks. Blend thoroughly; add nuts to the chocolate mixture. Fold the stiffly beaten egg whites into the chocolate and nuts. Divide batter into two nonstick 9-inch cake pans. Bake for 30 minutes in a preheated 350 degree oven. Frost when cool.

To make frosting, beat margarine and sugar until smooth. Add melted chocolate and egg and beat again. Frost cake and garnish with chocolate shavings or curls. Serves 8 - 10.

Beverly Barak

Passover Wine Nut Cake (Pareve)

An excellent way to end a Seder.

12	eggs, separated
1	cup sugar
1	cup red wine
1	cup cake meal
1/2	teaspoon salt
1	teaspoon cinnamon
1	cup ground nuts

In a large bowl, beat egg yolks and sugar until very light. Add wine, cake meal, salt , cinnamon and nuts. Beat egg whites in a separate bowl until stiff; fold into yolk mixture. Pour into a 10-inch tube pan and bake in a preheated 325 degree oven for one hour. Invert and cool. Serve 8 - 10.

Mildred Pisarev Conradi

Decadent Chocolate Mousse Cake (Dairy)

Easy to make, freezes beautifully.

7   ounces semisweet chocolate bars
1/4   pound unsalted butter or margarine
7   eggs, separated
1   cup sugar
1   teaspoon vanilla extract

Melt chocolate and butter in a small pan. In a large bowl, beat the yolks and 3/4 cup sugar until fluffy (about 5 minutes). Slowly add the warm chocolate mixture and vanilla.

Beat egg whites and slowly add 1/4 cup sugar while beating until stiff peaks form. Fold the chocolate mixture into the egg whites. Pour 3/4 of the batter into a greased 9-inch springform pan.

Cover the remaining batter and refrigerate.

Bake the cake for 35 minutes in a preheated 325 degree oven.

Remove from oven and cool. (The cake will drop as it cools.) Remove the outside of the pan. Stir refrigerated batter to soften slightly and spread it on the top of the cake.

Refrigerate until firm. Garnish with chocolate leaves or chocolate shavings and chopped nuts. Serves 8 - 10.

Variation: To make this mousse pareve, use margarine in place of butter.

Ivy Liebross

Wine Nut Cake (Pareve)

My mother, Syd Cullen, made this dry, pareve cake for me as a child; it has been a family favorite ever since. It goes well with fruit salad.

7   eggs, separated
1   cup sugar
1/4   cup sweet red wine
1   cup chopped nuts
1/2   cup cake meal

In a large mixing bowl, beat egg yolks until lemon colored and very thick. Gradually beat in sugar and wine. Combine nuts and cake meal; add to yolk mixture.

Beat egg whites until stiff; fold into yolk mixture. Turn into an ungreased 10-inch tube pan and bake for 75 minutes at 325 degrees. Invert pan and let cool. Serves 8 - 10.

Variations: For a dairy meal, add freshly whipped cream in addition to the fruit. This cake can be used to make a trifle. Slice layers of cake, drizzled with wine and use Passover instant vanilla pudding (prepared according to directions), fresh berries and whipped cream arranged in layers. Top with whipped cream and slivered, toasted almonds.

Eleanor Botney

Sponge Cake (Pareve)

A very light, lemony, moist cake that my mother,
Rachel Morris, used to make with me.

12	eggs, separated
1 3/4	cups sugar, separated
3	heaping tablespoons cake meal, sifted
1/2	cup potato starch
	Juice from 1 1/2 medium lemons
1 1/2	teaspoons lemon rind, approximately

Do **not** preheat oven. In a large mixing bowl, beat the egg yolks very well. Gradually add 1 1/2 cups of sugar and continue beating until blended. Fold sifted cake meal and potato starch into the yolk mixture. Add the juice and lemon rind.

Beat the egg whites until stiff and slowly add remaining 1/4 cup sugar. Fold the egg whites into the yolk mixture. Pour batter into a 10-inch tube pan and place in a cold oven. Turn oven on to 350 degrees and bake for 1 hour. Invert and cool. Serves 8 - 10.

Suggestions: *Serve with fresh strawberries that have been drizzled with sweet wine. For a dairy meal, add whipped cream, too!*

Linda Spivack

Passover Date and Nut Bars (Pareve)

An easy, delicious, fat-free dessert.

3	eggs
1	cup sugar
2/3	cup, plus 2 tablespoons matzo meal
1	cup chopped dates
1	cup chopped nuts

In a large mixing bowl, beat the eggs well; add sugar and matzo meal. Add dates and nuts. Blend thoroughly. Pour into a greased 8 1/2-inch square pan. Bake for approximately 40 minutes in a preheated 350 degree oven until light brown. Cut into 2-inch squares with a sharp, wet knife while still very warm. Allow pan to cool thoroughly before removing squares to avoid crumbling. Yields 16 bars.

Gussie Cutter

Frozen Strawberry Meringue Torte (Pareve)

*This outstanding dessert is a welcome change
from sponge cake for dessert.*

Crust:

5	ounces almond macaroons (about 1 1/2 cups)
2	teaspoons melted margarine
1/2	cup chopped pecans or walnuts

Filling:

2	egg whites (room temperature)
1	cup sugar
2	cups sliced fresh strawberries
1	tablespoon lemon juice

Sauce:

1	10-ounce package frozen sliced strawberries
3	tablespoons frozen, undiluted orange juice concentrate
1	tablespoon currant jelly
1	cup sliced fresh strawberries

To make crust, process macaroons, margarine and nuts until mixture holds together. Press into a 10-inch springform pan and bake for 7-10 minutes in a preheated 350 degree oven. Cool.

In a bowl, beat on low speed the egg whites, sugar, strawberries and lemon juice until well blended. Increase speed to high and beat until stiff peaks form (about 10-15 minutes). Pour into cooled crust. Cover and freeze until firm (about 6 hours). Remove from freezer. (The crust with the filling may be frozen up to three weeks and served directly from the freezer.)

When ready to serve, puree sauce ingredients together and pour over each frozen slice of the torte. Serves 12.

Marla Gitig

Passover Kamish Bars (Pareve)

*My Canadian mother-in-law, Tillie Lasker, learned this recipe from
her mother, and it is a fourth-generation family favorite.*

2   cups sugar
6   eggs
2   cups oil
1 1/2 cups matzo meal
1/2   cup potato starch
1/2   teaspoon salt
2   teaspoons cinnamon
2   cups chopped walnuts

In a large mixing bowl, beat sugar and eggs until light in color. Add oil and beat. Add remaining dry ingredients. Fold in walnuts. Spread evenly into a greased 9x13-inch pan.

Bake for approximately 20 minutes in a preheated oven at 350 degrees, until golden brown. Cool. Cut into 1 1/2 by 2-inch oblong pieces.

After more cooling, place bars on a cookie sheet and dry them out in the oven until they are very crisp. For an electric oven, turn heat to 200 degrees, then to 150 degrees for drying out the baked bars. For a gas oven, set at "Warm" to dry out bars. Store in oven to retain crispness. Serves 12.

Jill Lasker

Chocolate Macaroons (Pareve)

*Delicious is the word for this special soft cookie,
which can really be used all year.*

1   6-ounce package semisweet chocolate chips
2   egg whites
1/4   teaspoon salt
1/2   cup sugar
1   8-ounce package coconut (2 2/3 cups lightly packed) *(can omit)*
1   teaspoon Passover vanilla

Melt chocolate chips in microwave oven. Cool.

Beat egg whites until stiff; gradually add salt and sugar. Beat well after each addition. Fold in melted chocolate. Fold in coconut and vanilla.

Bake one pan of cookies at a time. Drop dough by teaspoonsful on ungreased, foil-lined cookie sheet. Bake exactly 13 minutes in a preheated 325 degree oven.

Cool cookies completely before lifting them off the foil. Yields 3 1/2 - 4 dozen cookies.

Alice Pill

Fudge Brownies (Pareve)

A rich, chocolately brownie that is not overly sweet.

2-1 **ounces bittersweet chocolate bars**
1/2 **cup margarine**
4 **eggs**
1 1/3 **cups sugar**
1 **cup cake meal**
1 **cup chopped walnuts**

Melt chocolate and margarine in a double boiler.

In a large mixing bowl, beat eggs until thick and lemon colored. Gradually beat in sugar. Add the cooled chocolate mixture. Gradually add cake meal and beat until well blended. Stir in the chopped nuts. Spread the batter evenly in a well-greased 11x14-inch pan. Bake for 35 minutes in a preheated oven at 350 degrees.

Cut into 2-inch squares while still hot. Cool brownies after cutting. Yields approximately 3 dozen squares.

Variation: Diet bittersweet chocolate may be substituted for the regular chocolate.

Eleanor Einy

Passover Chocolate Chip Cookies (Pareve)

Cookieholics will love these!

3 **eggs**
1/2 **cup margarine**
1 **rounded cup sugar**
1 **cup cake meal**
1/4 **teaspoon salt**
1/2 **cup potato starch**
1 **10- to 12-ounce package chocolate chips**
3/4 **cup toasted walnuts or pecans**

Beat together eggs, margarine and sugar. Combine dry ingredients and add to egg mixture. Add chocolate chips and nuts; mix well. Drop by the spoonful on a greased cookie sheet. Bake for 10-15 minutes in a preheated 350 degree oven. Cookies should be a light golden brown.

Remove from pan quickly and cool. Store in an airtight container. These cookies freeze well. Yields 5 dozen.

Variation: Brown sugar may be used instead of regular sugar.

Adelaide Suplin

Passover Granola (Pareve)

Excellent as a breakfast cereal or snack.

16 ounces matzo farfel
4 eggs, beaten
1/2 cup brown sugar
1 teaspoon cinnamon, or to taste
2 cups nuts (almonds, pecans, walnuts), coarsely chopped
2 cups dried fruits (apricots, peaches, raisins), cut into small pieces

Mix all ingredients in a large bowl, except dried fruit. Grease large cookie sheet and spread farfel-nut mixture into single layer on sheet.

Bake for 45-60 minutes in a preheated 300 degree oven, stirring to break up when crisp. Remove from oven and cool. Add dried fruit and store in a covered container. Yields approximately 3 quarts.

Variation: Trail mix may be made by adding chocolate chips, chopped dates, coconut flakes or anything your family prefers.

Janet Weinstein Abelson

Pesach Candy (Pareve)

Children will have fun helping to form these bite-size goodies.

1 1/3 pounds dried apricots
1 1/3 pounds dried peaches
1 1/3 pounds dried pitted prunes
1/2 - 3/4 cup orange juice
1 pound ground walnuts

Finely grind the four pounds of assorted fruit in a processor or grinder. Add the orange juice.

With wet hands, roll into one-inch balls. Roll the balls in the ground nuts and place in a tightly covered can. Allow to mellow in the refrigerator for several days. Yields approximately 50 balls.

Eleanor Botney

Imberlach (Pareve)

A honey-gingered confection as addictive as peanut brittle.

6   cups matzo farfel
6   egg yolks
2   cups honey
1 1/2 cups sugar
1/2   cup chopped nuts
1 1/2 - 2 tablespoons
      ginger (to taste)
4   tablespoons sweet wine
      Chopped nuts

In a large bowl, mix farfel with egg yolks until coated.

In a large pot, boil honey and sugar. Add farfel immediately and stir constantly. Add nuts and ginger; continue cooking until honey does not stick to sides of the pan and is golden brown (pan sides will be "clean" as you mix).

Dampen a wooden board (15x18-inch) with cold water. Pour mixture on the board and flatten with the side of a dampened glass, until approximately 1/4-inch thick. Spread wine over candy. Add more ginger to taste, if necessary. With a very sharp knife, cut diagonal strips and then into diamond shapes. Dip each piece into a bowl of chopped nuts and place on a serving dish. Yields 80 - 100 pieces

Note: Cut candy immediately so that it doesn't harden. It is much more difficult when it is hard.

Adelaide Suplin

Ingberlach (Pareve)

This has been a favorite for many generations in our family; a "must" at the end of the Seder.

1   pound honey (1 1/3 cups)
2   tablespoons sugar
2   cups matzo farfel
1 1/2 cups finely chopped
      nuts
2   teaspoons ground
      ginger

In a saucepan, bring honey and sugar to a slow boil. Add farfel, nuts and ginger. Stir constantly until golden brown (about 10 minutes).

Spread the mixture on a dampened bread board.

Roll with a wet drinking glass until 1/4 inch thick. When hard, cut into squares or diamond shapes. Freezes well (layer between wax paper). This recipe doubles well. Yields about 36-40 one-inch diamond-shaped pieces.

Idele Deutsch

Appetizers

Appetizers cover a broad spectrum, from small tidbits to accompany drinks before meals, to first-course pastas, soups or salads. In addition, many appetizers work equally well as entrees when served in larger portions.

Appetizers are perfectly suited to a party — as casual or as elegant as your time and budget permit. For a lovely, less formal way to entertain, serve a variety of appetizers, cheeses, wines and nonalcoholic beverages, and you have a format that is appropriate for many different occasions, such as *havdalah* (the ceremony at the end of the Sabbath), *kiddush* (the midday luncheon following Saturday morning services), a reunion, bridal shower, reception or an adult birthday party.

This format works equally well for a small or large group. It is easy to prepare ahead, which makes it ideal for today's busy lifestyle.

HINTS

- If you are serving finger-food appetizers but want something more interesting than the traditional cracker, matzo or toast point to hold them, try stuffing cherry tomatoes, hard-cooked eggs, mushrooms, Belgian endive leaves or even dried fruits. For a first course served at the table, hollowed-out tomato, avocado, small cantaloupe halves or rings, or lemon or orange cups set on a lettuce leaf make attractive containers.

- As for garnishes, there is life beyond the parsley sprig! Roll soft cheeses in chopped nuts or interesting herbs for a more sophisticated flavor and presentation. To finger-held appetizers, add a bit of mint, cilantro, celery leaves, arugula, basil or chives for a variation in eye and taste appeal. Or try a thin slice of lemon, a few capers, some sliced olives or a bit of black, red or golden caviar — kosher, of course. The possibilities are truly endless.

Tex-Mex Dip (Dairy)

A crowd-pleaser; be sure guests leave room for dinner!

2	**4-ounce cans Jalapeño Bean dip**
3	**avocados**
1	**tablespoon lemon juice**
1/2	**teaspoon salt**
1	**cup sour cream**
1/2	**cup mayonnaise**
1	**package taco seasoning**
2	**cups green onions, chopped**
2	**2-ounce cans chopped black olives**
2	**cups chopped fresh tomatoes**
8	**ounces Cheddar cheese, shredded**
	Tortilla chips

Spread bean dip in large quiche dish or shallow bowl. Mash avocado well; add lemon juice and salt. Spread over bean dip.

Mix sour cream with mayonnaise and taco seasoning. Spread on the avocado layer.

Layer green onions on sour cream, then olives. Layer chopped tomatoes next, with shredded cheese spread evenly over all.

Refrigerate. Serve at room temperature with tortilla chips. Dig deep to get all of the flavors. Serves 12 - 15 generously.

Jill Lasker

Mushroom Appetizer (Dairy)

A rich and elegant dish for garlic lovers.

2	**pounds fresh mushrooms**
1/4	**pound butter or margarine**
1	**entire small bulb garlic, minced or pureed**
1	**cup Parmesan cheese**
1	**cup parsley, chopped**
1/4	**cup sauterne wine**

Slice mushrooms thinly; sauté mushrooms in butter, then add the rest of the ingredients. Mix thoroughly. Serve hot as a side dish or as an appetizer with toast points. Yields 2 cups.

Suggestion: *May be prepared in a microwave oven.*

Lynda Gentilcore

Mushroom Turnovers (Dairy)

An elegant and attractive recipe to make ahead and freeze.

Dough:

3	3-ounce packages cream cheese
1/2	cup butter
1 1/2	cups sifted flour

Mushroom Filling:

1/2	onion, chopped
2	tablespoons butter or margarine
1/4	pound fresh mushrooms, chopped
1/8	teaspoon thyme
1/4	teaspoon salt
1/8	teaspoon pepper
1 1/2	tablespoons flour
1/2	cup sour cream

Dough: Mix cream cheese and butter or margarine together. Cut in flour with a pastry blender until lumps are like small peas. Form dough into a ball. Wrap in plastic wrap and refrigerate overnight.

Mushroom Filling: Sauté chopped onions in butter or margarine until lightly browned. Add chopped mushrooms, thyme, salt and pepper. Cook for 5 minutes, stirring frequently to keep from burning. Sprinkle flour into mixture and stir well.

Reduce heat; stir in sour cream and cook until the mixture thickens. Cool, then chill.

To assemble: Cut pastry into 2 parts. Roll out pastry until 1/8 inch thick and cut into 3-inch rounds. Place about 1/2 teaspoon of filling on each round; wet the edges, fold over and press edges closed with a fork. Prick the top crusts with a fork. Chill.

Bake in a 425 degree oven for about 15 minutes. Yields approximately 30 - 40.

Variations: *Turnovers may be made and frozen on a cookie sheet. Package in airtight containers and bake as needed. If frozen, bake longer.*

Ruth King

Pickled Mushrooms (Pareve)

These will keep 6-8 weeks,
although they usually get gobbled up much sooner.

1/3	cup dry white wine
1/3	cup white wine vinegar
1/3	cup salad oil
1/4	cup green onion, finely chopped
2	tablespoons snipped parsley
1	clove garlic, cut up
1	bay leaf
1	teaspoon salt
	Dash pepper
1/4	teaspoon dried thyme, crushed
1	12-ounce can whole mushrooms, drained

In a saucepan, combine all ingredients except mushrooms. Bring to a boil. Add mushrooms and return to a boil. Simmer, uncovered, 8-10 minutes.

Cool and store in a covered container in the refrigerator until ready to serve. Yields 2 pints.

Elinor Einy

Herring Salad Appetizer (Pareve)

This recipe works equally well as an hors d'oeuvre or first course.

1	large red onion
3	ribs celery
1	green bell pepper
1	yellow bell pepper
1	red bell pepper
1/4	cup chopped parsley
2	cups "flat fillet" herring
4-5	hard-cooked eggs
1	tablespoon salad oil
2	slices rye bread, soaked in 2 tablespoons red wine vinegar
2	whole apples, preferably green
	Sugar, cinnamon, nutmeg, dill (optional) and salt, to taste

Chop vegetables. Add oil, bread, apple, herring and egg and continue chopping until mixture resembles a coarse relish. Add seasonings to taste. Mix well. Yields 5 - 6 cups.

Suggestions: *Serve with crackers, stuff in cherry tomatoes, or spoon into hollowed-out lemon cups set on a lettuce leaf for an attractive first course.*

Bebe Simon

Old-Fashioned Herring Salad (Dairy)

A German dish traditionally served at "Anbeissen"
(break-the-fast following Yom Kippur).

2	pounds (32 ounces) herring snacks in wine sauce
2	red potatoes, boiled and peeled
3	hard-boiled eggs
2	dill pickles
1	16-ounce can pickled red beets, drained
3	apples, cored and peeled
1	tablespoon sugar
1	cup walnuts, optional
12	ounces sour cream Additional diced beets, pickles and hard-boiled eggs

Dice all ingredients (if food processor is available, use a metal blade and "pulse" each item separately).

Mix all ingredients together in a large bowl and refrigerate overnight.

Before serving, decorate the top of the mixture with additional diced beets, pickles, hard-boiled egg whites and hard-boiled egg yolks, in pie-shaped wedges, alternating red, green, white and yellow. Yields 24 portions.

Bea Reynolds

Chopped Herring with Sour Cream (Dairy)

An old favorite that goes back at least three generations in my family.

Herring:

1	12-ounce jar wine snack fillets of herring
2	slices rye bread White vinegar (for soaking)
1	small onion, finely chopped
1	green apple, peeled and cored
1	hard-boiled egg

Rinse herring well under cold water. Soak rye bread in vinegar; squeeze out excess. Finely chop all ingredients together and mix well. Turn into a 4-cup serving dish.

Pour sauce on top and refrigerate. Yields approximately 3 cups.

Sam Wigoda

Sauce:
2/3	cup sour cream
1/3	cup white vinegar

Chopped Herring Appetizer (Pareve)

A traditional favorite.

1	pound jar herring fillets in wine sauce
2	dry small slices challah
2	hard-boiled eggs
1	small apple, peeled and cored
1	small onion, cut in quarters

Drain and save liquid from herring and soak bread in liquid. Put herring, eggs, apple and onion into a blender or food processor. Squeeze liquid from bread and add to the rest of the ingredients. Chop fine.

Refrigerate. Serve with party rye or crackers. Yields 2 1/2 cups.

Mona Lapides

Chinese Meatballs (Meat)

A nice chafing-dish recipe.

Meatballs:

1	egg
1/2	cup water
1/2	cup bread crumbs
1	cup water chestnuts, minced
2	tablespoons white horseradish
1	pound lean ground beef

Sauce:

2/3	cup apricot jam
1	clove garlic, minced
1/2	cup soy sauce
2/3	cup water
1	tablespoon lemon juice

Meatballs: Combine all ingredients. Form small balls and place in a baking dish. Bake at 350 degrees for 30 minutes.

Sauce: Combine all ingredients in a saucepan. Heat until the mixture comes to a boil, stirring constantly. Cook for 3 minutes.

Add baked meatballs to the sauce and heat for 15 minutes. Best if refrigerated overnight or for several hours before serving. Heat to serve. Yields approximately 30 1-inch meatballs.

Suggestion: To reduce salt content, light soy sauce can be substituted for regular soy sauce.

Ruth King

Oriental Chicken Wings (Meat)

Can be an hors d'oeuvre or a main dish.

2	pounds chicken wings
1/4	cup sugar
1	tablespoon ground ginger
1/4	cup soy sauce
1/4	cup oil
2	tablespoons molasses
2	cloves crushed garlic
	Salt to taste
1/2	teaspoon dry mustard or to taste

Put wings in pan in single layer. Mix remaining ingredients together and pour over wings. Bake, uncovered, in a 350 degree oven for about 60 minutes. Serves 3 - 4 as a main dish.

Ingrid Blumenstein

Sweet-and-Sour Meatballs (Meat)

Freezes well and can be prepared ahead.

Meatballs:

1 1/4	pound ground beef
1	medium onion, grated
1	egg
8	soda crackers, crushed
1/2-3/4 cup water	
	Salt and pepper, to taste
1	cup chopped onion
2	tablespoons margarine or oil

Sauce:

2	cups ginger ale
1	cup ketchup
1/2	cup brown sugar, or less

In a large bowl, combine beef, onion, egg, crackers and enough water to moisten cracker crumbs. Add salt and pepper to taste and roll into bite-size balls. Brown meatballs and chopped onion in margarine or oil in skillet and drain on paper towels.

In the same skillet, stir together ginger ale, ketchup and brown sugar. Add meatballs and onion. Simmer lightly for 50-60 minutes until sauce thickens and is reduced. Stir frequently to prevent burning. Yields 40 medium meatballs.

Diane Tapper

Chopped Liver (Meat)

A classic meat grinder recipe; serve it with party rye or assorted crackers.

1	pound calf's liver, broiled and sliced
3	medium onions, sliced
4	large hard-cooked eggs
1/4	cup oil
	Salt, pepper and garlic powder, to taste

Sauté sliced onions in oil until golden. Remove from pan.

When liver, onions and eggs are cool, grind together twice; season to taste with salt, pepper and garlic powder. Serves 8 - 10.

Dotty Simmons

Mock Chopped Liver (Pareve)

A classic Jewish favorite goes modern in this delicious version.

4   **medium onions, sauteed**
4   **eggs, hard-boiled**
1   **17-ounce can peas, drained**
1/2   **cup walnuts, chopped**
      Salt and pepper, to taste

Blend all ingredients in a food processor or in a chopping bowl by hand. Serve a scoop of the chopped liver on a lettuce leaf. Yields approximately 3 - 4 cups.

Bebe Simon

Artichoke Appetizer (Dairy)

Makes a nice first course or hors d'oeuvre if cut in smaller portions.

1/2   **pound sharp Cheddar cheese**
12   **soda crackers**
1/2   **cup parsley, packed**
1   **clove garlic**
2   **6-ounce jars marinated artichoke hearts, drained**
4   **eggs**
1/4   **teaspoon salt**
1/8   **teaspoon pepper**
      Dash cayenne pepper

Grate cheese and set aside. Process crackers and set aside. Process parsley and garlic and leave in the processor bowl. Add artichoke hearts and then rest of ingredients. Turn on and off until blended, but not smooth; mixture should have bits of artichoke.

Pour into a greased, 8-inch square pan. Bake for 30-35 minutes at 325 degrees. Cut into 2-inch squares. Serve hot or at room temperature. Yields 16 pieces.

Variation: Add 1/4 cup chopped raw or sautéed onion.

Ruth Nebron

Artichoke Dip (Dairy)

If you like garlic, you'll love this one.

2   **10-ounce packages frozen artichoke hearts**
1   **cup mayonnaise**
1   **cup grated Parmesan cheese**
6   **cloves garlic, minced, or 6 tablespoons garlic puree (or to taste)**
      Parmesan cheese for sprinkling

Steam artichokes until tender. Drain and cut into thirds or small pieces. Blend with mayonnaise, Parmesan cheese and garlic.

Place in oven-proof dish and bake for 20 minutes in a 350 degree oven or until hot and bubbly. Sprinkle with more cheese. Serve with crackers. Serves 4 - 6.

Suggestion: Can be made ahead and then popped in the oven just before serving. Watch out—this is really "hot" stuff!

Linda Krasnoff

Eggplant "Caviar" (Pareve)

An updated version of this Middle Eastern classic
that can be served as a salad, salad dressing or a dip.

1	large eggplant (1-2 pounds)
1	medium onion, chopped fine (about 1 cup)
6	tablespoons olive oil
2	large cloves garlic, minced (or more to taste)
1/2	cup green bell pepper, minced
1/4	cup tomato paste or 2 tomatoes, peeled and chopped
1	teaspoon lemon juice
1	teaspoon wine vinegar, or to taste
	Salt and pepper, to taste

Preheat oven to 400 degrees. Pierce eggplant with fork and bake for 1 hour or until soft.

Sauté onions in 3 tablespoons oil in a 10- or 12-inch frying pan until soft and golden. Add garlic and bell pepper. Cook until soft.

Peel eggplant and chop; add to pan. Add rest of the oil. Cook 15-20 minutes until thick. Add tomatoes and/or tomato paste, lemon juice, vinegar, salt and pepper. Refrigerate.

Serve with crackers, pita wedges or rye bread pieces. Yields 4 - 6 cups, according to the size of the eggplant.

Variation: Can use both tomato paste and tomatoes if you like a strong tomato flavor.

Eve Marcus

Egg/Caviar Appetizer (Pareve)

A glamorous party dish.

1 1/4	envelopes unflavored gelatin
3	tablespoons lemon juice
1	tablespoon vermouth
1/2	teaspoon anchovy paste
1	medium onion
1/2	teaspoon Diablo/ Escoffier sauce, optional
1	cup mayonnaise
9	hard-boiled eggs
1	4-ounce jar kosher black caviar
	Nonstick cooking spray

In a small bowl, sprinkle gelatin over lemon juice and vermouth. Add anchovy paste and stir over hot water.

Chop onion in blender or food processor. Add the rest of the ingredients, except caviar, and mix well. Do not process eggs too long.

Pour mixture into a 4-cup ring mold sprayed with nonstick cooking spray. Refrigerate until firm.

Unmold on a platter and serve with a bowl of caviar in the center. Serves 12 - 20.

Ann Lauterbach

Cheese Balls (Dairy)

A glamorous recipe that can be made ahead and frozen.

1	pound hoop cheese
2	eggs
3	tablespoons flour
2	tablespoons sugar
	Pinch of salt
16	graham cracker squares, crushed
1/4	pound margarine, melted
1	small bottle maraschino cherries
1	pint sour cream

Beat cheese, eggs, flour, sugar and salt until creamy. Refrigerate to chill well; at least one hour.

Mix crushed graham cracker crumbs with melted margarine and put aside in a flat dish. Bring 4 quarts of water to a boil. Wet hands and form cheese mixture into walnut-sized balls. Drop balls into boiling water and cook 3-5 minutes. Remove with a slotted spoon as soon as balls rise to the top of the water.

Roll in crumbs and margarine until well coated. Place coated balls in a greased, flat baking pan. Bake in the oven for 30-35 minutes at 350 degrees.

Sauce: Chop maraschino cherries and add to sour cream with sufficient maraschino juice to thin the sour cream to pouring consistency.

Remove balls from the oven and serve immediately with sauce. Yields 24 - 30.

Note: Cheese balls may be frozen after rolling in graham cracker crumbs and baked when needed. DO NOT THAW.

Ruth King

Eggplant Dip (Pareve)

Unusual spices make this a memorable dip.

1	pound eggplant
1	large clove garlic, minced
1	teaspoon cumin powder
1	teaspoon paprika
2	tablespoons cider vinegar
1	tablespoon olive oil
1	tablespoon ketchup
1	tablespoon chili powder
	Salt and pepper, to taste

Preheat oven to 400 degrees. Pierce whole eggplant with fork and place on the middle rack of oven and bake until very soft; cool.

Peel skin and mash the soft pulp with remaining ingredients in a food processor or with a fork. Serve with crackers, matzos or rye rounds. Yields approximately 2 - 3 cups.

Beverly Barak

Cheese Puffs (Dairy)

A quickie to make; may be frozen prior to baking.

1/2   **pound sharp Cheddar cheese**
6   **ounces cream cheese**
1/2   **pound unsalted butter**
4   **egg whites, beaten stiff**
1   **large loaf unsliced bread**

Melt cheeses and butter in double boiler. When cool, fold in beaten egg whites. Cut all crusts off bread and cut into 1-inch cubes. Dip bread in cheese mixture and place on ungreased cookie sheet. Refrigerate overnight.

Bake 10-12 minutes in a 400 degree oven. Serve warm. Yields approximately 10 - 12 dozen.

Variation: Different cheeses and breads vary the taste. Lots of fun with which to experiment.

Rosalie Weiner

Cheese Slices (Dairy)

May be prepared several days ahead of time.

1   **cup flour**
2   **cups shredded Cheddar cheese**
1/2   **cup margarine**
2   **tablespoons onion soup mix (pareve)**

Mix ingredients until blended. Form into a roll approximately 1 1/2 inches in diameter. Chill at least 2 hours.

Slice into 1/2-inch pieces and bake on an ungreased baking sheet at 325 degrees for 10-12 minutes. Yields approximately 24 - 30.

Wendy Winnick

Onion Cheese Puffs (Dairy)

Cheese mixture can be stored in a crock and baked when guests arrive.

1   **cup mayonnaise**
1   **cup Parmesan cheese, shredded**
1/2   **cup onion, grated**
1   **tablespoon milk**
  Rye crackers

Mix together first 4 ingredients and spread on crackers. Put under broiler for 2 minutes or in the oven at 350 degrees, until light brown. Yields approximately 2 cups.

Ingrid Blumenstein

Savory Cheese Puffs (Dairy)

*A wonderful do-ahead recipe to have in the freezer
for unexpected guests.*

8   ounces whipped cream
    cheese
2   eggs
2   teaspoons lemon juice
2   teaspoons frozen or
    dried chives, or fresh
    chopped
1   cup white Cheddar
    cheese, shredded
1   package frozen pastry
    shells
    Dash pepper
    Dash garlic powder
    Milk or beaten eggs

Combine cream cheese, eggs,
lemon juice, chives, pepper and
garlic powder; beat well. Stir in
Cheddar cheese; chill.

On floured board, roll each
pastry shell to a 8x4-inch rectangle. Cut into 2-inch squares (8 to
a shell). Top each square with
rounded teaspoon of filling.
Brush edges with milk or beaten
egg. Twist ends together to make
1-inch ball-shaped puffs. Brush
with egg or milk. Place on ungreased cookie sheet 1 inch apart.
Chill 2-3 hours or freeze (defrost
before baking). Bake at 450 degrees for 12-15 minutes until
golden. Yields 40 - 48 pieces.

*Variations: May add chopped
spinach, pimiento or chopped chilies.*

Elaine Brown

Greek Spinach Dip (Dairy)

A quick and easy, low-cholesterol recipe.

1   10-ounce package frozen
      chopped spinach
1   cup nonfat yogurt
1   teaspoon dry dill weed
1/2   teaspoon onion powder
1   tablespoon lemon juice

Thaw spinach. Press as much
liquid out of spinach as possible.
Combine it with other ingredients. Cover and refrigerate.
Serve with raw vegetables or
crackers. Yields 1 1/3 cups.

*Can add garlic powder or Tabasco
sauce if desired.*

Myra Newman

Tangy Vegetable Dip (Pareve)

An easy dip that is good with raw vegetables.

1/2	teaspoon dry mustard
1	cup mayonnaise
2	tablespoons chili sauce
2	tablespoons lime juice
1	tablespoon minced parsley
3	tablespoons minced pimiento-stuffed olives
3	tablespoons minced sweet pickles
1	tablespoon minced onion
1/4	teaspoon Tabasco sauce (more if desired)

Blend 2 tablespoons of mayonnaise with mustard. Mix together rest of ingredients, including remainder of mayonnaise. Yields approximately 2 cups.

Honey Katz

Ceviche (Pareve)

An easy-to-prepare dish that takes advantage of California's abundant fresh fish.

3	pounds halibut, fresh or frozen (if boneless, use about 1 1/2 to 2 pounds)
1	cup lime juice, fresh or bottled
1	pound canned tomatoes, broken into pieces, with juice
1	3-ounce jar pimiento-stuffed olives, drained
1	medium onion, chopped
1/2	cup ketchup
1/2	cup olive oil
1	teaspoon leaf oregano, crumbled
1	scant teaspoon bottled red pepper seasoning
1	teaspoon salt Avocado, if desired

The night before: Trim skin and bones from halibut. Cut into 1/2-inch cubes. Place in a deep bowl (glass or china). Pour lime juice over top to cover fish. Cover and chill overnight.

The next day: Drain fish; rinse under cold water; place in a large bowl. Add all other ingredients and toss lightly.

May be topped with avocado. Serve with tortilla chips. Serves 10 - 12.

Variation: *Fresh tomato may be added if desired. Red snapper, salmon or tuna can be substituted for halibut.*

Judy Breitstein

Pastels (Meat)

Taught to me by a lovely Moroccan lady.
They make an elegant appetizer and freeze well.

Filling:

1	**pound ground beef or lamb**
2	**cups water**
2	**bay leaves**
1	**medium onion, cut up**
1/2	**teaspoon salt**
2	**tablespoons lemon juice**
1/8	**teaspoon pepper**
3/4	**teaspoon ground cinnamon**

Dough:

1/2	**pound filo dough leaves**
	Melted margarine

Mix all filling ingredients together, except lemon juice and cinnamon. Put into a saucepan and cook, uncovered, stirring occasionally until water evaporates. Remove bay leaves.

Put mixture through a meat grinder or finely chop by hand. Add juice and cinnamon. Adjust seasonings. Cool.

To assemble: Fold a sheet of filo dough in half crosswise. Cut in 4 sections, horizontally. Cut the four sections in half. Place 1 teaspoon filling on one corner of each strip. Fold corner over to form triangle; continue folding over in form of triangle until entire strip is used. Place on cookie sheet. (At this point, Pastels may be frozen).

To bake, preheat oven to 400 degrees. Brush room-temperature or frozen Pastels with melted margarine. Bake for 15-20 minutes (20-30 minutes if frozen) until lightly golden brown. Yields 50 pieces.

Claire Gering

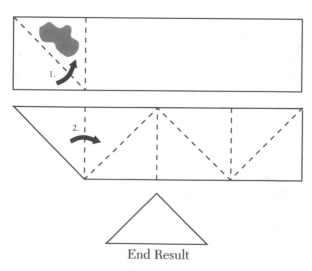

End Result

- - - - Indicates fold of pastry dough

Molly's Knishes (Pareve)

An easy adaptation of a traditional dish. Everyone loves them!
They freeze well, making them ideal for entertaining.

Dough:

4	cups flour
2	teaspoons baking powder
1/2	teaspoon salt
2	cups vegetable shortening
1 1/2	cups water
4	egg yolks

Potato Filling:

4	pounds potatoes
2-3	onions, finely cut
2-3	eggs, beaten (optional)
	Vegetable oil
	Salt and pepper to taste
1	heaping tablespoon pareve chicken soup mix (optional)
1	beaten egg
1	teaspoon water

Dough: Sift together flour, baking powder and salt. Cut shortening into flour mixture until crumbly. Beat water and egg yolks together and add to dry ingredients. Form dough into a large ball. Place in bowl and cover with plastic wrap. Refrigerate overnight.

Filling: Peel and cook potatoes for mashing. Meanwhile, sauté onion in the vegetable oil until very lightly golden brown. Drain onions well and save the oil. When potatoes are cooked, drain well and mash. Add onions, beaten eggs and seasonings to taste (1 heaping tablespoon pareve chicken soup mix adds a good flavor).

The next day divide dough into 6 parts, forming small balls. Roll each ball of dough very thin on a well-floured board, making a 15x15-inch square. Put filling along one edge of dough and roll, jelly-roll fashion, sealing to opposite edge of roll. Pinch each end to seal.

Cut into 1 1/2- to 2-inch pieces, using the side of your hand in a slicing motion. Using drained oil, grease hands to lightly cover knishes with the oil. Lightly brush tops of knishes with beaten egg mixed with one teaspoon water. Place, cut edge down, on ungreased pan and bake in a preheated oven at 350 degrees until golden brown (approximately 20-25 minutes). Yields approximately 90 small pieces.

Suggestion: *There are many fillings that can be substituted. Liver, cheese or potatoes are favorites. The dough also can be used for strudels.*
Commercially prepared puff pastry may be sustituted for dough.

Mary Kovshoff

Yaprakes, or Grape Leaves Stuffed with Meat and Rice (Meat)

A popular staple of Sephardic cuisine.
Traditionally served for Sukkot and at most life-cycle celebrations.

Grape Leaves:

1	**pound fresh, frozen or bottled grape leaves**
1	**pound lean beef or lamb, or both, browned**
1/4	**cup uncooked rice, washed and drained**
1/4	**cup tomato sauce or chopped fresh tomato**
	Salt to taste
	Pinch allspice
1/4-1/2	**cup chopped parsley**
1	**tablespoon oil**
1/4	**cup sauteed pine nuts (optional)**

Sauce:

	Water to cover
2	**tablespoons tomato sauce**
1	**tablespoon oil**
	Juice of 1-2 lemons

Rinse each grape leaf; remove tough stem; drape around edge of colander to drain. Mix together lightly the meat, rice, tomato sauce, seasoning, parsley, oil and nuts (too much handling makes the mixture tough). Spread out each grape leaf, bottom side up. Fill with about a tablespoon of the filling and roll loosely to allow rice to puff, tucking in sides. Place rolls in a pan lined with extra grape leaves. Arrange rolls close together to prevent them from falling apart. Over all, pour the mixture of water, tomato sauce and oil to cover 1/4 the depth of the pan. Cook slowly over low heat for 1 hour in a covered pan. If using a deep pan, place a heatproof plate over Yaprakes to keep them in place. Add more sauce if necessary, but not enough to make the Yaprakes soggy. After cooking slowly for 1 hour, add lemon juice and bake, uncovered, for 30 minutes in a 350 degree oven. Yields 30 Yaprakes.

Stella Rugeti

Soups

Soups are a model of versatility. Traditionally, they are the appetizer before a formal dinner, but they are often the hearty main course for a homey lunch or supper and can even be served as dessert, as in the case of cold fruit soup. They can be served in cups or mugs with a cracker or a round of bread, and offered to guests as a nice, nonalcoholic alternative start to a dinner party. From clear, delicate broth to hearty, rib-sticking stew, soups run the gamut from elegant to casual, from intricate to easy.

Some cooks feel they "can't be bothered" with home-made soups, yet they are really very easy to prepare, as well as inexpensive and more nutritious. Most use only one pot, require very little attention while simmering, taste better when prepared in advance and freeze beautifully. Some meat-based soups (like that Jewish classic, chicken soup) yield a bonus; the meat is cooked in the broth, then removed from the bones to be used another day while the bones are returned to the pot to flavor the soup. Most soup recipes are very flexible, so you can easily adapt them to reduce calories, sodium, fat or cholesterol, or to increase their fiber content. Many wonderful soups use inexpensive ingredients — cheaper cuts of meat, dried beans, grains or peas, root vegetables — which tenderize and taste divine after a long, slow cooking process. And few things smell as wonderful as a pot of soup, laden with savory spices, simmering on the stove on a chilly day.

Use the recipes here as a starting point only, because very few soups must be prepared precisely any one way to turn out well. Most of the fun in making soup is in "tinkering around" with it. Just remember your embellishments in case your family thinks it is the best soup you ever made or somebody asks you for the recipe!

My Mother's Chicken Soup (Meat)

A healthier version of the traditional chicken soup for
Shabbat and holidays, loved by one and all.
It is also famous as the "Jewish cure-all."

1	chicken (5-6 pounds), including feet, gizzard and heart
3 1/2	quarts cold water
1	onion, cut lengthwise in quarters
1	leek, sliced lengthwise and tied (white only)
2	carrots, sliced lengthwise
2	parsnips, sliced lengthwise
2	whole celery stalks, cut into 4 parts
	A few cut celery leaves
1	tablespoon salt
	Small bunch parsley, tied

Put chicken in pot with cold water. Bring to a boil, skimming off the foam. Add vegetables, except parsley. Cover pot and simmer for 45 minutes. Toward the end of the cooking time, add parsley. Continue cooking until chicken is tender; remove leek, parsley and onion. Refrigerate to harden fat.

Discard fat. Heat to serve. Serves 8 - 10.

Note: Some cooks prefer to add vegetables, including brown onions with the skin, the last half hour of cooking time to improve clarity, color and flavor.

Suggestion: Delicious served with matzo balls, kreplach, rice, noodles or any combination of the above.

Eleanor Kagan

Matzo Balls #1 (Pareve)

Cholesterol free, low sodium and low fat.
A Passover classic made healthier.

4	egg whites
1/2	cup matzo meal
2	teaspoons dried onions
1/2	teaspoon cinnamon
1	teaspoon dried parsley
1/4	teaspoon white pepper

In a mixing bowl, beat egg whites until stiff. Fold in mixture of matzo meal and seasonings. Let stand 15 minutes. Form in walnut-size balls, using mixture of water and oil to lubricate hands.

Drop balls in boiling salted water. Cover pot and simmer for 30 minutes. Remove from burner and let stand for 30 minutes. Remove from water with slotted spoon, add to soup and heat. Yields 10 medium-size balls.

Note: Matzo balls freeze well.

Ida Liberman

Matzo Balls #2 (Pareve)

A favorite of the family for Shabbat and all holidays.

2	tablespoons oil
2	eggs, slightly beaten
1/2	cup matzo meal
1	teaspoon salt
2	tablespoons kosher club soda
1	tablespoon parsley, finely minced

Mix oil with eggs. Add matzo meal and salt. Blend well. Add club soda and parsley. Cover and place in the refrigerator for at least 20 minutes.

Using a three-quart pot, bring salted water to a rapid boil.

Make balls by rolling batter in your hands, using water to moisten palms. Drop into boiling water. Lower heat and cover pot, tilting cover slightly, and cook for 30-40 minutes. Yields approximately 8 balls.

Variation: *For matzo balls lower in calories, omit oil.*

Note: *Leftover matzo balls may be served another time, browned in margarine or oil. They become a nice accompaniment to another meal. Refrigerate thoroughly before frying or they will fall apart.*

Dotty Simmons

Meat Kreplach (Meat)

This recipe can be easily duplicated with one exception; you have to add the memory of your own mother's kreplach on Rosh Hashanah.

Filling:

1/2	**pound ground meat**
1/4	**teaspoon black pepper, or to taste**
1/2	**teaspoon garlic salt, or to taste**
1/2	**teaspoon dill weed, or to taste**
1/4	**medium onion, finely chopped, optional**

Dough:

2	**eggs**
1/4	**cup water**
1/2	**teaspoon salt**
2	**cups all-purpose flour**

Beat eggs. Add water and salt. Add flour to egg mixture. Mix to blend. Knead into a soft dough. Roll out on a floured board to the thickness of poster board. Cut into 2-inch squares.

To make filling: Sauté onion in no-stick frying pan until glossy. Mix in ground meat, pepper, garlic salt and dill weed; set aside.

Place a teaspoon of filling in the center of each square and fold into triangles. Pinch edges together to seal. Press tine of fork around edges to extra-seal and decorate. (Kreplach can be frozen at this point. Place on a floured cookie sheet and when frozen, place in a plastic bag.)

To cook kreplach, bring 4 quarts of salted water to a boil. Cook kreplach for about 20 minutes. Remove and place directly into the completed chicken soup.

To serve as an appetizer or side dish, after boiling, drain on paper toweling. Place on a greased cookie sheet. Bake for 20-25 minutes at 350 degrees or until brown. Brush with melted pareve margarine. Yields approximately 36 kreplach.

Phyllis Sarto

Traditional Meat Kreplach (Meat)

A holiday favorite served with clear chicken soup.

Dough:

2	cups flour
2	eggs
1/2	teaspoon salt
2	tablespoons cold water

Filling:

1	pound beef (flanken or chuck), cut into large pieces
3	onions, chopped
2	cloves garlic, minced
1	teaspoon salt
1/4	pound chicken livers (approximately 2 livers)
3	tablespoons shortening: oil, chicken fat or pareve margarine
2	onions, chopped
	Salt, pepper
1	slice challah
1	egg

Dough: In a food processor bowl put flour, eggs and salt. Process while slowly adding water until a ball is formed. Wrap in plastic wrap and let rest for 30 minutes. Using a pasta machine, roll out as for thin noodle dough or roll out by hand to 1/8-inch thickness.

Filling: Put beef, 1 onion, 1 clove garlic and salt in heavy pot with 2 tablespoons water, tightly covered, and cook slowly for 2 hours on low heat until ingredients are very soft and liquid has cooked away, adding small amount of water only if necessary.

Brown livers lightly in pan with 1 tablespoon shortening.

Brown two onions in 2 tablespoons shortening. Cook until very soft. Add remaining garlic. Season with salt and pepper.

Cool all the filling ingredients and place everything, including any juices or gravy that may have formed, in food processor bowl. Process until coarse paste is formed. Add egg and challah; process until mixed. Adjust seasonings.

To make Kreplach: Cut dough into approximately 2-inch squares. Place 1 rounded teaspoon filling on each. Fold into triangle and pinch together to seal edges. Boil large pot of water with 1 tablespoon salt. Add 10-12 kreplach at a time. Boil 5-10 minutes, depending on thickness of dough. Repeat until all are done, adding water to pot as needed.

To serve, cook 1 minute in hot chicken soup until heated through or fry in shortening to serve as side dish. Yields 30 - 50 kreplach, according to size.

Note: Also freezes well.

Eve Marcus

75

Cockaleekie (Meat)

This is the Scottish version of "Chicken in the Pot."

1	**4-5 pound chicken, cut in quarters**
3 1/2	**quarts cold water**
1	**teaspoon salt**
1/2	**teaspoon white pepper**
3	**stalks celery, cut up**
1	**parsnip, whole**
2	**bay leaves**
1	**cup uncooked rice**
3	**large leeks, sliced (white part only; wash thoroughly to remove sand)**

Place chicken in a large pot and cover with cold water. Bring to a boil. Skim off foam. Add seasoning, vegetables and bay leaves. Simmer gently until chicken is tender (about 2 hours).

Remove chicken, vegetables and bay leaves from the pot. Refrigerate the broth to harden fat. Discard fat.

Heat broth; add rice and leeks. Cook for another 25 minutes. While soup is cooking, remove all the chicken from the bones and cut into small pieces. Discard skin, bones and vegetables. Add chicken pieces to soup and cook another 10 minutes. Taste to correct the seasoning. Serves 8 - 10.

Suggestion: *Freezes well.*

Marilyn Smith

Chicken in a Pot, Japanese Style (Meat)

This won rave reviews.

6	ounces dry Japanese noodles, either Soba (buckwheat) or Udon (wheat)
9	fresh black Chinese mushrooms or 2 ounces dried Chinese or European mushrooms
2	quarts strained, defatted chicken broth
12	ounces uncooked breast of chicken, skinned and cut into pieces, about 2x2 1/2 inches
1	cup carrots, thinly sliced
6	large leaves Napa (Chinese) cabbage, cut into 2-inch squares
1	8-ounce can bamboo shoots, drained
3	green onions, cut into 2-inch lengths
12	ounces firm tofu, drained, cut into 1-inch cubes
1	tablespoon dry Sherry Dash of pepper
1/2	cup chopped parsley
1	tablespoon soy sauce, optional (if stronger flavor is desired)

Cook noodles according to package directions, drain and set aside.

Prepare dry mushrooms according to package directions or cut fresh mushrooms in half. In a 6-quart pot, heat chicken broth and gently simmer raw chicken and carrots for 15 minutes. Add Napa cabbage, bamboo shoots, mushrooms and green onions. Simmer 5 minutes. Add tofu, noodles, sherry, pepper and soy sauce, if desired. Simmer uncovered for 10 minutes or until tofu and noodles are thoroughly heated.

Serve in large soup bowls, and sprinkle with 1 tablespoon chopped parsley. Serves 6.

Suggestion: *Serve with a crisp salad seasoned with vegetable oil and rice vinegar, as is the custom in Japan. Fresh fruit makes an ideal dessert.*

Eleanor Gold Hirsch

Bean Barley Soup (Pareve)

A family favorite from my daughter, Judy Rosen.

1 1/4	cups Great Northern beans, soaked 1 hour
1	cup pearl barley
1	onion, chopped
5	mushrooms, sliced
1/4	cup safflower oil
1/4-1/2	cup vegetarian chicken soup mix
10	cups water
1	leek, washed and sliced
1	carrot, sliced
1/2	cup chopped parsley
1	zucchini, cut in small chunks
1	tomato, sliced

In a large soup pot, add beans, barley, onion, mushrooms, oil and soup mix to the water. Bring to boil; lower heat and simmer 1 hour. Add leek, carrot, parsley and zucchini. Cook another 10 minutes. Stir in tomato just before serving. Serves 8 - 10.

Janet Arzt

Lentil Soup (Pareve)

This delicious vegetarian soup can be made in a pressure cooker or regular soup pot.

4	tablespoons oil
1	cup finely diced celery
1	cup finely diced carrots
1/3	cup chopped onions
2	cups lentils (thoroughly washed in a sieve under running water)
6	cups water
2 1/4	cups stewed tomatoes
2	teaspoons salt
2	teaspoons sugar
1/4	teaspoon black pepper
4	whole cloves
1	small bay leaf

Sauté celery, onion and carrots in oil in 6-quart pressure cooker, approximately 4 minutes. Add lentils with all the remaining ingredients. Cook at 15 pounds pressure for 40 minutes. Cool cooker quickly according to manufacturer's directions.

In a conventional soup pot, sauté the vegetables in oil until soft and translucent. Add lentils with remaining ingredients and cook over low heat for approximately 2 hours. Serves 8 - 10.

Variation: Add 4 sliced kosher franks or 1/2 to 1 cup sliced salami when serving as a meat dish.

Pearl Roseman

Harrira (Lentil-Lamb Soup) (Meat)

A Middle Eastern soup; thick, lemony and tasty.

2	tablespoons margarine
1	cup chopped onion
1	cup chopped parsley
1	tablespoon chopped celery leaves
1	teaspoon freshly ground black pepper
1	teaspoon turmeric
1/2	teaspoon cinnamon
1/2	pound lamb shoulder, cut into 1/2-inch cubes
	Wings, back and neck of one or two chickens
1/2	cup dried lentils, washed and drained
1	tablespoon tomato paste
1 1/2	quarts water
1/2	cup fine noodles
1/4-1/2	cup lemon juice
	Salt to taste

In a large soup pot, melt margarine and sauté onion, parsley and celery together with black pepper and turmeric for 3-4 minutes. Add cinnamon, lamb and chicken parts and cook until meat is lightly browned, turning frequently for approximately 15 minutes. Add lentils to pot with tomato paste and water. Bring to a boil, and cook over moderate heat until lentils are soft, 45 minutes to 1 hour.

Remove lamb and chicken parts from soup; discard skin and bones and return meat to pot.

Five minutes before serving, add salt and noodles, broken into small pieces. Cook three minutes longer. Add lemon juice; soup should have a definite lemon flavor. Serves 6 - 8.

Claire Gering

Dad Bloom's Onion Soup (Pareve/Dairy)

Tastes even better after second or third heating!

2	pounds onions, sliced thin
3	tablespoons margarine
1/4	teaspoon white pepper
3	tablespoons soy sauce
1	tablespoon Worcestershire sauce
3	beef bouillon cubes (pareve)
1/4	teaspoon liquid gravy enhancer (pareve)
4	quarts boiling water
1/2	cup wine, optional

In a large skillet, sauté onions in margarine until glazed. Transfer to a large soup pot; add boiling water. Add all other ingredients and adjust seasoning to taste. Serves 8 - 10.

Suggestion: *Soup may be made dairy. Made this way, it can be served in individual bowls topped with French bread and Jack cheese browned under the broiler.*

Linda Krasnoff

Cabbage Soup (Meat)

An Eastern European traditional favorite.

2 pounds shorts ribs or
   flanken with bones
1 large head cabbage,
   shredded
1 28-ounce can whole
   tomatoes
1 28-ounce can tomato
   puree
1 large onion, sliced
   Water to cover
1 tablespoon salt
1/2 teaspoon pepper
1/4 cup sugar
1 tablespoon sour salt or
   2 tablespoons lemon
   juice

Place meat and bones in large soup pot. Add remaining ingredients. Bring to a boil, covered, and then simmer approximately 3 hours. Adjust sweet and sour seasonings to taste. Serves 10 - 12.

Dorothy Zimmerman

Sweet Bouquet of Vegetable Soup (Pareve/Dairy)

Delicious low-cholesterol, low-calorie, hearty vegetable soup.

1 onion, chopped
1-2 ounces margarine or
   butter
8-10 cups water (may add
   pareve chicken soup
   mix or bouillon
   cubes)
6 carrots, sliced
1 tomato
2 parsnips
3 celery ribs, sliced
1/2 cauliflower, broken into
   pieces
1/2 bunch parsley
   Garlic salt and pepper
   to taste

Sauté chopped onion in margarine or butter. Add water or stock and remaining ingredients. Simmer covered, approximately 30 minutes or until vegetables are tender. Adjust seasonings to taste. Serves 6 - 8.

Theja Sommer

Mushroom Barley Soup (Pareve)

Good and hearty vegetarian soup.

1	**medium onion, peeled and quartered**
1	**pound mushrooms, rinsed and dried**
3	**tablespoons margarine**
6	**cups water**
1/3	**cup pearl barley, rinsed and drained**
1	**teaspoon salt, optional**
1/4-1/2 teaspoon black	**pepper**
	Thyme, to taste
1	**bay leaf**
1-2	**tablespoons soy sauce**
1/4	**cup parsley leaves, packed**

In food processor fitted with medium slicing disc, slice onion. Remove onion from bowl. Reinsert slicing disc and slice mushrooms. Leave in bowl.

Melt margarine in 3-quart pot. Add onion and cook over medium heat, stirring often, until onion absorbs margarine. Add mushrooms and cook over high heat, stirring constantly, about 5 minutes. Add water, barley, salt, pepper, thyme and bay leaf. Bring to a boil, stirring several times. Simmer covered until barley is tender, about 45 minutes.

Stir in soy sauce and simmer about 5 minutes longer to allow flavors to blend. Remove bay leaf. Chop parsley finely in dry food processor fitted with metal blade. Stir into soup and serve hot. Serves 6.

Janet Farber

Eternal Spring Soup (Meat)

Has a delicate, tender flavor.

2	**cups water**
2	**cups chicken stock**
1 1/2-2	**pounds Swiss chard, including stems (or any other green vegetable)**
1/2	**bunch parsley**
1	**8-ounce can peas, undrained**
	Garlic salt or powder

In a soup pot, bring water and chicken stock to a boil. Tear up Swiss chard and parsley. Add to boiling water and stock; simmer for about 20 minutes or until soft. Add peas. Puree in blender or food processor.

Serve hot, adding more water if needed. Season to taste with garlic salt or powder. Serves 6 - 8.

Theja Sommer

Creamy Zucchini Soup (Dairy/Pareve)

A lovely company soup from my cousin, Wini Drell, of Skokie, Illinois.

3	**medium onions, thinly sliced**
2	**cloves garlic, minced**
3	**tablespoons butter or margarine**
26	**ounces chicken broth, pareve**
4	**medium zucchini, sliced**
2	**stalks celery, with leaves, thinly sliced**
1	**tablespoon parsley, minced**
1	**teaspoon salt, or to taste**
1/2	**teaspoon dill weed**
1/2	**teaspoon basil**
	Freshly ground pepper
1	**cup milk or liquid nondairy creamer**

Sauté onions and garlic in margarine until tender. Do not brown. Combine broth and all ingredients except milk or nondairy creamer in large pot. Heat to boiling; stir in onions and garlic and simmer 30 minutes. Blend soup in 2 or 3 batches in food processor until slightly chunky. Return to pot and add milk or nondairy creamer.

Serve hot or cold. Garnish with lemon wedge, if desired. Serves 4-6.

Variation: Can be made with broccoli, spinach or cauliflower.

Marcia Abelson

Essence of Celery Soup (Pareve)

A surprising blend of fruit and vegetables becomes a delectable soup.

1	**large garlic clove**
2	**medium onions**
1	**pound celery, without tops**
6	**tablespoons unsalted pareve margarine**
1	**large pear, peeled, seeded, diced**
4	**teaspoons pareve chicken broth powder**
4	**cups water**

Cut up garlic, onion and celery; then chop finely in food processor. Melt margarine in a large soup pot and sauté vegetables and pear until cooked, about 30 minutes. Reprocess in food processor until finely pureed. Add chicken broth powder, then water; heat and serve. Serves 5 - 6.

Note: The mixture may be refrigerated or frozen after the chicken broth powder is added. When ready to use add, water and heat.

Claire Gering

Cream of Tomato Soup (Dairy)

A delicious soup that is even better the next day.

1 1/2	cups chopped onion
1	large clove garlic, crushed
1	tablespoon butter
1/2	teaspoon salt
1/2	teaspoon dried rosemary
1/2	teaspoon dried basil
	Ground black pepper, to taste
3 1/2	cups cooked tomatoes
3	tablespoons dry sherry
1/4	teaspoon honey
4	ounces cream cheese
	Fresh parsley

In a soup pot, cook onions and garlic in butter with salt until onions are soft and translucent. Add herbs and pepper; sauté a bit more. Add tomatoes, sherry and honey. Cover and simmer 30-40 minutes. Cut cream cheese into small cubes and add to hot soup. Continue cooking, stirring until smooth and cream cheese has thoroughly melted. Serve topped with freshly chopped parsley. Serves 3 - 4 people.

Note: Honey neutralizes the acidity of the tomatoes; 1/4 teaspoon baking soda can be used instead, if preferred.

Janet Weinstein Abelson

Borscht Cocktail Soup (Dairy)

This beautiful soup from Eastern Europe is traditional for Shavuot.

1/2	cucumber
1	32-ounce bottle borscht
1	pint sour cream
1 1/2	tablespoons chopped chives
1 1/2	tablespoons dill weed
1	cup beer

Peel and seed cucumber. Dice in 1/8-inch cubes. Mix all ingredients together. Chill and let flavors blend for several hours. Serves 8.

Claire Gering

Cold Berry Soup (Dairy)

A beautiful, unusual soup.
A Sukkot tradition; ideal for summer entertaining.

1	pint fresh strawberries or raspberries
1	cup ice water
1/2	cup sour cream
1/2	cup dry red wine
1/4-1/2	cup sugar
	Whole berries for garnish

Puree berries in blender or processor. Press through a fine sieve into a large, chilled bowl. Stir in water, sour cream, wine and 1/4 cup sugar. Taste and add more sugar if desired.

Refrigerate covered until cold and serve in chilled bowls. Serves 4.

Wini Drell

Gazpacho (Meat)

A beautiful cold soup from Spain that is a favorite in California.
Perfect for a hot summer day.

1   **16-ounce can tomato juice**
1   **cup chicken broth**
1/4   **cup oil (optional)**
2   **tablespoons wine vinegar**
1/2-1 **green bell pepper**
1/2-1 **peeled cucumber**
1-2   **stalks celery**
1/2   **onion**
1   **peeled tomato**
1/4   **teaspoon garlic powder**
2   **tablespoons Worcestershire sauce**
1   **tablespoon sugar (or equivalent sweetener)**
     Dash of pepper

Chop all vegetables in food processor and combine with all other ingredients. Chill before serving. Can be kept in refrigerator several days. Serves 6 - 8.

Variation: May be made pareve by using pareve chicken soup mix.

Eunice Berman

Gazpacho #2 (Pareve)

A healthful California adaptation of this Spanish classic.
Nice to serve while waiting for dinner.

4   **tomatoes, cut up**
1   **clove garlic**
2   **tablespoons wine vinegar**
1/4   **teaspoon ground pepper**
1   **cup tomato juice**
1   **cucumber, peeled and diced**
1   **green bell pepper, seeded and diced**
3   **scallions, finely sliced**

Process tomatoes in blender or food processor until smooth. Add the garlic, vinegar and ground pepper; process again. Pour this puree into a container; add tomato juice and stir well. Chill.

Serve in small chilled bowls with bread sticks. Add cucumber, green pepper and scallions for garnish. Serves 4.

Note: There is no oil in this recipe, and low-salt tomato juice will reduce sodium content more. There are only 53 calories per cup.

Variations: Add 1 cup green chile salsa and 1/4 teaspoon Tabasco sauce to make the soup hotter; chopped zucchini and chopped celery can also be used as garnish.

Ida Liberman

Minestrone Soup (Pareve/Dairy)

A filling soup; almost a meal by itself.

2	15-ounce cans kidney beans
1	tablespoon olive oil
2	medium cloves garlic, minced
1/4	teaspoon pepper
1/4	cup chopped parsley
1	small unpeeled zucchini, diced
2	stalks celery, chopped
1	small carrot, diced
2	green onions, chopped
4-5	chard leaves, chopped (broccoli leaves or spinach may be used)
3	tablespoons butter or margarine
1	8-ounce can tomato sauce or 1 pound canned tomatoes
2 1/2	cups water
1/2	cup dry sherry
1/4	cup uncooked elbow macaroni
	Grated Parmesan cheese

Place beans in 3-1/2-quart pot. Mash until 2/3 of beans are broken. Add oil, garlic, pepper and parsley; stir. Then add all vegetables, butter, tomatoes and water. Simmer 1 hour. Add sherry; cook 10 minutes. Add macaroni; cook 10-15 minutes more. Sprinkle with cheese to serve. Makes 12 cups. Serves 6 - 8.

Note: The only salt in this recipe is in canned beans and tomatoes, or you may use low-salt products.

Variations: Add a few leaves of basil or 1/2 cup grated or diced potatoes or use tomatoes instead of tomato sauce. Also, add more water if soup is too thick.

Eve Marcus

Italian Vegetable Soup (Meat)

This soup is best when made a day ahead.

1	pound soup meat with bone
5	quarts cold water
3	teaspoons salt
1	cup dried red kidney beans
2	tablespoons oil
2	cloves garlic
1	medium onion, minced
1/2	cup snipped parsley
1/2	pound ground beef
1/4	teaspoon pepper
1	cup celery, diced
2	cups cabbage, finely shredded
1 1/2	cups carrots, diced
1	28-ounce can tomatoes
1 1/2	cups pasta (spaghetti, shells or macaroni)
1 1/2	cups zucchini, thinly sliced
1	10-ounce package frozen peas
	Salt and pepper to taste

In a large kettle, place soup meat with bone, water, salt and beans. Bring to a boil; skim; cover. Simmer 3 hours.

In oil, sauté garlic, onion, parsley, ground beef and pepper until the onion is tender; discard garlic.

Remove bone from soup; cut off meat. Add the meat to soup, along with onion mixture, celery, cabbage, carrots and tomatoes. Cover and simmer for 20 minutes.

Refrigerate several hours or overnight.

Skim fat from the soup. Bring the soup slowly to a boil. Add spaghetti, zucchini and peas. Cook, covered, for about 10 minutes. Add salt and pepper to taste. Makes approximately 7 - 8 quarts.

Note: *Substitute canned kidney beans and adjust cooking time accordingly.*

Judy Rosen

Tortilla Soup (Meat)

A taste of Mexico and an excellent way to use leftover cooked chicken and/or broth.

2	tablespoons vegetable oil
4	corn tortillas, cut into strips
1	cup chopped onion
2	teaspoons minced garlic
2-4	tablespoons chopped jalapeño chile peppers
7-8	cups chicken broth
2	cups chopped cooked chicken
1	cup whole kernel corn
1/2	cup chopped red bell pepper
1/4	cup chopped cilantro
1	tablespoon fresh lime juice
2	teaspoons cumin

In a heavy soup pot, heat oil over medium high heat. Add tortilla strips and cook until crisp, 2-3 minutes. Remove with slotted spoon and drain on paper towels. Add onion, garlic and chile peppers to pot and cook 3 minutes. Add remaining ingredients and simmer 10 minutes.

Spoon into bowls and top with tortilla strips. Yields 9 cups.

Pearl Roseman

Mexican Fish Soup (Dairy)

Very tasty and very easy, served with home-fried tortilla chips.

2 1/2	cups fish stock (may use liquid from poaching salmon)
1/4	cup tomato sauce
2	tablespoons diced celery
2	tablespoons diced onion
2	tablespoons diced green bell pepper (or one chopped serrano chile)
2	tablespoons diced tomato
1	clove garlic, minced
1	teaspoon oregano
	White pepper to taste
1	bay leaf
1/4	pound Monterey Jack cheese, in strips or grated
1/4	pound Cheddar cheese, in strips or grated

In a 2-quart pot, combine fish stock and all ingredients, except cheeses and chips. Add salt, if desired. Bring to a boil, lower heat and simmer 20-30 minutes. Serve soup in bowls; lay strips of Jack and Cheddar cheese on top.

Home-fried tortilla chips or corn chips may be served with the soup. Yields 3 - 4 cups.

Variations: Omit salt for a low-salt recipe. Amounts of vegetables may be increased, if desired.

Eve Marcus

Cioppino (Pareve)

Low fat, low salt and low in cholesterol.

2	large onions, diced
2	cloves garlic, minced
1	green bell pepper, chopped
2	cups tomato juice
1/2	cup burgundy wine
1	28-ounce can tomatoes
1	teaspoon dried oregano
1	teaspoon dried parsley
1/2	teaspoon dried basil
1/4	teaspoon pepper
1	pound halibut, cut in chunks
2	potatoes, peeled and diced

In a large pot, cook onions, garlic, bell pepper, tomato juice, wine, tomatoes and seasonings until vegetables are tender. Cover and cook an additional 10 minutes. Add fish and potatoes; cover and cook 15 minutes longer or until potatoes are done. Uncover and cook an additional 5 minutes. Serves 6.

Ida Liberman

Lorie's Hot and Sour Szechuan Soup (Meat)

A spicy soup to warm one on a cold winter day!

4	dried Chinese mushrooms
1/2	cup dried fungus, optional
1/2	cup veal, chicken or turkey
1/2	cup bamboo shoots, cut
1	teaspoon salt, optional
1	tablespoon cornstarch
2	tablespoons oil
6	cups chicken broth
7	ounces tofu bean curd, cut in 3/4-inch cubes
3	tablespoons dark soy sauce
1/2	teaspoon pepper
3	tablespoons white vinegar
2	tablespoons cornstarch dissolved in 4 tablespoons water
3	whole eggs, beaten (or egg whites)
1/2-1	teaspoon sesame oil

Cover mushrooms and fungus separately with boiling water. Let soak 3-4 hours or overnight.

Julienne meat, bamboo shoots, fungus and mushrooms.

Mix meat with 1/2 teaspoon salt and cornstarch. Heat oil in wok or frying pan and sauté meat mixture; set aside.

Add chicken broth to wok or pan and bring to boil. Add bamboo shoots, mushrooms, fungus, meat and bean curd; add soy sauce, 1/2 teaspoon salt, pepper and vinegar. Thicken mixture with dissolved cornstarch. Add beaten eggs (or egg whites), stirring quickly for 1 minute. Add sesame oil.

Serve hot. Serves 3 - 4 as a main dish.

Suggestion: *May be frozen without bean curd. Reheat and add bean curd; taste for seasoning.*

Min Leonard

Salads

Californians' love affair with salads is no doubt encouraged by the tremendous selection of fruits and vegetables available in ever-increasing variety in our supermarkets and restaurants. Fruits and vegetables considered exotic not too long ago quickly have become California favorites, and several new varieties seem to appear each season from around the world.

Creative cooks, influenced by a constant shower of cookbooks, television cooking shows and a never-ending variety of ethnic restaurants, have all encouraged our experimentation with un-usual combinations of salad greens, seasonings and dressings. And then there is Sephardic Jewish cooking; due to the influence of the year-round variety of crops growing around the Mediterranean, it has always emphasized fruits and vegetables. Add to that our rapidly growing appreciation for healthy living, and the impor-tance of salads in California cuisine is assured.

In California a platter of fresh fruits nearly always accompanies any menu — as a salad if not as the dessert. Salads are often the main dish, and even the entire meal, as in the very popular Chinese chicken salads.

In this section you will find salads featuring fruit, vegetables, pasta, legumes, fish, poultry and meat — just some of the endless possibilities available. Use these recipes as a starting point, add whatever is fresh and beautiful in your market (or garden), and create your own terrific concoctions.

Hearts of Palm Salad (Pareve)

An impressive salad for special occasions.

2 tablespoons vegetable oil
1 tablespoon sesame oil
1 tablespoon rice vinegar, unseasoned
Salt and pepper to taste
1 bunch fresh spinach leaves
1 14-ounce can hearts of palm, sliced
8-10 cherry tomatoes, halved
1 tablespoon finely minced green onion
2 teaspoons finely minced capers
2 teaspoons finely minced celery

In a small, deep bowl, whisk oils into vinegar, stirring constantly. Season with salt and pepper.

Arrange spinach on platter. Top with hearts of palm and tomatoes. Sprinkle with green onion, capers and celery. Pour dressing over all and serve immediately. Serves 6.

Cirel Blitz

Mediterranean Meat Salad (Meat)

From my friend Claudia Wolff, a perfect one-dish meal for
a warm evening in the Sukkah, but delicious any place,
any time! Multiply as desired.

4-6 ounces cooked lamb or beef (broiled or roasted, and sliced)
8 small red potatoes
1 tablespoon olive oil
1 small eggplant, thinly sliced
1 green bell pepper, cubed
1 red bell pepper, cubed
6 green onions, chopped
2 cloves garlic, minced
1 bay leaf
2 tablespoons lemon juice
2 tablespoons chopped parsley, optional
1/2 teaspoon ground pepper
1/2 teaspoon ground turmeric
1/2 teaspoon paprika

In medium-sized saucepan over medium heat, bring potatoes and enough water to cover to a boil. Reduce heat to medium-low; cover and cook 10 to 15 minutes, or until tender. Cool slightly; slice into quarters and set aside.

Meanwhile, heat oil in large skillet over medium heat. Stir in eggplant, bell peppers, onions, garlic and bay leaf. Cook 5 to 10 minutes, or until vegetables are tender-crisp, stirring often. Remove bay leaf and stir in lemon juice. Add potatoes, lamb or beef, parsley, ground pepper, turmeric and paprika. Toss gently. Serve warmed or at room temperature. Serves 4 as a salad or 2 - 3 as a main dish.

Susan Brandes

Middle East Rice Salad (Dairy)

*This rice salad from my niece Wendy Winnick is a real hit.
Multiplies easily to serve a crowd.*

3	cups hot cooked rice (1 cup raw rice)
1/4	cup vegetable oil
2	tablespoons lemon juice
3/4	teaspoon seasoned pepper
1/2	teaspoon each: salt, crumbled rosemary leaves, oregano leaves and minced garlic
1/4	teaspoon mint leaves, crumbled
1	small zucchini, thinly sliced
1	medium tomato, peeled, seeded and chopped
4	ounces Feta cheese, cut into small cubes (about 2/3 cup)

Spoon rice into large mixing bowl. Blend oil, lemon juice, seasoned pepper, salt, rosemary, oregano, garlic and mint. Stir into rice. Cover and let cool. Add zucchini, tomato and cheese, stirring lightly. Serve at room temperature or chill before serving. Serves 6.

Diane Tapper

Tabouli Salad (Pareve)

*This Middle Eastern salad is an excellent and unusual way to
incorporate whole grains in the menu.*

Salad:

1	cup cracked wheat (also known as bulgur)
1	cup minced fresh parsley
1	cup minced fresh mint
1	cup minced green onion
4	tomatoes, cut into 1/2-inch cubes
1	cup cubed cucumber (optional)

Dressing:

1/3	cup lemon juice
1/3	cup olive oil
	Salt, pepper to taste

Put wheat in bowl and add enough boiling water to cover. Wait at least 1 hour. Add other salad ingredients.

Combine dressing ingredients and toss with salad. Chill before serving. Serves 6 - 8.

Variations: *If desired, add green or black olives, celery, cheese (makes dish Dairy) or corn to taste.*

Dotty Simmons

Greek-Style Tomato Salad (Dairy)

Tangy Feta cheese enlivens this salad.
From my Florida friend, Ruth Lederman.

6	medium tomatoes, sliced
1/4	pound Feta cheese, crumbled
1	small onion, thinly sliced
1	3 1/2-ounce can pitted black olives, drained and sliced
1/2	cup olive oil or salad oil
1/4	cup red wine vinegar
2	tablespoons minced parsley
4	teaspoons sugar
1/2	teaspoon basil
1/4	teaspoon salt
1/4	teaspoon cracked black pepper
	Lettuce leaves

Prepare 2 1/2 hours before serving or even the day before. Layer tomato slices, Feta cheese, onions and olives in 13x9-inch baking dish. In a small bowl, whisk together olive oil, vinegar, parsley, sugar, basil, salt and pepper. Pour over tomatoes. With rubber spatula, gently lift tomato slices to coat with dressing. Cover dish and refrigerate.

To serve, line a platter with lettuce leaves and arrange tomatoes on top. Serves 8.

Marcia Abelson

Caesar Salad (Dairy)

As close as you can get to the original Caesar Salad.

1	clove garlic
4	ounces olive oil
1/2	cup fresh sourdough croutons (see below)
2	eggs
2	heads Romaine lettuce—torn, washed, dried and chilled
1/2	teaspoon freshly grated black pepper
1/2	teaspoon salt (or to taste)
6-8	tablespoons freshly grated Parmesan cheese
	Juice of 1 medium lemon

Three days before serving, peel a garlic clove and add to olive oil. One day before serving, purchase sourdough bread; cover bread and allow it to sit, unrefrigerated, until ready to use.

On the day of serving, cube and toast the day-old sourdough bread to make croutons. Cook eggs for 1 minute in boiling water; remove and set aside. In a large salad bowl, VERY GENTLY toss lettuce, pepper, salt and oil. Add eggs, Parmesan and lemon juice; toss again very gently. Add croutons and serve immediately. Serves 4 - 6.

Variation: Add anchovies, if desired, and omit salt. (There were no anchovies in the original recipe; they were added a few years later.)

Elaine Brown

Garlic Coleslaw (Pareve)

An unusual variation that's good with Mexican food.

Garlic Vinaigrette:

2	tablespoons vinegar
2	teaspoons salt (or less)
1	teaspoon black pepper (or less)
3	small cloves garlic, crushed
6	tablespoons vegetable oil

Salad:

1	medium head cabbage, shredded
2	tablespoons chopped fresh cilantro
2	tomatoes, chopped
1	cucumber, peeled and chopped

To make garlic vinaigrette, mix all dressing ingredients and let stand several hours to blend flavors.

To assemble salad, place cabbage in a large bowl. Add vinaigrette and cilantro; mix. Add tomatoes and cucumbers. Serves 8.

Eve Marcus

Black Bean Salad (Pareve)

A bold mix of colors adds to the appeal of this dish.

1 1/2	cups cooked black beans OR 1 15-ounce can black beans, drained and rinsed
1	small green bell pepper, cut into small strips
1	small carrot, coarsely shredded
1	tablespoon chopped red onion
2	tablespoons vegetable oil
1/4	teaspoon grated lime rind
2	tablespoons lime juice
1/8	teaspoon ground cumin
1/8	teaspoon ground red pepper
	Lettuce or cabbage leaves, optional

In a bowl, combine beans with green pepper, carrot and onion. In a screw-top jar combine oil, lime rind, lime juice and spices. Cover and shake well. Pour over beans; toss and chill. Arrange on lettuce or cabbage leaves. If uncooked beans are used, use a scant 3/4 cup dry beans to make 1 1/2 cups. Cook 2 1/2 to 3 hours or until tender and add 1/2 teaspoon salt, or to taste. To decrease cooking time, presoak beans in water. Serves 3 - 4.

Pearl Roseman

Vermicelli Salad (Dairy)

Best prepared a day ahead so that flavors blend.

1	16-ounce package vermicelli
1/2	pound Feta cheese
8	ounces Italian salad dressing
1/4	cup mayonnaise
6-8	finely sliced green onions, or to taste
2	tablespoons Dijon mustard
8	ounces frozen tiny green peas, uncooked
1	red bell pepper, cut into small pieces
1	15-ounce can whole black olives, sliced (or a 3 1/2-ounce can sliced black olives)
1/3-1/2 cup pine nuts (optional)	

Cook vermicelli according to directions on package; drain and rinse. Place vermicelli in large bowl. Mash feta cheese with fork; add to vermicelli. Add all other ingredients except pine nuts. Just before serving, add pine nuts, if desired. Serves 12 - 14 for a main dish.

Adelaide Suplin

Mushroom-Zucchini Salad (Pareve)

For a taste of summer, year 'round.

1/2   pound sliced fresh
      mushrooms (2 1/2
      cups)
1   zucchini, thinly sliced
1   tomato, diced
1/4   cup sliced green onion
2   tablespoons olive oil
2   tablespoons white
      vinegar
1   teaspoon salt
1/2   teaspoon coarsely
      ground pepper
1/2   teaspoon marjoram,
      crumbled
      Lettuce leaves

Combine mushrooms, zucchini, tomato and green onion. Combine remaining ingredients; pour over vegetables. Toss gently. Serve on lettuce-lined plates. Serves 6.

Rosalie Weiner

Sweet-and-Sour Cucumber Salad (Pareve)

This salad was made famous at Trader Vic's restaurant.
It's best made a day ahead.

1/4   cup sugar
1/4   cup water
1/2   cup white vinegar
1/2   teaspoon salt
2   cucumbers or 1
      hothouse cucumber,
      thinly sliced
2   teaspoons dehydrated
      parsley flakes

On the day before, mix all ingredients except cucumbers; refrigerate. Peel and score cucumbers. (Hothouse cucumber need not be peeled but should be scored.) Put in plastic bag and refrigerate.

Mix dressing and sliced cucumbers together one hour before serving. Serves 6 - 8.

Debra Gordon

Avocado-Orange Salad (Pareve)

My mother-in-law, Jacquelyn Gordon, serves this quite often.

Salad:
1   head of Boston or butter lettuce
1   avocado, cut up
1   11-ounce can mandarin orange sections, drained (reserve syrup)
2 or 3 slices of red onion

Dressing:
1   package Italian salad dressing mix
2   tablespoons of mandarin orange juice
1/4   cup white champagne vinegar
2/3   cup salad oil
1/8   cup slivered almonds

Make dressing mix according to package directions, using 2 tablespoons mandarin orange juice instead of water. Refrigerate.

Tear lettuce into small pieces; add avocado, mandarin orange sections and onion. Toss together and add dressing as desired, reserving balance for future use. Sprinkle slivered almonds on top. Serves 3 - 4.

Variation: Substitute sliced fresh navel oranges and juice for mandarin oranges and juice.

Debra Gordon

Onion Salad Dressing (Pareve)

Grated onions add the "zing."

1/3   cup catsup
2/3   cup oil
1/3   cup vinegar
1/2   cup sugar
1/4   cup grated onion
            Salt to taste

Mix together and shake well. Yields approximately 2 cups.

Ingrid Blumenstein

Curried Tuna Salad (Dairy)

A main-dish salad with a crunchy Oriental touch.

2	6 1/2-ounce cans tuna, drained
1	10-ounce package frozen peas, thawed
1	cup thinly sliced celery
1	8-ounce can water chestnuts, sliced
3/4	cup mayonnaise (or a little less)
1/2-1	teaspoon curry powder
1	tablespoon lemon juice
1/8	teaspoon garlic salt
1	cup chow mein noodles
1/2	cup roasted peanuts

Break tuna into chunks; combine with peas, celery and water chestnuts. Cover and chill well.

Combine mayonnaise, curry powder, lemon juice and garlic salt. Add chow mein noodles to tuna mixture; toss lightly. Add mayonnaise mixture; toss again.

Serve on bed of crisp salad greens. Sprinkle with nuts. Serves 5 - 6.

Doris Goodman

Fruited Tuna Salad (Pareve or Meat)

Served in a half papaya or cantaloupe,
this makes a lovely luncheon or supper dish.

1	6 1/2-ounce can tuna or
1	cup cooked chicken
1/2	cup drained pineapple tidbits
1/2	cup seedless grapes
1/2	cup diced celery
1/4	cup chopped pecans
3	tablespoons thinly sliced stuffed olives
1/4-1/3	cup salad dressing or mayonnaise
	Lemon wedges
	Pecans

Drain and break tuna or chicken into chunks. Combine with remaining ingredients.

Serve on lettuce; garnish with lemon and pecans. Serves 3.

Idele Deutsch

97

Tuna Pasta Salad (Dairy)

A whole "meal-in-a-bowl."

3	quarts boiling water
1	tablespoon salt (or less)
2	cups pasta (rotini or rotelle)
1 1/2	cups finely sliced celery
1/2	cup chopped green bell pepper
1/2	cup chopped sweet pickle
1/2	cup chopped red bell pepper (optional)
2	cups frozen peas, uncooked
2	6 1/2-ounce cans tuna, drained and flaked
2	tablespoons honey
1/2-3/4	cup mayonnaise (regular or light)
1/2	teaspoon salt (optional)
1	cup cubed cheddar cheese

Cook pasta in boiling salted water until "al dente."

Rinse in cold water and drain.

Toss vegetables and pasta together with tuna. Add salt, if desired. Combine honey and mayonnaise; add to salad. Add cheese just before serving. Serves 6 - 8.

Note: Flavor is enhanced when made the day before.

Barbara Deutsch

Hot Spinach Salad (Pareve)

A different twist on a popular salad.

8	cups fresh spinach, cut up
1	small red onion, sliced thin
1	8-ounce can sliced water chestnuts, drained
1	8-ounce can mandarin oranges, drained
1/2	cup sliced almonds, toasted
1/2-3/4	cup Italian dressing
2	hard-cooked eggs, cut up

Wash and drain spinach; remove stems. Add onions and mix. Add water chestnuts, oranges and almonds; toss lightly. Heat salad dressing. Pour over tossed salad just before serving. Sprinkle eggs over salad and serve immediately. Serves 6 - 8.

Ruth King

Tangy Potato Salad (Pareve)

*An updated version of the classic favorite
from my niece Wendy Winnick.*

1/4	cup minced onion
1 1/2	teaspoons salt, or to taste
1/4	teaspoon pepper
2	tablespoons vinegar
2	tablespoons sweet pickle relish
1	quart (approximately 2 pounds) cooked potato slices
2/3	cup mayonnaise
1/2	cup chopped celery
1	tablespoon prepared mustard
2	tablespoons chopped fresh parsley
1/2	teaspoon celery seed
1	tablespoon capers
	Paprika

Combine onion, salt, pepper, vinegar and relish; add potatoes; mix lightly. Allow to cool. Combine mayonnaise, celery, mustard, parsley, celery seed and capers; mix into cooled potatoes. Sprinkle with paprika. Chill several hours. Serves 6 - 8.

Diane Tapper

Molded Gazpacho Salad (Pareve)

An unusual, low-cal twist on a California hot-weather favorite.

1	6-ounce package low-calorie lemon gelatin
1 1/2	cups boiling water
1 1/2	cups vegetable juice cocktail
4	tablespoons low-calorie Italian salad dressing
8	teaspoons red wine vinegar
1	cup sliced cauliflower florets
1	cup chopped tomatoes (seeded, if preferred)
1	cup chopped celery
1/2	cup chopped green bell pepper
	Vegetable oil spray

In a large bowl, dissolve gelatin in boiling water. Stir in vegetable juice cocktail, salad dressing and vinegar. Chill until partially set.

Fold in cauliflower, tomato, celery and green pepper. Turn into 6-cup mold sprayed with vegetable oil. Chill several hours. Serves 8 - 10.

Trana Labowe

Pineapple-Mandarin Orange Mold (Pareve)

*A refreshing combination, especially good served
with Chinese chicken salad.*

3	cups boiling water
2	3-ounce packages orange gelatin
1	3-ounce package lemon gelatin
1	8-ounce can mandarin oranges, drained
1	20-ounce can crushed pineapple, drained (reserve juice)
8	ounces (or more) pareve whipping cream, whipped

In a large bowl, dissolve both gelatins in boiling water. Pour reserved pineapple juice into 1-cup measure; add enough cold water to make 1 cup. Add to dissolved gelatins and stir. Refrigerate until partially thickened. Fold in whipped cream until thoroughly blended. Fold in pineapple and oranges. Pour into 10-cup mold and refrigerate. May be made 2 to 3 days prior to use. Serves 16 - 20.

Beverly Barak

Chinese Coleslaw (Pareve)

*Everyone loves this crunchy and delicious
coleslaw when Cousin Shellie serves it.*

Dressing:

1/4	cup sugar
1/2	teaspoon white pepper
1	teaspoon salt
1	cup oil
6	tablespoons rice vinegar

Salad:

2	tablespoons oil
1/2	cup sliced almonds
1/4	cup sesame seeds
8	green onions, sliced
1	head cabbage, finely chopped
2	3-ounce packages Top Ramen noodles, broken up

Combine dressing ingredients; set aside. Finely chop cabbage using food processor (or by hand).

Heat 2 tablespoons oil in skillet and toss in almonds and sesame seeds; cook until just lightly brown. Combine with everything else. Chill. Serves 4 - 6.

Marcia Abelson

Marinated Tomato Salad (Pareve)

Easy and festive; works beautifully for any occasion.

5	large tomatoes, thickly sliced
1	red onion, thinly sliced
1/2	cup chopped fresh parsley
1/4	cup red wine vinegar
1/2	cup salad oil
1	tablespoon sugar
1	teaspoon freshly ground black pepper

Place tomatoes and onions in alternating layers in decorative serving dish. Mix remaining ingredients together; pour over layered vegetables. Marinate several hours in refrigerator. Serves 5 - 6.

Linda Krasnoff

Luscious Lemon Chicken Salad (Meat)

Makes a lovely luncheon dish.

Salad:

6	cups (1 large head) iceberg lettuce, shredded
2	cups cooked chicken breasts, chunked
1	cup sliced water chestnuts
1	cup julienned carrots
1	6-ounce package frozen Chinese pea pods, thawed
1/2	cup sliced radishes
1/2	cup sliced green onions
5	ounces chow mein noodles or rice sticks

Dressing:

1/4	cup salad oil
3	tablespoons low-salt soy sauce
3	tablespoons lemon juice
3	tablespoons rice vinegar
1	tablespoon brown sugar (or substitute)
1	tablespoon dry sherry or water
1	teaspoon garlic powder
1/2	teaspoon sesame oil
1/2	teaspoon minced fresh ginger

Combine all dressing ingredients; refrigerate. In large bowl combine all salad ingredients except noodles. Chill thoroughly.

Just before serving, toss gently with dressing. Top with noodles. Serves 6 - 8.

Elaine Brown

Sesame Chinese Chicken Salad (Meat)

*My family and friends enjoy this dish after attending synagogue
services the second day of Rosh Hashanah.*

Salad:

1	**pound boneless and skinless chicken breast**
1/2	**teaspoon garlic powder**
1	**large head lettuce, shredded**
4-5	**tablespoons sesame seeds, toasted**
4-5	**tablespoons slivered almonds, toasted**
1/3-1/2	**package rice noodles (6 3/4 ounces) or**
2-3	**cups chow mein noodles**
2	**cups (approximately) oil for frying**

Dressing:

1/2	**teaspoon Chinese mustard powder**
1	**tablespoon hoisin sauce**
2	**tablespoons rice vinegar**
2	**tablespoons sugar**
1	**teaspoon light soy sauce**
2	**teaspoons sesame oil**
4	**tablespoons vegetable oil**

Blend dressing ingredients and set aside. Season chicken with garlic powder, wrap in foil and bake in a 350 degree oven for 30 to 40 minutes. Cut into strips or small pieces. Mix together with lettuce. Toss with dressing and add sesame seeds and almonds. Add the noodles, which have been fried in hot oil, or the Chow Mein noodles at the very end. Serves 5 - 6.

Hint: The ingredients can be prepared a day in advance, but toss together just before serving.

Beverly Barak

Oriental Tuna Salad (Pareve)

*A great party dish—multiplies easily. May be prepared a day ahead,
adding beans and noodles just before serving.*

1	**10-ounce package frozen Italian green beans**
1	**6 1/2-ounce can tuna, drained**
1	**cup thinly sliced celery**
1/2	**cup mayonnaise**
1	**tablespoon lemon juice**
1 1/2	**teaspoons soy sauce, or to taste**
	Dash garlic powder
1	**cup chow mein noodles**

Steam beans according to package directions. Drain and cool; reserve. Mix all the ingredients except the beans and noodles. Just before serving add beans and noodles to the mixture. Serves 4 - 6.

Shirley Green

Fruited Chinese Chicken Salad (Meat)

A California interpretation of an Oriental favorite.

Salad:

2	large whole cooked chicken breasts
	oil for frying
4	ounces rice sticks
1	head iceberg lettuce
1	8-ounce can sliced water chestnuts
1	cup seedless green grapes
1	cup mandarin oranges, drained
1/2	red bell pepper, chopped
3 - 4	green onions, chopped

Sesame Soy Dressing:

3	tablespoons rice vinegar
1	tablespoon mild soy sauce
2	tablespoons salad oil
2	tablespoons sesame oil
1/2	teaspoon ground ginger

Blend all dressing ingredients and set aside. Shred or dice cooked chicken and set aside. Deep fry sticks (for approximately 1/2 to 1 minute per side) a small amount at a time (they puff up in frying pan). Turn over once. Drain on paper towels and set aside.

Shred lettuce, combine with chicken, water chestnuts, grapes, mandarin oranges, red pepper and green onions.

When ready to serve, blend all dressing ingredients thoroughly, and toss with chicken mixture and rice sticks. Sprinkle with sesame seeds and serve immediately. Serves 4-5.

Ruth King

Wendy's Oriental Salad Dressing (Pareve)

A delicious variation for Chinese chicken or tuna salad.

1 1/2	teaspoons dry mustard
6	tablespoons sugar
2	tablespoons soy sauce
3	tablespoons sesame oil
3/4	cup oil
9	tablespoons rice vinegar, seasoned

Mix all ingredients together in a blender or by hand with a whisk. Yields approximately 1 1/2 cups.

Wendy Scott

"Tink Un" Salad and Dressing (Pareve)

An original recipe from "favorite aunt" Clara, who served this juicy vegetable salad to her grandchildren—they would dip into ("tink un") it with egg bread and loved it. Make as much or as little as desired.

1   can stewed tomatoes with juice
Vegetable oil
Salt and pepper, to taste
Onion and garlic powder, to taste
Assortment of raw, cut-up vegetables, e.g.: celery, lettuce, raw sweet onion, radishes, cucumber, green or black olives, etc.

Mix all dressing ingredients well and pour over vegetable mixture.

Annette Masler

Cholesterol-Free Blender Mayonnaise (Pareve)

Wonderful for the dieter or cholesterol-shy.

1/3   cup cholesterol-free egg product
1/2   teaspoon dry mustard
1/2   teaspoon sugar
1/4   teaspoon paprika
2   tablespoons white vinegar
1   cup corn oil

Blend first four ingredients with 1/2 cup oil in blender on medium-high speed just until mixed. Without turning off blender, pour in remaining oil in slow, steady stream. If necessary, use rubber spatula to keep mixture flowing into blades. Continue blending until oil is completely incorporated and mixture is smooth and thick. Keep mayonnaise refrigerated and use within 2 weeks. Makes 1 1/2 cups.

Ruth Elcott

Breads

Homemade bread makes a wonderful gift for many occasions. The "quick" breads are especially nice to add to party trays or to wrap in cellophane and add to *"Shalach Manot"* or *"Mishloah Manot"* (Purim gift baskets). Oat bran muffins are a thoughtful gift for the cholesterol conscious.

The *challah*, or braided egg bread, is the centerpiece of the Shabbat celebration in Jewish homes and is a popular bread the world over. Our recipes are easily adaptable to the lovely round version for Rosh Hashanah and Yom Kippur, or they can be made into smaller or extra-large loaves as desired.

Many other kinds of breads and rolls are all delicious ways to add variety and good nutrition to one's diet.

Helpful hints for making bread:

- Rapid-rise yeast is a good time saver and works well.

- A cooking or candy thermometer is helpful for testing or "proofing" yeast before mixing your ingredients to make bread. This is done by dissolving the yeast in 1/2 cup of the water or milk needed in the recipe, which has been warmed to approximately 115 degrees and allowing it to stand for 5 minutes. If the yeast-water combination has doubled, your yeast is good and you can proceed with the recipe.

- **Bread machines:** Bread machines are a wonderful time and money saver. Be sure the quantity of ingredients does not exceed your machine's capacity and set it to achieve desired results. Use the machine to make and knead the challah dough. Braid the loaf by hand and bake in a conventional oven.

Hints for Making Challah

Proof yeast: Sprinkle yeast in 1/2 cup of the total warm water with sugar or honey. In 5-7 minutes it will double and be ready to use.

Top braid falling: When challah is baking in the oven, the top braid often slips off. To prevent slippage, fasten the top braid with toothpicks to the lower braid.

White areas of challah: When the challah is about finished baking, it may have risen more since the egg yolk was "painted" on. It is possible to "paint" additional egg yolk on parts that need it and continue baking.

To prepare challah on Thursday night: Make the challah dough and place it in the refrigerator in an oiled bowl covered with a towel. The dough will rise in the refrigerator. (Do not place in the coldest part of the refrigerator.) In the morning, remove the dough and place it in an oiled, room-temperature bowl, punch out the air, and cover with a warm, moist towel. Let it rise about 1 1/2 hours, then continue with process.

Freezing challah: Challah may be frozen after it's baked and cooled. Defrost when ready to use. Reheat in 350 degree oven for about 15 minutes.

Blessing over challah before baking: It is traditional to remove a small piece of dough and put it next to the challah before baking in the oven. This piece of kneaded dough is a symbolic contribution of a loaf given to the High Priests in the days of the Temple, as commanded in the Bible.

The following blessing is said before placing challah in the oven:

"Baruch Atah Adonai, elohaynu melech ha-olam, asher kidshanu b'mitzvotov, v'tsivonu l'hafrish challah."
"Blessed art Thou, O Lord our God, King of the Universe, who has sanctified us by Thy commandments and commanded us to separate the challah."

Braiding Challah

1. Basic Three-Strand Braid: Divide dough into three parts. Roll each into a long rope of even thickness. Pinch together the ends and braid.

2. Braiding with a crown: For long challah, place smaller braid on top of the long three-strand braid. Divide original dough into four parts, rather than three. For round challah, form unbraided dough into a circle.

Place a small three-strand braid in a circle on top of the round, if desired.

3. Round challah: Form a three-strand braid into a spiral form and pinch the ends together.

4. Four-strand braid: Basic rule: Under 2, over 1, alternating outermost strands on the right and left.

A Word About Challah

With today's two-career couples, it is difficult, if not impossible, to fit bread-baking into a family's busy schedule. Many bakeries and supermarkets carry challah, however, a store-bought loaf can't compare to a hot, fragrant loaf just pulled from the oven. Luckily, many supermarkets now carry frozen, pre-shaped challah dough. Let the frozen dough rise several hours on a cookie sheet, then brush the loaf with a beaten egg for a beautiful glaze, and sprinkle it with sesame or poppy seeds.

The chief beauty of baking your own challah, whether you make the dough or buy a frozen loaf, is that it allows the cook to perform a special mitzvah. Since the destruction of the second Temple in Jerusalem in 70 C.E., Jews have pulled a small piece of dough, about the size of an olive, off the uncooked challah loaf and burned it in the oven while the challah bakes. This act recalls the loaves that were left for the Temple priests to eat, and it also reminds us of our sorrow after the Temple's destruction. The act of making the temple offering, called challah, lent its name to the bread. (You can do this mitzvah with a store-bought loaf, discarding a small piece, but it doesn't have the same emotional appeal.)

Challah #1 (Pareve)

My grandmother's recipe, modified for today,
makes one beautiful large loaf.

1	**package yeast**
5	**cups sifted flour**
3	**eggs**
3	**tablespoons sugar**
2	**tablespoons oil**
2	**teaspoons salt**
1/2	**teaspoon vanilla extract**
1	**cup warm water**
1/2	**cup raisins, optional**
1	**egg yolk, beaten**
	Sesame seeds

Mix yeast with 1/4 cup of the warm water. Cover and set aside for 5-10 minutes.

Put flour, and raisins if desired, in a bowl and push to sides to make a well.

Add yeast, eggs, sugar, oil, salt, vanilla and balance of water. Stir until ingredients are well mixed.

Flour a board and knead dough until soft and elastic.

Place dough in an oiled bowl, cover with a damp cloth and let rise 1 hour. Punch down, cover and let rise again until double in bulk (about 45 minutes).

Separate dough into 4 sections on floured board. Form 3 sections into long, thick rolls and braid on a piece of heavy-duty foil. Separate the fourth piece into 3 smaller sections and make a braid to place on top of the larger braid. Cover and let rise about 1/2 hour or until double in bulk.

Mix egg yolk with 1-2 tablespoons water and brush on challah. Sprinkle with sesame seeds. Bake in a preheated oven at 350 degrees for about 1 hour or until bottom is well browned. Yields 1 loaf.

Barbara Deutsch

Rabbi Shira's Challah (Pareve)

A slightly different and delicious challah. Make this one the night before and allow to rise overnight in the refrigerator.

5   cups flour
      (approximately 4 cups
      unbleached white and
      1 cup whole wheat)
1/2   cup sugar (scant)
1 1/2 teaspoons salt
1   package yeast
1   cup warm water
1/2   cup margarine, melted
3   eggs, beaten lightly
1   egg white, optional

In a large bowl, mix 4 cups flour (3 cups white and 1 cup whole wheat) with the sugar and salt.

In a small bowl, dissolve yeast in the water and add to dry ingredients. Add the beaten eggs and margarine. Mix very well, and add enough flour until the dough leaves the sides of the bowl. Place on a floured board and knead un-. til smooth, adding enough flour so the dough does not stick to the board. A good test for kneading is to punch your finger into the dough; when the depression bounces back, it is ready.

Place dough in an oiled bowl and turn it so that it is all lightly oiled. Cover dough with a damp towel and set it in a warm place (I put it in my pilot-lit oven or outside in a sunny spot), and allow it to rise one to two hours. Punch it down and let it rise again. This second rising can take place in the refrigerator overnight if you like.

Punch down again. Shape or braid into 2 medium-sized loaves or 1 large loaf and place on oiled baking pan. Bake in preheated 350 degree oven for about an hour or until golden brown. A glaze, consisting of the beaten egg white and poppy or sesame seeds (or sugar and cinnamon for Rosh Hashanah) can be added before or during the baking period. If desired, you may double the recipe to make 2 large challot for Shabbat. Yields 1 loaf.

Ruth Elcott

Challah #2 (Pareve)

The whole family looks forward to this Shabbat treat.

2	packages dry yeast
2	cups very warm water
1/2	cup sugar
1/2	cup oil
1	teaspoon salt
2	eggs, beaten
6-7	cups flour, approximately
1	cup raisins, optional
1	egg for glaze
	Poppy or sesame seeds, optional

Using an electric mixer with the dough hook at #2 speed, dissolve the yeast in water with sugar. Mix well. Add 4 cups of the flour and the salt, mixing well. Add beaten egg and mix. Add oil and mix. Fold in raisins, if desired. Add 2 cups flour and knead, adding additional flour as necessary. Continue kneading until dough is soft and elastic, not sticky. Place dough in a large, warm greased bowl, turning over to grease all sides; cover with towel and let rise 1-2 hours or until doubled in bulk.

Remove from bowl, punch down and shape into two loaves (either plain or braided).

Preheat oven to 350 degrees. Glaze with beaten egg. If desired, sprinkle with poppy or sesame seeds. Bake 30-40 minutes until challah is golden brown and sounds hollow when tapped. Yields 2 loaves.

Sharon Blumenstein

Corn Rye Bread (Pareve)

Ideal for sandwiches.

2		packages yeast
2		cups warm water
2		tablespoons honey
1		tablespoon salt, optional
2		tablespoons shortening
3	1/2	cups rye flour
3		cups all-purpose or bread flour
1-3		tablespoons caraway seeds
		Cornmeal

Dissolve yeast in 1/2 cup of water with honey. In about 5-7 minutes it will rise to a full cup. Then pour into the mixing bowl.

Add remaining water, shortening and salt, if desired. Add rye flour and beat with mixer for about 5-7 minutes. Change to dough hook, if available, and add caraway seeds and white flour, approximately 1/2 cup at a time. Knead with dough hook for about 4 minutes or knead by hand about 8-9 minutes on a floured board. If necessary, add more flour to make a smooth, elastic dough.

Lightly coat the inside of a bowl with oil. Place dough in bowl, turning to coat all over. Cover with plastic wrap or damp towel and let rise 1-1 1/2 hours until double in size.

Remove dough from bowl, punch out air, and turn out on a floured board. Cut in half and shape into 2 loaves. Can be baked in 6 or 7 inch cake pans (sides greased) or on a cookie sheet. Sprinkle pan bottoms with cornmeal. Let rise in pans a second time for about 35-45 minutes, until doubled in size.

Brush with egg white. Do not let egg white touch the pan. Bake in a preheated 375 degree oven for about 40-50 minutes. Yields 2 loaves.

Rosalie Weiner

Pumpernickel Bread (Dairy/Pareve)

I've baked this forever—makes 3 nice loaves!

2	packages yeast
3 1/2	cups warm water
2-3	tablespoons honey
1/4	cup dark molasses
2	squares unsweetened chocolate, melted
1	tablespoon butter/margarine
9	cups all-purpose bread flour
3	cups rye flour
1	cup whole bran cereal
3/4	cup yellow corn meal
2	cups mashed potatoes, (instant, if desired) at room temperature
2	tablespoons caraway seeds, optional Cornmeal

Dissolve yeast in 1/2 cup water with honey. When bubbly (5 minutes), put in mixer bowl. Add the remaining water, molasses, chocolate and butter. Combine flours and mix 2 cups with cereal and corn meal. Add to liquids and beat 2 minutes, scraping bowl. Add potatoes, 1 cup flour mixture or enough to make a thick batter. Beat 2 minutes, scraping bowl as needed. Stir in caraway seeds and enough flour to make a soft dough. Turn out on a floured board. Cover dough with towel and let rise 15 minutes. Knead in remaining flour (more if necessary) until smooth and elastic. Cover in oiled bowl and let rise until doubled, about 1 hour.

Punch down. Shape into 3 loaves. Place in 8 or 9 inch round pans, or on cookie sheets, that have been greased and sprinkled with corn meal. If using round pans, also grease the sides. Let rise until doubled; about 45 minutes. Bake in preheated 350 degree oven for 50 minutes.

After baking, remove from pans in approximately 10 minutes (if on cookie sheets, remove right away). Yields 3 loaves.

Rosalie Weiner

Sandwich Delight (Dairy)

This has been in my files for years! I've changed it constantly to suit either the ingredients on hand or my desires.

2	packages yeast (1 tablespoon)
1/2	cup warm water
2	teaspoons honey
1	cup evaporated milk
2	cups water
1/2	cup molasses
2	tablespoons butter or margarine
1	tablespoon salt, optional
2 1/4	cups rye flour
2 1/4	cups wheat flour
4 1/2	cups white flour
	Egg yolk or melted butter

Combine yeast with water and honey and proof (see p. 106 for instructions on proofing yeast). Add milk, water, molasses, butter, salt, rye flour and wheat flour to make a thick batter. Beat 2 minutes, scraping bowl as needed. Add enough white flour to make a smooth, elastic ball. Should take about 10 minutes of kneading.

Let rise in an oiled bowl, covered, for 1 hour or until doubled. Punch down and shape into desired loaf size. Slash tops and let rise again until doubled.

Brush with either melted butter, or 1 egg yolk mixed with 2 teaspoons water. Bake in preheated 375 degree oven for 40 minutes using a 9x5-inch or 8x4-inch or a round pan. Yields 2 - 3 loaves.

Rosalie Weiner

Zucchini Bread (Pareve)

An easy, quick bread recipe that can serve as a substitute for cake. Especially appealing when spread with cream cheese.

2	cups flour
1	tablespoon ground cinnamon
2	teaspoons baking soda
1	teaspoon salt
3	eggs, beaten
2	cups sugar
1	cup vegetable oil
1	tablespoon vanilla extract
1	cup chopped nuts (or less)
2	cups zucchini, unpeeled and grated

Preheat oven to 350 degrees. Sift together flour, cinnamon, baking soda and salt. Combine eggs, sugar, oil and vanilla. Stir into flour mixture until well blended. Add zucchini and nuts.

Pour into 2 greased loaf pans. Bake for approximately 60 minutes. Yields 2 loaves.

Zachary Lasker

Swedish Limpa Bread (Dairy/Pareve)

This popular bread is always a hit with everyone.

2	packages yeast
1 1/2	cups tepid water
2	tablespoons brown sugar
2 1/2	cups rye flour
2 1/2	cups white, unbleached flour
1	teaspoon anise seed or
1	tablespoon grated orange peel
1	tablespoon salt (or less)
1/4	cup molasses
2	tablespoons butter or margarine
	Cornmeal

Proof yeast in 1/2 cup of tepid water with 2 tablespoons brown sugar. Wait 5-7 minutes until yeast rises to the top of cup.

Combine flours. Mix 1 2/3 cups of flour mixture, anise seed (or orange peel) and salt. Add yeast mixture with remaining warm water, molasses and butter gradually to dry ingredients. Beat for 2 minutes at medium speed.

Add 1 cup of flour mixture or enough to make a thick batter and beat at high speed for 2 minutes, scraping bowl occasionally.

Knead in just enough additional flour to make a soft dough, adding more white flour as necessary for the desired consistency.

Turn out on a floured board and knead until smooth and elastic, approximately 8-10 minutes, with some slapping around of the dough. If using a bread hook, this step may be done by the machine.

Place in a greased bowl and turn to coat the ball of dough.

Cover and let rise in a warm place, free from drafts, for 1 hour until double in bulk.

Punch down and turn out on lightly floured board. Divide into 2 equal round, slightly flattened, loaves. Place the loaves on greased baking sheets sprinkled with cornmeal.

Cover and let rise until double (about 35 minutes).

Bake in a preheated 400 degree oven for 25 minutes or until the loaves sound hollow. Cool in pans for 5 minutes, then cool on racks. Yields 2 loaves.

Rosalie Weiner

Anadama Bread (Dairy/Pareve)

No kneading is necessary for this easy-to-make bread.

1/2	cup yellow cornmeal
3	tablespoons butter/margarine
1/4	cup molasses
2	teaspoons salt (or less)
3/4	cup boiling water
1	package yeast
1/4	cup warm water
1	tablespoon honey
1	egg, beaten
3	cups flour
1	tablespoon cornmeal
1/4	teaspoon salt, optional

Combine 1/2 cup cornmeal, butter, molasses, salt and boiling water in a bowl. Let stand until lukewarm. Then mix well.

Dissolve yeast in 1/4 cup warm water with honey. Add yeast, egg and 1 1/2 cups flour to cornmeal mixture to make a soft dough. Stir in remaining flour to form a smooth dough.

Place dough in a greased 9x5-inch loaf pan. Cover and let rise in a warm place until the dough reaches the top of the pan, 2-2 1/2 hours. Sprinkle top with corn-meal-salt mixture.

Bake in a preheated 375 degree oven for 35-45 minutes or until well browned. Remove from pan and cool before slicing. Yields 1 loaf.

Rosalie Weiner

Natural Bread (Pareve)

A heavy, country-style whole wheat bread.

1	package dry yeast
2	cups warm water
2	teaspoons salt
2	tablespoons caraway seeds
2 1/2	cups rye flour
2 1/2	cups whole wheat flour
1	egg, beaten
	Cornmeal

Sprinkle yeast into warm water, using a large bowl. After yeast starts to foam, about 10 minutes, add salt and caraway seeds.

Add flour, 1 cup at a time, stirring with a wooden spoon until dough starts to come away from the bowl. Remove from bowl to floured board and knead, adding more flour as needed. Knead about 10 minutes, until dough is smooth and elastic; not too sticky or too hard, but firm.

Place dough in a lightly oiled bowl, turning to coat all over. Cover bowl with damp cloth and let rise in warm place, 2 hours or more, until about double in size.

Turn dough onto lightly floured board and knead for 1 minute. Pat into oval shape and brush with a beaten egg for crispness.

Put into 9 1/2x5 1/2x2 3/4-inch loaf pan that has been oiled and sprinkled with corn meal.

Let dough rest in pan for about 5 minutes.

Preheat oven and bake 60 minutes at 400 degrees. Remove from pan and cool before cutting. Yields 1 loaf.

Note: *Store flours in a cool place such as a refrigerator, as flour can turn rancid.*

Janet Arzt

Shepherd's Bread (Dairy)

A classic country white bread.

2	packages yeast
1	cup warm milk
1 1/2	cups warm water
1/4	cup margarine
1	tablespoon salt (or less)
2	tablespoons honey
7	cups flour

Variation: Bread may also be baked in a greased cast-iron Dutch oven. Bake, covered, for 12 minutes in a 375 degree oven or uncovered for 30-35 minutes.

Proof yeast in 1/2 cup of the total water and honey (wait 5-7 minutes until yeast rises to the top of cup).

In a mixing bowl, combine yeast, remaining water, milk and margarine (does not need to melt completely). Add salt and 2 1/2 cups of flour. Mix for 2 minutes at medium speed, scraping bowl occasionally.

Add 1 cup of flour, or enough to make a thick batter. Beat on high speed for 2 minutes, scraping bowl when needed. Stir in enough flour to make the dough come away from the sides of the bowl. Knead in mixer for 3 minutes. Then knead in rest of the flour by hand and slap the dough about for 5 minutes until smooth and elastic.

Place in a greased bowl, turning to coat dough ball entirely. Cover with plastic and let rise in a warm place free from draft, until double in size (about 1 hour).

Punch down and turn out onto a lightly floured board. Cover and let rise for 15 minutes.

Divide dough in half and shape into two balls. Place on greased baking sheet, cover and let rise until doubled again (about 1 hour).

Bake in a preheated 400 degree oven for 25-30 minutes or until bread sounds hollow when thumped. Yields 2 loaves.

Rosalie Weiner

Oatmeal Muffins with Fruit and Veggie Variations (Dairy)

I created this recipe when I had to go on a low-cholesterol, low-fat diet.

1/2	cup wheat flour
1/2	cup unbleached white flour
1	teaspoon baking powder
1/4	teaspoon salt
1	cup uncooked oats
3	tablespoons sugar
3	tablespoons vegetable oil
3/4	cup nonfat milk
1/3	cup egg whites (about 3 medium or 2 large eggs)

Preheat oven to 425 degrees and insert paper or aluminum foil muffin cups into a 12-muffin pan. Sift flour, baking powder and salt together. Stir in oats.

In a separate bowl, mix sugar, oil and milk. Lightly whisk egg whites and add to liquids. Quickly combine all ingredients until just mixed.

Divide into 12 muffin cups. Bake 18-20 minutes or until lightly browned. Use a toothpick to test. Yields 12 muffins.

Variations: Add all fruits and vegetables just before baking. Carrot or zucchini muffins: add 1 teaspoon grated orange peel and 3/4 cup lightly packed, grated carrots or zucchini.
Blueberry muffins: add 2/3 cup washed, drained, fresh blueberries or unthawed frozen berries.
Apple muffins: add 1 teaspoon cinnamon to dry ingredients and stir in 2/3 cup diced, unpeeled, fresh apple.

Eleanor Gold Hirsch

117

Oat Bran Muffins (Dairy)

A better-tasting muffin for the low-cholesterol bound.

Dry Mix:

2 1/4	cups apple/cinnamon-flavored oat bran cereal (used for hot cereal)
2	teaspoons baking powder
1-1 1/2	teaspoons ground cinnamon
1/3	cup white raisins
1-1 1/2	large apples, unpeeled and diced
	Grated rind of medium-size orange
	Grated rind of 1/2 lemon

Wet Mix:

2	eggs, beaten (may use yolk of 1 egg only and 2 whites)
1	cup nonfat milk
1	teaspoon vanilla
1/2	cup honey
2	tablespoons vegetable oil
	Cinnamon and sugar for topping

Preheat oven to 350 degrees. Lightly mix dry and wet ingredients together. Fill lightly oiled 12-cup muffin tin. Sprinkle top of muffins with cinnamon and sugar mixture.

Bake for 20 minutes or until lightly browned. Yields 12 muffins.

Suggestion: If apple/cinnamon oat bran is not available, use plain oat bran and increase cinnamon to 1 1/2 teaspoons and add 1 more small apple. Pineapple or other fruits may be substituted for the apple.

Pearl Roseman

Banana Nut Oat Bran Muffins (Dairy)

An easy, low-cholesterol, nutritious breakfast or snack.

2 1/4	cups oat bran cereal (used for hot cereal)
1	tablespoon baking powder
1	tablespoon cinnamon
1/4	cup brown sugar
1/4	cup chopped walnuts or pecans
1/4	cup raisins, optional
1 1/4	cups skim milk
2	very ripe bananas (the riper the better)
2	egg whites
2	tablespoons vegetable oil

Preheat oven to 425 degrees. Mix dry ingredients in a bowl. Mix milk, bananas, egg whites and oil in a blender or food processor. Add to dry ingredients and mix.

Line 12-cup muffin pan with paper baking cups and fill with batter. Bake for 17 minutes. Muffins do not get brown. Yields 12 muffins.

Helyn Friedman

Persimmon Bread (Dairy)

An elegant holiday bread, delicious with cream cheese.

2	cups persimmon pulp
2	teaspoons baking soda
2	cups sugar
4	tablespoons margarine, melted
1-2	cups walnuts, chopped
1	cup white raisins
3	cups flour
1-2	teaspoons ground cinnamon
1/2	teaspoon ground cloves
1	teaspoon ground nutmeg
1	teaspoon salt
1/2	cup milk
1/2	cup brandy*

Preheat oven to 325 degrees. Mix baking soda into persimmon pulp. Add sugar, melted margarine, nuts and raisins.

Mix together flour and spices. Separately mix together milk and brandy. Add flour and liquid alternately to pulp mixture. Pour into 2 well-greased loaf pans.

Bake for approximately 70 minutes, or until toothpick comes out dry. Yields 2 loaves.

*Variation: *May use less brandy and more milk or all milk and no brandy.*

Doris Goodman

Date and Nut Bread (Pareve)

A lovely version of an old favorite.

2	cups boiling water
1	cup dates, cut up
4	tablespoons margarine
2	teaspoons baking soda
1	cup brown sugar, firmly packed
2	eggs, beaten
4	cups flour
1/4	teaspoon salt
1	teaspoon vanilla
1/2	cup walnuts, chopped

Preheat oven to 350 degrees. Pour boiling water over dates, margarine and baking soda and stir. Add brown sugar and beaten eggs. Add remaining dry ingredients, vanilla and nuts. Mix well.

Grease four 20-ounce cans. Divide batter into the 4 cans. Loaf pans may be substituted. Bake 50-60 minutes. Yields 4 loaves.

Suggestion: May be served with cream cheese. Freezes well.

Edythe Merkow

Banana Bran Nut Bread (Pareve)

A good, quick bread to have in the freezer for unexpected company.
Also makes a lovely gift loaf

2   eggs, well beaten
1 1/2 cups mashed banana
       (4-5 medium)
1/4   cup shortening, melted
1   cup bran
1 1/2 cups sifted flour
2 1/2 teaspoons baking
       powder
1/2   teaspoon baking soda
1/2   cup sugar
1/2   cup chopped nuts

Preheat oven to 350 degrees. Combine eggs, mashed bananas, shortening and bran. Sift flour, baking powder, soda and sugar together. Add dry mixture to banana mixture and mix only enough to blend. Add nuts. Place in a 8 1/2x4 1/2x3-inch greased loaf pan. Bake for 45-60 minutes, or until toothpick comes out dry.

Delicious with cream cheese and jam. Yields 1 loaf.

Shirley Azaren

Kugels & Pasta

Kugels are among the best loved dishes in Jewish cuisine. If a kugel popularity contest were held, however, dairy kugels would probably be the "sweepstakes" winner. At Hanukkah and Shavuot, when it is traditional to serve dairy dishes, a kugel is often featured, if not two or three.

Although most kugels are dairy they are also made in many other varieties. There are noodle kugels, potato kugels and kosher-for-Passover kugels. There are kugels for dinner, brunch and *kiddush* (the traditional luncheon following the Sabbath or holiday morning service) and — if you are lucky — leftover kugels for breakfast.

Pareve, or meat kugels, which use chicken fat or beef broth, make appealing side dishes at a meat meal. Potato kugels are almost as popular as their noodle cousins, and the special kugels made with matzos are favorites at Passover.

All the kugel recipes that follow survived our testers' rigid evaluations. And all of them are, to a kugel, delicious.

Min's Noodle Kugel (Dairy)

Irresistible. Don't plan on having "just one bite" of this classic dish!

8	ounces wide noodles
4	ounces butter or margarine
6	eggs
1	cup sour cream
1	cup cottage cheese
1/2	cup sugar
1/2	cup milk
1/2	cup golden raisins, optional
1/2	pound dried apricots, optional

Topping:
1	cup corn flake crumbs
1	cup brown sugar
1/4	cup butter, melted

Cook noodles in boiling salted water until tender. Drain and add butter. Set aside. Beat together eggs, sour cream, cottage cheese, sugar and milk. Add raisins or apricots or both. Add mixture to noodles. Pour into buttered 8x12-inch baking dish. Mix together topping ingredients. Sprinkle over kugel. Bake at 350 degrees for one hour. Serves 10 - 12.

Hint: *To reduce calories and cholesterol you can reduce margarine to 2 tablespoons, use light sour cream, liquid egg substitutes, skim milk and sugar substitutes.*

Min Leonard

Cheesy Noodle Pudding (Dairy)

Hungarian classic version. Wins raves from everyone!

8	ounces wide noodles
4	ounces butter, melted
1/2	cup sugar
	Dash salt
1	lemon rind, grated
16	ounces cottage cheese
8	ounces farmer or hoop cheese
8	ounces cream cheese
6	eggs, lightly beaten
8	ounces sour cream
2	cups milk

Topping:
1	cup corn flake crumbs
1/4	cup butter, melted
1/2	cup slivered almonds
1	cup brown sugar

Cook noodles and drain. In a large bowl, mix noodles with butter. Add sugar, salt, lemon rind and cheeses. Mix lightly. Add eggs. Fold in sour cream and milk. Place in greased 10x14x2 1/2-inch pan. Mix together topping ingredients and sprinkle over noodles (all ingredients may be increased to taste). Bake at 325 degrees for 1 1/2 hours. Serves 12 - 14.

Claire Schneider

Easy Noodle Pudding (Dairy)
Crushed pineapple makes this kugel a little different.

2 cups milk
8 ounces medium egg noodles
4 eggs, beaten
1/2 cup sugar
1 large red apple, peeled and chopped
1/2 cup golden raisins
8 ounces cottage cheese
1/2 cup crushed pineapple, drained
2-4 ounces butter or margarine

In a stew pot, cook together milk and noodles; bring to a boil. Add eggs, sugar, apple, raisins, cottage cheese and pineapple. Pour melted butter or margarine into an 8x8-inch casserole. Add noodle mixture and bake at 350 degrees for approximately 1 hour or until browned on top. Serves 6 - 8.

Elinor Einy

Lemon Noodle Pudding (Dairy)
Fresh lemon distinguishes this dish.

16 ounces medium, flat noodles, cooked and drained
6 eggs
16 ounces sour cream
8 ounces butter or margarine, melted (reserve 5 tablespoons for topping)
1 cup sugar (reserve 5 tablespoons for topping)
Rind and juice of 1 lemon (mix together)
2 cups corn flakes

In a large bowl, mix noodles with eggs, sour cream, butter or margarine, sugar, lemon rind and lemon juice. Pour into 9x13-inch pan. Mix together corn flakes with reserved butter or margarine and sugar. Sprinkle over all. Bake at 350 degrees for one hour. Serves 12.

Ingrid Blumenstein

Apricot or Cherry Noodle Pudding (Pareve)
Pareve kugel recipes are hard to find; this one is delicious.

4	ounces unsalted margarine, melted
16	ounces wide noodles, cooked
4	eggs, beaten
1/2	cup sugar
1	teaspoon vanilla extract
1	20-ounce can pineapple, crushed and drained
10	ounces apricot jam or one 20-ounce can cherry pie filling

Melt margarine; pour into noodles. Add eggs, sugar, vanilla and pineapple; mix together. Pour 1/2 noodle mixture into greased 3-quart pan. Spread with filling, then cover with rest of noodle mixture.

Mix together corn flakes, sugar and cinnamon; sprinkle over top. Dot with margarine. Bake at 350 degrees for 40 minutes. Serves 10 - 12.

Ingrid Blumenstein

Topping:
1	cup corn flakes
1	tablespoon sugar
1	teaspoon cinnamon

Apricot Sour Cream Kugel (Dairy)
A very different method and combination of flavors for this popular dish.

1	12-ounce package noodles, cooked and drained
4	eggs
3	ounces cream cheese
4	ounces butter, melted
1/4	cup sugar
1	cup apricot nectar
1	teaspoon vanilla extract
8	ounces sour cream

Place cooked noodles in a 9x13-inch baking dish. Combine rest of ingredients and pour over noodles.

Mix cinnamon, sugar and corn flakes; sprinkle on top. Dot with remaining 4 ounces of butter. Bake at 350 degrees for one hour. Serves 10 - 12.

Cirel Blitz

Topping:
1	teaspoon cinnamon
1/4	cup sugar
2	cups corn flakes, crushed
4	ounces butter

Cherry Kugel (Dairy)

Cherry pie filling gives this traditional dish a delicious new twist..

12	ounces medium noodles	
1/4	pound butter	
3	eggs, beaten	
16	ounces cottage cheese	
8	ounces sour cream	
3/4	cup milk	
1/2	cup sugar	
	Pinch salt	
1	20-ounce can cherry pie filling	

Cook and drain noodles. Melt butter in oven in 10x12-inch glass baking dish, then pour off into noodles. Add rest of ingredients (except cherry filling) to noodles and mix. Pour into baking dish and bake at 350 degrees for 40 minutes. Cover with pie filling and bake an additional 30 minutes. Serves 10 - 12.

Ruth Nebron

California Kugel (Dairy/Pareve)

Fresh orange juice and apples are the secret that make this kugel different!

10	ounces medium egg noodles
2	tablespoons butter or margarine, melted
4	eggs
2	cups fresh-squeezed orange juice (not frozen), including pulp
1/2	cup sugar
1/2	teaspoon salt
1/3	cup golden raisins
3	medium tart apples, cored, peeled and grated
2	teaspoons lemon juice

In a large pot, cook noodles and drain. Return to pot and toss with butter. In a second bowl, beat eggs; add orange juice, sugar, salt and raisins. Pour over noodles and mix. Mix apples and lemon juice; add to noodle mixture and mix. Pour into 8x10-inch greased pan. Bake at 350 degrees for one hour. Serves 8 - 10.

Janis Weiss

Aunt Rollie's Noodle Kugel (Dairy)

From my husband's Aunt Rollie; a special family treat.

1   16-ounce package wide
     noodles
3   eggs, well-beaten
1   large Red Delicious
     apple, peeled and
     chopped
1   8-ounce carton cottage
     cheese
1   16-ounce carton sour
     cream
1   teaspoon sugar
     (if desired)
1   cup raisins
4   ounces margarine,
     melted

In a large stew pot, cook noodles and drain. Return noodles to pot; mix together with all remaining ingredients. Bake at 350 degrees in well-oiled 8 1/2x11-inch baking dish for one hour. Serves 10.

Suggestions: May use fewer raisins, add cinnamon to taste and /or use less margarine, if desired.

Shirley Izenstark

Kugel (Dairy)

For best results, prepare this tasty dish a day in advance.

1   16-ounce package wide
       noodles
1/4   pound melted
       margarine
7   eggs
1   pint sour cream
1   pint cottage cheese
3/4   cup milk
1/2   teaspoon salt
1/2   cup sugar
1   cup golden raisins

Topping:
1 1/2 cups corn flakes,
       crumbled
1   cup sugar
2/3   cup margarine

In a large pot, cook noodles and drain. Return to pot, add margarine and set aside. In a large mixing bowl, beat eggs; add remaining ingredients and stir. Add to noodles and blend. Put in a greased 9x15-inch pan. Mix topping ingredients and spread on top of kugel. Cover and refrigerate overnight. Remove from refrigerator one hour before baking and bring to room temperature. Bake at 325 degrees for 1 to 1 1/4 hours, uncovered. Serves 12 - 16.

Sue Ann Levine

Spinach-Noodle Kugel (Pareve)

A quick and easy side dish with chicken, fish or meat.

8   ounces noodles, cooked
1   10-ounce package frozen, chopped spinach, defrosted and drained well
1/2 cup liquid nondairy creamer
3   eggs, beaten
1   packet onion soup mix
2   tablespoons pareve margarine

Mix all ingredients well and place in a 9x13-inch well-greased baking dish. Bake at 350 degrees for 45 minutes. Serves 8.

Suggestion: *Egg substitutes work well with this recipe.*

Walter Richheimer

Tortellini with Tomato Vinaigrette (Dairy)

Beautiful colors add to the appeal of this West Coast favorite.

1   cup sun-dried tomatoes
3   tablespoons Dijon mustard
1/2 cup red wine vinegar
1   tablespoon sugar
1   teaspoon crushed garlic
1/2 teaspoon salt
1/2 teaspoon freshly ground pepper
1/2 cup olive oil
1/2 cup coarsely chopped fresh basil, plus 1 1/4 cups, julienned
18   ounces fresh tricolored, cheese-filled tortellini
1   cup fresh Roma tomatoes, diced
     Salt and freshly ground pepper to taste
1/4 cup Parmesan cheese

To make vinaigrette, soak sun-dried tomatoes in 1 cup boiling water for 5 minutes. Coarsely chop reconstituted tomatoes and place in blender or food processor with next 6 ingredients. Process until smooth. While mixing, slowly add oil until all is emulsified into dressing. Stir in chopped basil. Adjust seasonings.

Cook tortellini according to package instructions, until al dente. Cool. In large mixing bowl, combine with vinaigrette, julienned basil (reserve 1/4 cup for garnish) and Roma tomatoes. Mix well. Season with salt and pepper. Serve chilled and garnished with remaining 1/4 cup julienned basil and Parmesan cheese. Serves 8 - 10.

Pearl Roseman

Fresh Tomato Sauce with Basil (Pareve)

*A versatile sauce that makes use of California's
year-round supply of fresh herbs and tomatoes.*

2	**large tomatoes or 10 Roma tomatoes, peeled if desired**
2	**tablespoons finely chopped onion**
1-3	**cloves garlic, minced**
	Salt and pepper to taste
2	**tablespoons olive oil**
2	**tablespoons chopped fresh basil**
1/4	**teaspoon dried oregano, optional**
1/8	**teaspoon dried thyme, optional**
1	**teaspoon parsley, optional**

Chop tomatoes coarsely. Heat medium skillet, add oil and sauté onion and garlic until soft. Add tomatoes and cook gently for about 10 minutes. If sauce is too thick or needs more volume, add small amount of tomato juice or tomato sauce. Add seasonings to taste. Pour over hot cooked and drained pasta. Can also use sauce on fish or chicken. Serves 2.

Suggestion: Best with summer tomatoes.
Variation: For a richer sauce, add 1 tablespoon butter or margarine. If fresh herbs are available, use greater quantities.

Eve Marcus

Mushroom Tetrazzini (Dairy)

This vegetarian spaghetti casserole will appeal to mushroom lovers.

1	**16-ounce package spaghetti**
12	**ounces Provolone cheese, cut into small pieces**
4	**tablespoons butter or margarine**
1/2	**pound fresh mushrooms, cut in thick slices**
1	**medium onion, sliced**
3	**tablespoons flour**
1 1/2	**teaspoons salt**
	Dash pepper
2	**cups milk**
1/4	**cup cooking or dry sherry**
1/3	**cup chopped parsley**

Cook spaghetti and drain. Set aside 1/2 cup cheese for topping. In 3-quart saucepan, heat butter or margarine over medium to high heat. Sauté mushrooms and onions for 5 minutes (or until golden). Stir in flour, salt and pepper. Gradually add milk and sherry. Add cheese (all but 1/2 cup) and parsley. Cook and stir until mixture is thick and cheese is melted.

Place hot spaghetti in large casserole dish. Pour sauce over spaghetti and sprinkle with remaining 1/2 cup cheese. Broil until cheese melts. Serves 6 - 8 as a main dish; 8 - 10 as side dish.

Suggestion: May be reheated in microwave.

Marcia Abelson

Vegetarian Lasagna (Dairy)

Use uncooked noodles for this absolutely delicious dish.

16   ounces small-curd
      cottage cheese
16   ounces mozzarella,
      grated (use only 1/3
      of this in the sauce)
2   eggs
2   10-ounce packages
      chopped frozen
      broccoli, defrosted
      and completely
      drained
1   16-ounce box of lasagna
      or wide noodles,
      uncooked
1   32-ounce jar spaghetti
      sauce
      Dried oregano, salt and
      pepper, to taste

Do not cook noodles. In a large bowl, mix all ingredients except noodles and 2/3 of the grated mozzarella.

Grease 9x13-inch baking pan; cover with thin layer of sauce on the bottom. Add 1/2 of the noodles, then 1/2 of the remaining sauce. Repeat, using up noodles and sauce. Top all with remaining mozzarella.

Refrigerate overnight. Before baking, pour 1 1/2 cups cold water around edges of pan (not in center).

Bake, lightly covered, at 350 degrees for 1 hour and 15 minutes, then let set for 15 minutes. Serves 10 - 12.

Variation: Other vegetables, such as spinach or zucchini, may be used.

Pearl Leonard

129

Vegetable Pasta Bake (Pareve)

My great niece passed this recipe to me from her grandmother.
An interesting side dish with fish.

1	16-ounce package orzo or small pasta shells
1	cup chopped green peppers, fresh
1	cup chopped onion
6	ounces mushrooms, sliced thin
4	ounces margarine
2	bouillon cubes
1	cup boiling water
	Nonstick vegetable spray
1	2.8-ounce can fried onion rings

Cook pasta until al dente and drain. Sauté peppers, onions and mushrooms in margarine till tender. Dissolve bouillon cubes in boiling water and mix with shell mixture. Add vegetables and mix gently.

Prepare 9x13-inch glass pan with vegetable spray. Layer 1/2 pasta mixture, then spread onion rings over top. Layer pasta mixture again, ending with onion rings. Bake 45 minutes at 350 degrees. Serves 8 - 10.

Freda Balsham

Tuna Lasagna (Dairy)

A rich, easy main dish for family or company.

1	8-ounce package lasagna noodles
3	tablespoons butter or margarine
1/2	cup onion, chopped
1/2	cup green bell pepper, diced
2	6- to 7-ounce cans tuna, drained
1	10 3/4-ounce can cream of celery soup
1/2	cup milk
1/2	teaspoon dried oregano
1/2	teaspoon salt
1/4	teaspoon pepper
1/2	pound Cheddar cheese, grated
1/2	pound mozzarella cheese, grated

Prepare noodles according to package directions. Drain. In a large skillet, sauté onion and green pepper in melted butter. Add tuna, soup, milk, oregano, salt and pepper. Simmer 10 minutes.

In a 3-quart shallow baking dish, layer 1/2 each of the lasagna, tuna sauce, Cheddar and mozzarella; repeat. Bake in a 350 degree oven for 30 minutes. Serves 8.

Cirel Blitz

Spinach Lasagna (Dairy)

My sister, Laurian Ross, gave me this recipe; a good luncheon dish.

2   eggs, beaten
13   ounces Monterey Jack cheese
4   ounces butter, melted
1   teaspoon parsley flakes
2   pounds large-curd cottage cheese
    Dill weed, to taste (optional)
    Garlic salt, to taste
    Salt and pepper to taste
1   8-ounce package lasagna noodles, cooked and drained
1/2   cup Parmesan cheese, plus more for sprinkling
2   10-ounce packages frozen chopped spinach, cooked, drained and squeezed dry

Mix together eggs, Jack cheese, butter, parsley, cottage cheese, dill, garlic salt, and salt and pepper. Grease a 9x13-inch baking dish. Cover bottom with 1/3 of noodles. Add 1/2 of the Parmesan cheese and 1/2 of the spinach. Pour over 1/2 of the cheese mixture. Add another 1/3 of the noodles. Repeat, ending with noodles. Sprinkle more Parmesan on top. Bake for 1 hour in a preheated 350 degree oven. Serves 12.

Suggestion: Can be frozen. To serve, partially thaw and bake 1 1/2 hours.

Phyllis Sarto

Savory Tuna Pasta Sauce (Pareve)

A quick and easy pasta sauce.

1	clove garlic, minced
1	tablespoon chopped Italian parsley (2 large sprigs)
1	tablespoon chopped fresh basil or 1 teaspoon dried basil
1/4	cup olive oil
1/4	teaspoon hot red pepper, crushed Salt (optional)
1	6 1/2-ounce can chunk tuna, drained and flaked
2	heaping tablespoons tomato paste
1/2	cup dry red wine
2	cups canned, peeled Italian tomatoes
12	ounces pasta, any shape, cooked and drained

Combine garlic, parsley and basil; set aside 1/2 of the mixture. In a medium saucepan, sauté other 1/2 of the mixture in oil (do not brown). Add red pepper and salt (optional); cook 1 minute. Add tuna and tomato paste; stir with wooden spoon 1 minute more. Add wine and stir over high heat until paste is dissolved. Add tomatoes and cook 5 minutes more. Adjust seasonings to taste.

Remove from heat and add remaining herb mixture. Pour over hot cooked pasta. Serves 3 - 4 as a main dish, 6 as a side dish.

Eleanor Botney

Eggs & Cheese

The ever-handy egg serves many functions in kosher homes and kitchens. Eggs are *pareve*, or neutral, under Jewish dietary law, so they can be used freely in cooking. Eggs also play a symbolic part in certain Jewish traditions. A roasted egg (representing the festival sacrifice) appears on the Seder table at Passover. Hard-boiled eggs (representing the continuity of life) are part of the mourning ritual and eggs wrapped in dough (representing the captivity of the evil Haman) are given as gifts by Sephardic Jews on Purim.

The combination of eggs, cheese and vegetables form the basis of a host of delectable dairy dishes. Some of these recipes, adapted from other cultures, require creativity on the part of kosher cooks, who must follow strict guidelines regarding the separation of meat and dairy dishes. For this reason many California Jews have enthusiastically adopted Mexican and Southwestern-type cuisine, since in most cases it requires very little to convert these recipes to dairy dishes.

For those following strictures of cholesterol and/or fat intake, egg and cheese dishes may appear less frequently on the table than they did a generation ago. But when you feel the urge to splurge, here are some terrific dishes to try.

HINT

- Liquid egg substitutes are available in almost all grocery stores for those who wish to reduce the cholesterol and fat content of egg and cheese recipes. These substitutes also work well in baked goods, with little if any change in flavor or texture.

Cheese Blintzes (Dairy)

A universal favorite!

Crepes:

4   eggs
1 1/2 cups flour
1 1/2 cups milk
4   tablespoons margarine

Filling:

1   package (about 2 1/2 pounds) hoop cheese
5   eggs
1/4   pound margarine
1   tablespoon salt
9   tablespoons sugar or equivalent of sugar substitute

Crepes: Beat eggs. Gradually sift in flour (if batter becomes too thick, thin with small amount of milk, and continue sifting in flour). When all flour is absorbed, add remaining milk. Heat frying pan; butter lightly. Pour a small amount (about 2 tablespoons) of batter into pan, tilting to make a thin crepe. Cook approximately 45 seconds until set and barely golden. Slide each pancake onto a towel. Repeat until all the batter is used.

Filling: In an electric mixer beat all ingredients until smooth. Place a heaping tablespoon of filling in the center of each crepe, folding sides in and rolling over to enclose filling. (Blintzes may be frozen at this point.)

Fry blintzes lightly in butter several minutes on each side until they are crisp and light brown. Or bake, arranging them in one layer in a shallow, buttered baking dish, brushing the tops with melted butter, in a preheated 425 degree oven for 15-20 minutes. Serve with sour cream and preserves. Yields approximately 36 blintzes.

Variation: Add 1/2 cup golden raisins to filling.

Min Leonard

Blintz Casserole (Dairy)

This casserole is served often during Shavuot and Hanukkah and for elegant brunches or dairy meals the year round. Note variations.

10	eggs, beaten
3	cups sour cream
6	tablespoons sugar or equivalent of sugar substitute
4	tablespoons vanilla extract
1/2	teaspoon salt
1/2	pound margarine
36	blintzes (see p. 134)
	Sugar and cinnamon to sprinkle on top

Blend eggs, sour cream, sugar, vanilla and salt. Melt margarine in two 9x13-inch glass baking dishes. Divide blintzes between the two dishes and place on melted margarine. Pour sour cream mixture over blintzes. Sprinkle with sugar and cinnamon. Bake at 350 degrees for 30-45 minutes (may take a little longer if using frozen blintzes). Serve immediately. Serves 12 - 16.

Note: Casserole may be made with commercially prepared frozen cheese or fruit-filled blintzes.

Variations: Cut orange into quarters and remove seeds. Place in a food processor or blender and whir until liquefied. Add to sour cream mixture. Or add 2-3 teaspoons of cinnamon to sour cream mixture.

Min Leonard

Chile Relleno Casserole (Dairy)

Serve with salsa for an authentic touch.
A quick and easy dish to assemble.

2	16-ounce cans vegetarian beans, mashed or 2 16-ounce cans vegetarian refried beans
1	teaspoon chili powder
2	4-ounce cans diced green chilies
1	pound Monterey Jack cheese, grated
4	eggs, beaten
4	tablespoons flour
1	cup milk

Mash beans and season with chili powder. Spread over bottom of a greased 9x13-inch baking dish. Layer chilies, then cheese. Mix together eggs, flour and milk; spread on top. Bake at 350 degrees for 30-45 minutes, or until set and slightly brown. Serves 8 - 10.

Shirley Moore

Huevos con Tomat y Queso:
Eggs with Tomato and Cheese (Dairy)

*A traditional dish for Sephardic families for the meal preceding the
fast at Tisha B'Av. An excellent brunch, luncheon or light supper meal.*

4-5	**fresh tomatoes, peeled and diced, or 1 (#2 1/2) can diced or cut-up stewed tomatoes**
1	**tablespoon oil**
	Pinch sugar
	Salt and pepper to taste (some kinds of cheese are saltier)
4-6	**eggs**
1/4	**cup grated cheese (Kaskaval, Romano or Parmesan) or 4-6 slices solid cheese (Feta, Kaskaval or Provolone), cut into small pieces**

Choose an appropriate-size pan for the number of eggs you are using. Place tomatoes in the pan with oil, sugar and salt; allow to simmer 3-4 minutes. Add half the cheese. Break eggs (as for poaching) into sauce. Sprinkle balance of cheese on eggs. Cover and simmer slowly until yolks are cooked. Serves 2 - 3.

Suggestion: *Serve hot with plenty of French or Greek sesame bread for dipping in the sauce.*

Susan Brandes

Corn, Chile and Cheese Casserole (Dairy)

Should be made a day ahead to allow flavors to blend.

1	**17-ounce can cream-style corn**
1	**4-ounce can diced green chilies**
1	**4-ounce jar diced pimientos, drained**
1/2	**cup melted butter**
2	**eggs, beaten**
1/2	**cup cornmeal**
1/2	**teaspoon salt**
1	**cup sour cream**
2	**cups diced Monterey Jack cheese**

Place all ingredients in a large bowl and mix thoroughly. Turn into buttered shallow 1 1/2 quart baking dish. Bake, uncovered, in a preheated 375 degree oven for 40 minutes or until set. Serves 6 - 8.

Trana Labowe

Tortica Rustica (Dairy)

A gourmet party dish that elevates a sandwich to elegance.

2	loaves frozen bread dough, thawed (or fresh dough may be used)
3/4	pound Cheddar cheese, sliced
1	16-ounce can asparagus tips
1	8-ounce can chopped green chilies, drained
2	2 1/4-ounce cans chopped olives, drained
1/2	pound fresh mushrooms, sliced
3/4	pound Jarlsburg cheese, sliced
1	egg white plus 1 tablespoon water

Omelet Layer:

1	tablespoon butter
3	eggs, beaten
1	clove garlic, minced
1/4	teaspoon dried tarragon
1/4	teaspoon salt
1/4	teaspoon pepper

Roll or shape one loaf of bread dough with hands, to fit in bottom and up sides of an oiled 10- to 12-inch springform pan. If dough is too elastic to retain shape as you work it, let it rest a few minutes, then try again.

Set all ingredients out, ready to layer, leaving omelet for the next-to-last layer. To prepare the omelet; melt butter in a large pan. Combine other ingredients and pour into hot butter. Cook on medium heat, lifting edges to allow uncooked portion of the egg to flow underneath to cook. Cook until set.

Press each layer down as you assemble torta in the following order: Cheddar, mushrooms, chilies, olives, Jarlsburg, omelet and cover with asparagus.

Roll or shape remaining dough and fit on top of torta. Pinch edges of dough together at sides, sealing well. Brush with egg white/water mixture.

Bake 1 hour at 350 degrees until brown and the crust pulls away slightly from the sides of the pan. To serve warm, allow to cool slightly. May also be refrigerated and served cold. Cut into wedges to serve. Serves 16 - 20.

Variations: *This recipe can be varied as desired with spinach, marinated artichoke hearts, broccoli, etc.*

Rosalie Wiener

Mexican Cheese Strata (Dairy)

*A Southwest adaptation of a classic strata
that is best assembled a day ahead.*

4	cups broken cheese-flavored tortilla chips
2	cups shredded Monterey Jack cheese
6	eggs, beaten
2 1/2	cups milk
1	4-ounce can chopped green chilies
1/4	cup finely chopped onion
3	tablespoons ketchup
1/2	teaspoon salt
1/4	teaspoon hot pepper sauce
	Whole tortilla chips and halved tomato slices for garnish

Sprinkle the broken tortilla chips evenly over the bottom of a greased 12x7x2-inch baking dish. Sprinkle with the cheese.

In a medium bowl using a rotary beater, combine the eggs, milk, green chilies, onion, ketchup, salt and hot pepper sauce. Pour over cheese. Cover and refrigerate overnight. Take out 1/2 hour before baking. Bake uncovered in a preheated 325 degree oven for 50-55 minutes or until set and lightly browned. Garnish with tortilla chips and tomato slices. Serves 6.

Ruth King

Spinach-Cheese Bake (Dairy)

Don't be fooled; there is supposed to be twice as much pepper as salt!

1/2	pound sharp Cheddar cheese
1	10-ounce package frozen chopped spinach, thawed and drained well
1	16-ounce carton cottage cheese
3	eggs, slightly beaten
3	tablespoons flour
1/4	teaspoon salt
1/2	teaspoon black pepper
1/8	teaspoon garlic powder

Cut Cheddar cheese into small cubes. Combine all ingredients in a large bowl. Spoon into a greased 8-inch square baking dish. Bake for 45 minutes in a preheated 375 degree oven or until set. Let cool 10 minutes before serving. Serves 4.

Variations: Top with 2 ounces shredded mozzarella cheese and 2 tablespoons slivered almonds; or 2 tablespoons Parmesan cheese; or sautéed onions.

Trana Labowe

Chile Relleno Crustless Quiche (Dairy)

A Southwest quiche that's always a hit.
It's a dairy meal with a difference.

1/4	pound butter or margarine, melted
10	eggs, well beaten
1/2	cup flour
1	teaspoon baking powder
1/2	teaspoon salt
1	7-ounce can diced green chilies
2	cups small curd cottage cheese
1	pound Monterey Jack cheese, grated

Melt margarine in a 9x13-inch glass baking dish. Coat bottom and sides of pan well. Pour off excess butter into a small container and set aside.

Mix all ingredients, except eggs, lightly. Then add beaten eggs and mix through. Pour into baking dish. Drizzle remaining melted butter over mixture. Bake in a 350 degree oven for 45 minutes until lightly brown and bubbly. Let set for 5-7 minutes before cutting and serving. Serves 10 - 12.

Note: *This can be made the day before and refrigerated until baking. Take out and bring to room temperature approximately 1 hour before baking.*

Ruth King

Proznick (Dairy)

A good, cheesy, vegetarian luncheon dish.

2	pounds cottage cheese, small curd
6	eggs
6	tablespoons butter, melted
6	tablespoons flour
2	cups (8 ounces) Cheddar cheese, shredded
1	10-ounce package frozen chopped broccoli or spinach, defrosted

Combine all ingredients. Pour into a greased 9x13-inch pan and bake, uncovered, at 350 degrees for 1 hour. Serves 8 - 10.

Variations: *May be used as an appetizer by cutting into smaller pieces. Egg substitutes may be used.*

Niki Schwartz

Broccoli Cheese Soufflé (Dairy)

A rich dish for special occasions.

6	slices bread, with crusts trimmed
1	pound Cheddar cheese, shredded
8	eggs, beaten
1 1/2	teaspoons salt
1	teaspoon dried mustard
4	cups milk
1	tablespoon chopped onion
1	10-ounce package frozen broccoli, cooked and drained
	Paprika

Arrange bread in bottom of a 9x13-inch greased casserole dish. Mix together cheese, eggs, salt, mustard, milk, onion and broccoli. Pour over bread. Refrigerate overnight.

Remove from the refrigerator 45 minutes before baking. Sprinkle with paprika. Bake, uncovered, in a preheated 350 degree oven for 1 hour or until brown and bubbly. Serves 8 - 10.

Thanya Shulkin

Leek-Corn Quiche (Dairy)

From a specialty shop in the East.

1 1/2	cups thinly sliced leeks
2	cups corn (3-4 ears or one 10-ounce package frozen corn)
1/4	cup butter
1/4	cup white wine
1	cup grated Emmenthaler cheese
4	eggs, beaten
2	cups whipping cream
1/2	teaspoon salt
1/8	teaspoon pepper
1	10-inch pie shell, unbaked

Cook leeks and corn in butter until tender (approximately 10 minutes). Remove from heat; add wine and set aside. Sprinkle cheese over pie shell and top with cooked mixture. Stir together eggs, cream, salt and pepper and pour over mixture. Bake at 350 degrees in a preheated oven for 40-45 minutes or until knife inserted in center comes out clean. Serves 8.

Rosalie Weiner

Easy Onion Quiche (Dairy)

An easy, do-ahead delicious quiche.

1	9-inch deep-dish frozen pie shell
1	cup sour cream
2	cups Swiss cheese, grated
3	eggs, beaten
1/2	teaspoon salt
1	2.8-ounce can fried onion rings (approximately 1 1/2 cups)

Pierce pie shell with fork many times. Bake shell for 10 minutes at 400 degrees. Turn down oven to 300 degrees.

Mix remaining ingredients; pour into baked shell. Bake for 1 hour or until slightly brown. Serves 6.

Note: Reheats in a microwave oven very successfully. Use 70% power for best results.

Trana Labowe

Artichoke Squares (Dairy)

Artichokes give this dish its personality.

2	14-ounce cans artichoke hearts, well drained
6	tablespoons unsalted butter
1/2	cup bread crumbs, fresh or dried
2	medium onions, chopped
9	eggs, beaten
1/4	teaspoon cayenne pepper, or to taste
	salt to taste
1/2	teaspoon crumbled oregano, or to taste
1	pound sharp Cheddar cheese, shredded
2	tablespoons minced parsley

Coarsely chop artichoke hearts and place in a bowl. Melt butter in a 10-inch skillet. Mix about 2 tablespoons of the butter with the bread crumbs and reserve for the topping.

Sauté onions in remaining butter until just cooked. Combine onions and the remaining ingredients with artichoke hearts; mix well.

Pour into a 2-quart oblong baking dish. Top with buttered crumbs. Bake in a preheated 350 degree oven for 35-40 minutes or until light brown. Let stand for 10 minutes. Cut into squares. Serves 10 - 12.

Fay Auerbach

Scrambled Eggs for 24 People

This will hold a long time. Excellent for company brunch.

Eggs:

3	**dozen eggs**
1 1/3	**cups half & half**
3	**teaspoons salt**
	Pepper to taste
2	**ounces butter**

White Sauce:

4	**tablespoons butter, melted**
4	**tablespoons flour**
2	**cups hot milk**
	Chopped parsley

In a large bowl, beat eggs lightly with half & half and seasonings. Melt 2 ounces butter in a very large skillet; pour in eggs and cook slowly, stirring occasionally, until almost set.

In a medium saucepan, melt 4 tablespoons butter. Remove from heat and stir in flour thoroughly. Return to heat and cook for a few minutes, being careful not to let butter burn. Very slowly stir in hot milk; cook and stir until sauce thickens.

Fold in hot white sauce while eggs are still creamy. Keep hot in 200 degree oven or place over hot water. Sprinkle with chopped parsley.

Ruth Nebron

Fish

Long a main staple for the calorie- and health-conscious, fish has recently gained popularity in the American diet. There is much evidence, however, that fish has always been part of Jewish cuisine. Each culture has traditional fish dishes that have been handed down from generation to generation: gefilte fish and herring dishes for those Jews from Eastern European countries, and poached or fried fish with egg-lemon sauce for those from the Mediterranean region. Fish has always been popular with those keeping kosher, since it is *pareve* and may be served in combination with dairy foods.

To be acceptable under kosher guidelines, a fish must have fins and scales that can be removed from the fish skin. This means, for example, that catfish is not kosher because it has no scales. No predator fish, such as shark, is acceptable under the rules of *kashrut*.

Here in California, fish is available in many varieties and can be prepared in many ways. With just a change in the sauce, fish crosses ethnic boundaries instantly: with a salsa, it's Mexican; under a marinara sauce, it's Italian; add honey, ginger and soy sauce for the beginning of a Polynesian dish; soy sauce and a variety of thinly sliced vegetables give it an Oriental flavor.

Our collection of fish recipes covers a variety of options. With them as your starting point, let your creativity and whatever is in the refrigerator guide you in creating some memorable and healthy dishes.

HINTS

- Baked, broiled, poached or fried fish is cooked perfectly by allowing 10 minutes of total cooking time for each one inch of thickness. If you are using a microwave oven, refer to the manufacturer's directions, since microwaves vary in power.

- To protect its quality and flavor, fresh fish can be frozen indefinitely by placing it in a container a little larger than it is and filling with water to cover. To thaw, simply place the container in the refrigerator until the ice melts.

Grandma's Gefilte Fish (Pareve)

A classic recipe for this popular and traditional dish for holidays, kiddushim *and other occasions, too!!*

1   **pound pike**
1   **pound carp or sea bass**
1   **pound whitefish**
2   **tablespoons matzo meal or bread crumbs**
2   **eggs, beaten**
2   **onions**
1/2   **cup water**
1   **teaspoon salt, or to taste**
     Dash pepper
2   **carrots, scraped**
1   **stalk celery**

Skin and bone fish, saving skin and bones for later use. Put fish and 1 onion through the finest blade of a food chopper, or chop finely. Add beaten eggs, matzo meal, water and seasonings. Mix well. Using wet hands, form into balls the size of a lemon. Slice the other onion, carrots and celery and put in a large, heavy pot. Add to this the skin and bones of the fish. Over them, gently place the fish balls. Cover with cold water and bring to a boil. Skim off any foam that forms, and simmer for 1 1/2-2 hours.

Remove fish balls and continue to cook broth until it is reduced to about 1/3 of its original volume. Strain broth through several layers of cheesecloth and return fish balls and carrots to broth. Cool. Serves 6 - 8.

Suggestion: Fish balls may be made smaller to serve as appetizers.

Claire Gering

Leslie's Mexican Gefilte Fish (Pareve)

This southwestern version of the traditional favorite rates rave reviews every time!

Patties:
1 1/2   **pounds ground fish (any combination whitefish, carp, pike, etc.)**
2   **onions, finely chopped**
1   **carrot, grated**
1   **egg**
1/4   **cup matzo meal**
1/4   **cup ice water**

Sauce:
1   **16-ounce can stewed tomatoes**
1/2   **teaspoon sugar**
1   **bay leaf**

Fry onions in oil until dark brown. Combine 1/2 fried onions with fish, carrot, matzo meal, egg and water. Form into patties; fry in oil (brown both sides) and put in 9x13-inch baking dish. Mix remaining fried onions with sauce ingredients and pour over fish. Bake at 350 degrees for 1 hour. Serves approximately 6 - 8.

Suggestion: May use unsweetened frozen fish loaf available in most kosher markets.

Paddi Bregman

Halibut Ragout (Pareve)

*A hearty stew that's great over steamed rice
with a crusty French bread.*

2	pounds fresh or frozen halibut or any firm fish or combination of fish
1/2	cup chopped onion
1	large clove garlic
1/4	cup chopped green bell pepper
3	ribs celery, sliced diagonally
3	carrots, julienned
	Oil to sauté vegetables
2	1-pound cans stewed tomatoes
1	cup water
2	teaspoons pareve chicken soup mix
1	teaspoon salt
1/8	teaspoon pepper
1/4	teaspoon thyme, or to taste
1/4	teaspoon basil, or to taste
3	tablespoons minced parsley

Thaw halibut, if frozen, and cut into 1-inch pieces; set aside.

In a 2 1/2- to 3-quart pot, sauté the onion, garlic, green pepper, celery and carrots in oil. Add tomatoes, water, chicken soup, salt, pepper, thyme, basil and 2 tablespoons parsley. Cover and simmer 20 minutes. Add halibut. Cover and simmer 5-10 minutes longer. Sprinkle with remaining parsley. Serves 6.

Emma Schlesinger

Lemon-Baked Fish (Pareve)

*My mother, Evelyn Goodstein, invented this. Good for any fish steak
or fillet. Can serve 1 to 100, depending on the amount of fish.*

1	pound firm-fleshed fish fillets
1	teaspoon (approx.) dry chicken-flavor soup mix (pareve)
	Grated rind of 1 lemon
	Juice of 1 lemon

Dip fish in lemon juice to coat both sides. Place fish in baking pan. Pour in balance of lemon juice. Sprinkle with lemon rind. Sift a light dusting of soup mix over fish. Bake at 350 degrees for 10-20 minutes, depending on the thickness of the fish. Serves 4.

Claire Gering

Salmon En Croute (Pareve/Dairy)

*This simple yet elegant entree can be assembled
and then chilled in the refrigerator a day ahead.
Bake just before serving and collect the compliments.*

1	**package frozen puff pastry sheets (2 sheets)**
8	**3-ounce pieces salmon fillets (skin removed)**
1/2	**cup lemon butter dill sauce (available at most fish counters)**
1	**egg white, lightly beaten**

Allow frozen pastry to thaw. On a lightly floured board, roll one sheet at a time into a large, thin, oblong sheet. Cut each sheet diagonally into 4 triangles. Place a piece of salmon on each triangle and brush with lemon butter dill sauce. Fold pastry triangles to completely encase salmon in any fashion that forms a tidy little package. End with folded edges on top of package (to add visual interest). Brush with beaten egg white.

Bake at 375 degrees in a preheated oven for approximately 35-40 minutes. Crusts will puff up and should be a deep golden brown. Serves 8.

Donna Gould

Savory Poached Salmon (Dairy)

An easy and quick gourmet way to poach salmon — serve chilled.

6	**salmon steaks (1 inch thick) or approximately 3 pounds center-cut salmon fillets**
1	**4-ounce package dry vegetable soup mix (pareve)**
2 1/2	**cups water**
1	**cup dry white wine**
1	**cup sour cream**
1 - 2	**tablespoons prepared horseradish**
1 - 2	**tablespoons lemon juice**
	Lemon slices
	Parsley sprigs

In a large skillet stir together soup mix, water and wine. Bring to boil over medium-high heat; add salmon. Reduce heat and simmer 15 minutes or until fish flakes easily. Remove salmon carefully; cover and chill. Retain poaching liquid. Boil poaching liquid over high heat for 10 minutes or until reduced to about 1 cup. Cool. Add sour cream, horseradish and lemon juice. Pour into small bowl and chill. Serve salmon on lettuce leaves and garnish with thinly sliced lemon and parsley. Serve sauce on side. Serves 6.

Elaine Brown

Foil-Poached Salmon (Pareve)

An easier way to poach salmon; a great "special occasion" dish!

3	pounds whole or half salmon
1	cup water
1/4	cup lemon juice
1/2	cup chopped onion
1/2	teaspoon basil
1/4	teaspoon rosemary
1/4	teaspoon tarragon
2	lemon slices
1/2	teaspoon salt, optional
	Lemon or cucumber slices for garnish
	Parsley sprigs or fresh dill for garnish
	Heavy-duty aluminum foil

In a medium saucepan, combine all ingredients except salmon and simmer gently for 20 minutes. Wash salmon. Place heavy-duty aluminum foil on a sturdy cookie sheet or in a large pan (use enough foil to wrap fish and poaching liquid). Bring up edges of foil; pour poaching liquid over salmon. Crimp the foil to seal tightly.

Bake at 375 degrees for 9-10 minutes per pound of salmon, for a minimum of 30 minutes. Remove from oven; allow to stand 5 minutes before opening foil. Remove skin; transfer to serving plates or platter and decorate with lemon or cucumber slices, parsley or dill, as desired. May be served hot or chilled. Serves 6 - 8.

Beverly Barak

Festive Broccoli Sauce (Dairy)

A delicious side sauce for poached salmon or any fish dish.
Works equally well as a vegetable dip.

1	10-ounce package frozen chopped broccoli
2	cups sour cream (regular or low fat)
1/2	cup mayonnaise (regular or light)
1	package dry pareve vegetable soup mix
1	8-ounce can water chestnuts, finely chopped

Thaw broccoli and drain on a paper towel. In a medium mixing bowl, stir together sour cream, mayonnaise and soup mix. Stir in broccoli and water chestnuts. Cover and refrigerate at least 2 hours. Stir before serving. Sauce may be stored in refrigerator for up to 3 days. Yields 4 cups.

Variations: Plain, nonfat yogurt may be substituted for all or part of sour cream. Using low-fat mayonnaise and light sour cream (or yogurt) makes this a very light dressing or dip.

Elaine Brown

Salmon Salad Molds (Pareve)

A nice first course or luncheon dish from my mother, Esther Volk.

1	**16-ounce can salmon**
1	**envelope unflavored gelatin**
1	**pareve vegetable bouillon cube**
1/4	**cup minced celery**
1	**tablespoon capers**
1	**tablespoon lemon juice**

Drain salmon, reserving liquid in measuring cup. Add enough water to liquid to equal 1/2 cup. Sprinkle gelatin on liquid. Dissolve bouillon cube in 1/2 cup boiling water and add to salmon liquid, stirring until gelatin is dissolved.

Flake salmon gently and toss with celery, capers and lemon juice. Add salmon liquid mixture. Spoon into greased mold or molds. Chill until set and unmold onto lettuce leaves. Serves 4 - 5.

Alexandra Volk Levine

Hot Salmon Melts (Dairy)

Makes a nice luncheon dish or lots of appetizers.

2	**7-ounce cans Alaska red salmon**
1/3	**cup light mayonnaise**
2	**tablespoons minced onion**
2	**tablespoons minced parsley**
2	**tablespoons drained chopped pimiento**
2	**teaspoons lemon juice**
	Dash pepper
3/4	**cup shredded sharp Cheddar cheese**
	8 slices French or whole-grain bread, or split English muffins
	Dash cayenne pepper, if desired

Drain salmon and break into chunks in a large mixing bowl. Add mayonnaise, onion, parsley, pimiento, lemon juice and pepper. Toss gently to mix. Fold in 1/2 cup cheese. Spread about 1/4 cup mixture on each slice of bread. Place slices on large, heatproof baking dish or cookie sheet. Sprinkle remaining cheese over slices. Broil about 6 inches from heat for 3-4 minutes or until cheese melts and tops are golden. Serves 6 - 8.

Suggestion: For appetizers, slice bread into 1x2-inch strips or cut muffins into quarter wedges.

Elaine Brown

Gravlax (Pareve)

A memorable, classic dish that can be used any way that lox is served.

1	piece of center-cut salmon (3-3 1/2 pounds)
1/2	cup Kosher salt
4	tablespoons sugar
1 - 2	tablespoons coarse ground pepper
1	large bunch fresh dill

Purchase salmon 2-3 days before you plan to serve the Gravlax; ask fish seller to leave skin on but to split salmon and remove backbone and little bones surrounding it (or remove the bones yourself; it is really easy).

Place fillet skin side down on counter top or large cookie sheet. Mix the salt, sugar and pepper together in a small bowl and spread over the exposed salmon flesh. Reserve some dill for decoration; place the rest of the dill on one half of salmon and cover with the other half, with skin up.

Wrap salmon in foil and place on plate, then weigh down with a weight (such as canned goods).

Refrigerate for 36-48 hours; turning over each day to cure evenly.

At end of curing period, remove fish from the refrigerator and scrape away dill and seasonings. Dry with paper toweling.

Just prior to serving place on platter and surround with reserved sprigs of dill. Slice on the diagonal, detaching the flesh from the skin. Serve with mustard sauce (see below). Leftover skin can be brushed with butter and broiled. Serves 6 - 10 as an entree.

Paddi Bregman

Mustard Sauce (Pareve)

To accompany Gravlax.

1/2	cup prepared mustard
2	teaspoons dry mustard
4 - 6	tablespoons sugar
4	tablespoons white vinegar
4 - 6	tablespoons fresh dill
2/3	cup oil
2	egg yolks

Place ingredients in a food processor bowl or blender with the metal blade and make a thin mayonnaise. Place in a bowl and refrigerate until serving time. Yields approximately 1 1/2 cups.

Paddi Bregman

Fish-Spinach-Cheese (Dairy)

Another winner. An elegant, rich dish;
serve with green salad for a complete meal.

1   pound any firm-fleshed white fish fillets
    Seasoned flour to coat fish (1/4 cup flour and any seasonings you like; salt, pepper, paprika, garlic powder, etc.).
3   cups shredded cheese (Cheddar, Swiss or a mixture of both)
2   10-ounce packages frozen spinach, thawed and drained well
1   large onion, chopped and sauteed
8   ounces fresh mushrooms, sliced and sauteed
    Paprika

Remove all bones from fish and note thickness. Coat fish with seasoned flour and place in buttered or oiled 9x13-inch baking dish. Cover fish with 1 1/2 cups shredded cheese. Mix sauteed onion and mushrooms with spinach and 1 tablespoon flour. Spread spinach mixture over cheese. Cover with remaining 1 1/2 cups cheese. Sprinkle paprika over all.

Bake at 375 degrees for 5 minutes for each 1/2 inch of thickness of fish. Allow to cool for 5 minutes before serving. Serves 5 - 6.

Walter Richeimer

Sole Fillets Tarragon (Pareve)

Entree and vegetables cook together in one dish; serve with rice or
pasta for a complete meal.

1   pound sole fillets, or any white fish
1/4   cup onion, chopped
1   10-ounce to 16-ounce package of frozen broccoli, cauliflower and carrots
      Pepper to taste
1   teaspoon tarragon
1   tablespoon margarine
1/4   cup white wine
      Lemon wedges

Combine onion and vegetables. Spread in a single layer over the bottom of a baking dish. (Fish comes in various sizes. Choose appropriate size pan.) Place fillets on top of vegetables. Sprinkle with pepper and tarragon. Dot with margarine. Pour wine over fish.

Bake covered at 400 degrees for 15-20 minutes or until fish flakes with a fork. To serve, lift the fish and vegetables onto a serving platter, using a slotted spoon. Garnish with lemon wedges, if desired. Serves 2 - 4.

Shirley Moore

Red Snapper Olé (Pareve)

This is from Chuck Dell'Ario, an Oakland attorney.

1 1/2 pounds red snapper fillets, cut into 2-inch pieces
1 tablespoon olive oil
1 medium onion, coarsely chopped
4 medium ripe tomatoes, diced
6 small tomatillos, husked and cut into eighths
2 hot chili peppers, seeded and minced, or 1 4-oz. can of green chilies
1 bay leaf
1/2 cup minced fresh cilantro
1 clove garlic, minced
1/2 - 1 teaspoon ground cumin (or to taste)
1/2 teaspoon salt (or to taste)
1 teaspoon pepper (or to taste)
1 cup black olives, sliced

Heat oil in medium-large skillet or sauté pan over medium heat. Add onion and sauté until translucent, about 5 minutes (do not brown). Add tomatoes, tomatillos, chilies and bay leaf. Simmer, covered, for 5 minutes. Add cilantro, garlic, cumin, salt and pepper. Simmer, covered, for 10 minutes more. Sauce should be slightly thickened. Correct seasoning, if necessary.

Add snapper and olives to sauce. Simmer, covered, until snapper is just cooked through, stirring occasionally, about 8 minutes. Serves 4 - 6.

Note: Any firm white fish may be used. If fresh or canned tomatillos are not available they may be omitted.

Patricia Elias

Slim Salmon Loaf (Dairy)

A classic favorite made lighter.

2 7 3/4-ounce cans salmon, drained
2 eggs
1 cup mashed potatoes, made with skim milk
1 tablespoon minced onion
1 tablespoon chopped parsley
1/2 teaspoon salt
Pepper

Preheat oven to 375 degrees. In a medium bowl combine salmon, eggs, potatoes, onion, parsley, salt and dash of pepper. Mix with a fork until well blended. Spread in a nonstick or greased 9x5-inch loaf pan or individual baking molds. Bake at 375 degrees; 40 minutes in the loaf pan or 20 minutes in individual molds. Serves 5.

Trana Labowe

Fish Stew Picante (Pareve)

Makes a delicious, low-cholesterol, complete meal served with a salad and crusty, heated French bread. A theme can be achieved by serving in large pottery bowls on a red and white checkered table cloth with red candles in green bottles. Neapolitan love songs may be played in the background.

1 1/2 - 2	pounds firm, fresh fish, preferably several varieties, cut into pieces, approximately 1x1 1/2-inches
1	tablespoon vegetable oil
1	cup thinly sliced white onion
1	clove garlic, finely minced, (optional)
3/4	cup celery, thinly sliced diagonally
1/2	cup diced green bell pepper
2/3	cup sliced carrot coins (rounds)
2	cups fresh tomatoes, diced, or one 16-ounce can tomatoes, broken up
2	medium zucchini (optional)
2	cups cubed, unpeeled red potatoes
1	cup dry white wine
1	cup water
1	cup tomato juice
1	tablespoon lemon juice
1	teaspoon dried orange peel
1	teaspoon dried basil leaves, crushed
1	teaspoon salt
1/8	teaspoon dry fennel seeds
1/4	teaspoon red pepper, or to taste

In a 4-quart heavy cooking pot, sauté onion, garlic (if desired) celery, pepper and carrots in oil. Add tomatoes, potatoes, wine, water, tomato juice, lemon juice and all seasonings. Cover and simmer slowly for 30 minutes, or until potatoes are tender.

Add fish; gently cook stew uncovered for about 12 minutes or until fish flakes. Do not overcook. Fish pieces must remain intact. Add zucchini, cut into thick round slices, if desired. For sharper flavor, increase red pepper to 1/3 or 1/2 teaspoon. Serves 6.

Eleanor Gold Hirsch

Fillet of Sole Veronique (Dairy/Pareve)

Red or green grapes add color to this classic, delicate dish.

6 - 8	sole fillets (1 1/2 pounds)
	Salt and pepper
1	tablespoon lemon juice
1	onion, chopped
1/2	cup white wine
2	tablespoons butter or margarine
1	tablespoon flour
1	cup seedless grapes (canned or fresh)
2	tablespoons milk
	Paprika
	Parsley

Sprinkle fish with salt, pepper and lemon juice. Grease a medium-size baking dish; sprinkle onions over bottom. Roll up each fillet and place on onions in dish. Pour wine over fish and cover with aluminum foil.

Bake in 350 degree oven for 30 minutes.

Melt butter in a small saucepan; stir in flour until smooth. Pour liquid from fish into flour mixture; stir well. Bring to boil and simmer 2-3 minutes.

Add grapes and milk and pour over fish. Sprinkle with paprika; decorate with parsley. Serves 6.

Suggestion: *If using canned grapes, liquid from grapes can be substituted for milk.*

Eunice Berman

Halibut Florentine (Dairy)

My mother, Esther Volk, frequently served this dish for company.

Sauce:

1/4	cup butter or margarine
2	tablespoons flour
1	cup milk
1	cup sour cream
1/4	teaspoon white pepper
1 1/2	teaspoons dry mustard
3	tablespoons white wine (optional)
1/2	cup shredded Cheddar or Monterey Jack cheese
	Juice of 1/4 lemon
1	10-ounce package frozen chopped spinach, thawed and drained

Fish:

6	fillets of halibut
6	slices of Swiss cheese

In a large skillet, melt butter and blend in flour. Gradually blend in milk. Cook and stir until thickened and smooth.

Blend in sour cream, pepper, mustard, wine, shredded cheese and lemon juice. Cook over low heat until cheese melts. Stir in spinach.

Broil fish fillets 5-6 minutes on each side or until fish flakes with a fork. Top each piece of fish with a slice of cheese. Cook 1-2 minutes or until cheese melts.

Arrange on a platter and pour sauce over fish. Serves 6.

Alexandra Volk Levine

Harold's Southwestern Barbecued Salmon

(Pareve/Dairy)

Salmon with a typical California barbecue flavor!

1 1/2-2	pounds fillet of salmon or salmon steaks
1/4	teaspoon ground cumin
1/4	teaspoon ground coriander
1	tablespoon olive oil
1	clove crushed garlic
1/2-1	teaspoon lemon juice
	Dash of pepper

Mix all the seasonings together and brush lightly on one side of salmon.

Spray fish basket with vegetable cooking spray. Broil over hot coals or in hot broiler 5-6 minutes per inch of thickness of fish or to taste. Serves 4 - 5.

Eve Marcus

Brown Sugar Baked Salmon (Dairy)

This version of teriyaki sauce makes a wonderfully sweet and different fish.

Fish:

6	salmon steaks, 1 inch thick, or 2-3 pounds salmon fillet in one piece

Marinade:

1/2	cup brown sugar, packed
4	tablespoons melted butter
3	tablespoons soy sauce
2	tablespoons fresh lemon juice
2	tablespoons dry white wine or water

In a small bowl combine all marinade ingredients. Place salmon steaks or fillet in a glass baking pan that holds fish snugly in one layer. Pour marinade over fish. Cover and marinate in refrigerator from 30 minutes to 6 hours.

Uncover pan. Place on middle rack of preheated 400 degree oven. Bake 15-20 minutes or until fish is done, basting every 5 minutes. Do not turn fish. Serve immediately. Serves 6.

Janis Weiss

Poultry

Kosher dietary laws forbid the eating of many kinds of birds, including all birds of prey. To be acceptable, poultry, like meat, must be carefully selected, humanely killed by a specially trained *shochet* (ritual slaughterer) and properly soaked and salted. Poultry, like meat, may not be cooked or served with any dairy products under the laws of *kashrut*.

With the growing interest in nutrition and concern for healthier foods, chicken and turkey make frequent appearances as the entrees on Jewish tables.

Chicken, in fact, may now be the most frequently used meat in kosher cooking. To make that frequency welcome, Jewish cooks have developed and adapted a broad repertoire of interesting and varied recipes, from the simple roast chicken — served most often for *Shabbat* and holiday dinners — to sumptuous adaptations of dishes using other kinds of meat and from other ethnic backgrounds.

HINTS

- Turkey also has grown in popularity as its availability has increased. It is a healthy alternative to beef in chili, meatballs, meat loaf, spaghetti sauces and patties.

- Ground turkey tends to look very white when cooked in meat loaf or meatballs. Adding ketchup, tomato paste or paprika will improve its appearance and taste.

Chicken Artichoke Casserole (Meat)

An elegant company dish.

8	chicken cutlets, cut into 1 1/2-inch pieces
1	cup flour
2	teaspoons salt, optional
1/4	teaspoon pepper
3	tablespoons margarine or oil
2 1/4	cups chicken broth
3/4	cup dry white wine
1-3	tablespoons tomato paste
1/4	teaspoon rosemary
1/2	pound fresh mushrooms, sliced
2	10-ounce packages frozen artichoke hearts, cooked and drained
3	tablespoons chopped scallions

Put flour, salt and pepper in a plastic bag. Add chicken and shake until chicken is coated.

In a skillet, heat margarine or oil; sauté chicken until opaque and slightly brown (add margarine or oil as needed). Place chicken in a casserole.

In a separate bowl, mix broth, wine, tomato paste and rosemary. Pour over chicken. At this point, casserole may be refrigerated if being prepared ahead of time. Bring to room temperature before proceeding.

Bake, covered, at 350 degrees for 30 minutes. Add mushrooms, artichokes and scallions. Bake covered for 15 minutes more. Serves 6 - 7.

Suggestion: Can be served with rice or noodles.

Lois Rothblum

Balsamic Chicken (Meat)

An unusual combination of flavors makes this special.

5	pounds chicken, cut into pieces
1/4-1/2	cup vegetable oil
1/2	cup balsamic vinegar
3	tablespoons sugar
3	tablespoons ketchup
1	tablespoon Worcestershire sauce
2	medium scallions, minced (including tops)
1	teaspoon salt
1/2	teaspoon cracked pepper
1	teaspoon dry mustard
1	medium clove garlic, minced
	Tabasco to taste

Combine all ingredients and pour over chicken. Coat thoroughly. Allow to marinate in refrigerator for 8 hours or more. Turn chicken occasionally.

Bake for 60 minutes in a 325 degree oven or until tender. Serves 4 - 6.

Variation: Chicken may be baked in a 325 degree oven for 30 minutes, removed from marinade and then barbecued for 4 - 5 minutes on each side to brown. Baste chicken with marinade while barbecuing.

Janis Weiss

Chicken Breasts Wellington (Meat)

A glamorous and elegant presentation. Can be assembled early in the day and refrigerated until ready to bake and serve.

6	ounces long-grain and wild rice
2	tablespoons grated orange peel
3	tablespoons vegetable oil
6	skinless, boneless chicken breast halves freshly ground pepper, to taste
1/4	pound mushrooms, sliced
2	eggs, separated
1	package (10-ounce) frozen, puffed pastry shells, thawed and rolled out to six 7-inch rounds

Sauce:

16	ounces whole berry cranberry sauce
2	tablespoons orange liqueur
2	tablespoons lemon juice
1/4	teaspoon dry mustard

Cook rice according to instructions on package for firmer rice. Add orange peel and let cool.

In a large frying pan, heat oil over medium heat. Add chicken breasts and cook until browned, about 4 minutes a side. Remove with tongs and season with pepper. Add mushrooms to remaining oil and cook until tender, about 3 minutes.

Beat egg whites until soft peaks form. Add cooked rice and mushrooms; mix well.

On each pastry circle, place 1/3 cup rice mixture and top with chicken. Moisten edge with water, press to seal edges together. Place seam side down on a large ungreased baking sheet.

In a small bowl, beat egg yolks lightly with 1 tablespoon water; brush over dough. Bake uncovered for 35 minutes in a 400 degree oven.

For sauce, combine cranberry sauce, orange liqueur, lemon juice and mustard in a small saucepan. Heat over low heat until warmed. Serve over chicken. Serves 6.

Ceil Halperin

Raisin Chicken Santa Fe (Meat)

A taste of the Southwest! Best prepared one or two days in advance.

4-5	chicken breast halves, skinned and boned
1-2	tablespoons olive oil
4	cloves garlic, minced
1	onion, chopped
1	red bell pepper, sliced into strips
1	green bell pepper, sliced into strips
1 1/2	cups defatted chicken broth
1	cup golden raisins
1/4	cup tomato paste
2	oz. canned green chilies, diced
1	teaspoon ground coriander
	Salt, pepper (optional)

Cut chicken into wide strips. Cook chicken in oil over medium heat in large skillet until lightly browned, If necessary, add more oil. Turn once. Remove from pan and set aside. Add garlic, onion and peppers to pan and sauté 2 minutes, or until soft and transparent.

Mix in broth, raisins, tomato paste, chilies and coriander. Return chicken to mixture. Bring to a boil, then reduce heat and simmer, covered, 10 minutes.

Uncover and cook approximately 10 minutes more, or until chicken is tender and sauce is slightly reduced. Season to taste with salt and pepper, if desired. Serves 3 - 4.

Variations: A low-fat recipe — may also use "salt-free" tomato paste and chicken broth.

Doris Goodman

Chicken with Apricots (Meat)

Tender, moist and delicious.

3	pounds chicken, cut into pieces
1	cup flour, seasoned with salt and pepper
4	tablespoons oil or pareve margarine
2	onions, chopped
12-18	dried apricots (more, if desired)
1	cup dry sherry (more, if desired)
1	cup orange juice (more, if desired)

Roll chicken in seasoned flour. Brown chicken in oil or margarine in skillet. Remove chicken and sauté onions lightly. Remove onions. Place chicken in casserole and cover with layer of onions and layer of apricots.

Mix together orange juice and sherry and add to casserole. Bake, covered, at 350 degrees for one hour. Uncover for 15 additional minutes so sauce thickens. Serves 4.

Janet Weinstein Abelson

Pollo Verde (Meat)

A south-of-the-border dish that is really different and easy to prepare.

1	cup fresh cilantro leaves
1	pound tomatillos, fresh, or 1 16-ounce can, drained
1	cup onion, chopped
1	clove garlic, chopped
	Salt and pepper, to taste
1	cut-up broiler or fryer (3-4 pounds)

Wash and chop cilantro leaves. Husk, wash and chop tomatillos. In food processor or blender, process cilantro, onion, garlic and tomatillos until pureed. Add salt or pepper. Put chicken in a heavy pot; add pureed sauce. Bring to a boil. Cover and cook over low heat for one hour. Remove chicken. May add water to prevent burning, or (if necessary) sauce can be reduced after cooking.

Serve with rice and tortillas. Serves 4.

Variation: Tomatoes may be substituted for tomatillos, but it won't be verde!

Eve Marcus

Sweet-and-Sour Chicken (Meat)

Elegant and delicious.

2 or 3	chickens, cut into pieces
1	bottle Russian dressing
1	package dry onion soup mix
1	10-ounce jar apricot preserves

Combine all ingredients and pour over chicken. Bake uncovered in a 325 degree oven for 1 1/2 hours. Serves 4 - 6.

Variation: A 16-ounce can of whole cranberry sauce may be substituted for apricot preserves.

Wini Drell

Orange Chicken (Meat)

Tasty and different; easy to make.

6-8	small chicken breast halves (remove skin)
1 1/2	cups orange juice
1	egg, slightly beaten
1	teaspoon salt
1/2	cup crushed corn flakes
1/2	cup shredded coconut
1/4	cup melted pareve margarine
1	orange, thinly sliced for garnish

Make marinade by mixing orange juice, beaten egg and salt together. Pour over chicken breasts. Allow to marinate at least 1-2 hours.

Mix corn flakes and coconut; roll chicken in mixture. Place chicken in baking dish, reserving marinade. Add the melted margarine to the marinade and pour over chicken (should be approximately 1/2 to 3/4 inches deep). Cover with foil and bake for 30 minutes at 350 degrees. Remove foil and bake 15-30 minutes longer or until chicken is nicely browned. Garnish with orange slices. Serves 4 - 6.

Suggestion: Salt may be omitted by using ginger and garlic powder instead.

Marcia Schlesinger

Barbecued Lemon Chicken (Meat)

Fast and easy.

4	chicken breasts, boned and skinned
	Juice of 2 lemons
1	pinch of pepper
4	cloves of garlic, crushed
2	tablespoons fresh chopped dill weed

Arrange chicken in a medium baking dish. Combine remaining ingredients and pour over chicken. Marinate for 20 minutes or longer. This recipe is best barbecued. Grill chicken for 5-10 minutes on each side, basting with lemon marinade. Serves 4.

Suggestion: Chicken can also be baked, broiled or microwaved. Marinade can be used on firm-fleshed fish such as halibut or salmon.

Judy Hailpern

Plum Chicken (Meat)

A deliciously different dish.

2	chickens, cut into pieces
1/2	cup soy sauce
1/2	cup plum jam
1/4	cup honey
1/4	cup orange juice
1	clove garlic, crushed

Combine all ingredients and pour over chicken. Bake, uncovered, in a 350 degree oven for 60-75 minutes, basting occasionally. Serves 4 - 5.

Myra Newman

Ebony Chicken (Meat)

My daughter, Donna Chapman,
gave me this simple but delicious company dish.

2 1/2-3 pounds chicken, cut into pieces	
1/4	cup lemon juice
1 1/4	cup sherry wine
3	tablespoons olive oil
1	clove garlic, crushed
1	teaspoon tarragon
1 1/2	teaspoons salt
	Paprika

Arrange chicken in a shallow 9x12-inch baking dish. Combine remaining ingredients, except paprika, and pour over chicken. Marinate in refrigerator for about 3 hours, turning frequently. Sprinkle with paprika before baking. Bake at 375 degrees for 1 hour or until fork-tender. Serves 4.

Alice Spilberg

Sesame Chicken (Meat)

One of our favorites.
May be assembled in advance and baked just before serving.

3 1/2-4 pounds chicken, cut into pieces, patted dry	
1/2	cup apricot or plum jam or honey
1/2	cup mustard (Dijon or French)
2-4	tablespoons untoasted sesame seeds (or more if desired)

Mix jam or honey with mustard. Spread mixture on chicken. Coat with sesame seeds and place in a 9x13-inch baking dish. Bake uncovered in a 350 degree oven for approximately 1 hour or until tender and golden brown. Serves 4 - 6.

Eleanor Botney

Chicken with Mustard Sauce (Meat)

A no-fail dish that can be prepared ahead of time; great for entertaining.

8   chicken breast halves

Marinade:
1/2   cup dry sherry
1/2   cup soy sauce
3/4   cup vegetable oil
1/4   cup light brown sugar
2   large cloves garlic, crushed
1/4   teaspoon ground pepper

Mustard Sauce:
1/2   cup mayonnaise
1/3   cup Dijon-style mustard
1   teaspoon Worcestershire sauce
1/2   teaspoon hot pepper sauce

Marinate chicken for two hours. Barbecue or broil chicken pieces as desired. Serve with mustard sauce. Serves 6 - 8.

Variation: Any chicken parts may be substituted.

Laura Schoor

Dijon Dill Chicken (Meat)

This is one for mustard lovers.

4   pieces of chicken (about 1 1/2 pounds)
1/4   cup Dijon mustard
1   tablespoon honey
2   tablespoons onion, chopped
1   clove garlic, crushed
1   teaspoon dill weed

In a small bowl, combine mustard, honey, onion, garlic and dill weed. Remove skin from chicken. Place chicken in a lightly greased 9-inch square baking dish. Spread with mustard sauce.

Bake at 350 degrees for 40-50 minutes or microwave, covered, on full power for 12 minutes. Serves 2 - 3.

Debra Gordon

Lo-Cal Marsala Chicken (Meat)

Herbs and wine flavor this delicious, tender chicken.

3	chicken breast halves
3	chicken legs
3	chicken thighs
1/4	teaspoon garlic powder
1/4	teaspoon paprika
1/4	teaspoon pepper
1/4	teaspoon dried thyme leaves
1/2	cup seasoned bread crumbs
4	sprigs fresh parsley, minced
1/3	cup water
1/3	cup Marsala wine

Remove skin from chicken. Place all seasonings and crumbs in a plastic bag. Shake chicken, a few pieces at a time, in the mixture.

Place coated chicken pieces in a baking dish. Carefully pour water in the pan around the chicken. Bake, uncovered, at 350 degrees for 45 minutes.

Pour wine over chicken. Cover pan with foil and bake 15 minutes more. Remove foil and bake 10 minutes more. Serves 6.

Sylvia Levine

Chicken Cacciatore (Meat)

A food processor makes this a simple dish to do,
for family or company.

2-2 1/2	pounds frying chicken, cut into 8 pieces
1/4	cup vegetable oil
4	sprigs parsley
1	clove garlic, peeled
1	medium onion, quartered
1	16-ounce can whole tomatoes
1	teaspoon salt
1/2	teaspoon oregano
1/4	teaspoon basil
1/8	teaspoon pepper

Make sauce in food processor or blender. Process parsley, garlic and onion until medium fine. Add tomatoes and seasoning and process just to break up the tomatoes. In a 12-inch skillet, brown chicken in hot oil over medium-high heat. Drain off excess fat.

Pour sauce over chicken. Cover and simmer 45 minutes or until tender. Serves 4.

Suggestion: *Can be prepared without any salt for low-sodium diets. Slices of zucchini, mushrooms, chopped green bell peppers and eggplant can be added during last 10 minutes of cooking time.*

Muriel Kaplan

Chicken Adobe (Meat)

Use an entire bulb of garlic in this excellent dish!

8	thighs or 2 pounds chicken, skin removed
1	bulb of garlic, separated into cloves and peeled
1/4	cup light soy sauce
1/4	cup white vinegar
	Black pepper to taste

Combine all ingredients and pour over chicken. Marinate overnight or at least half a day (the longer, the better). Turn several times.

Place marinated chicken and sauce in a heavy pot and bring to a boil. Simmer approximately 30 minutes or until more than one-half cooked.

Remove sauce. Brown chicken and garlic. Pour off excess fat; add sauce and heat. Serves 4 - 5.

Suggestion: Serve with rice.

Greta Grunwald

Chasen's Chicken Breasts (Meat)

This famous Hollywood recipe was given to me many years ago by the niece of the restaurant owner.

8	boned small chicken breasts, seasoned to taste
4	tablespoons margarine
1	cup flour
1	cup cold liquid nondairy creamer
4	eggs, beaten
1	cup seasoned bread crumbs
	Oil for frying

Pound chicken breasts and fold each in half. Place 1/2 teaspoon margarine in fold. Dip each piece into flour, followed by nondairy creamer, eggs and bread crumbs; then eggs and bread crumbs again. Refrigerate overnight.

Deep-fry in hot oil (cover chicken one third of its depth) until golden brown. This can be done in advance.

Heat or reheat on cookie sheet in 400 degree oven for 20 minutes before serving. Serves 6 - 8.

Shirley Izenstark

Moussaka (Meat)

*An updated, low-calorie and low-cholesterol
version of the Greek classic.*

1	large eggplant
1 1/2	pounds ground turkey meat (white meat is even lower in calories)
2	onions, sliced
1	6-ounce can tomato paste
1	cup water
1	cup dry wine
3	tablespoons parsley
1/2	teaspoon cinnamon
1/2	teaspoon ground nutmeg
1/4	teaspoon ground pepper
1	cup toasted sourdough bread crumbs (can make your own)

Peel and thinly slice eggplant. Soak eggplant slices in heavily salted cold water for 1 hour. Drain and pat dry.

Brown turkey in large nonstick skillet, breaking turkey into bits. Skim off fat, if any. Add onions, tomato paste, water, wine, parsley, cinnamon, nutmeg and pepper. Cover and simmer for 1 hour. Stir in 1/2 cup bread crumbs.

Cover the bottom of a 8x12-inch baking dish with some of the turkey mixture. Arrange a layer of eggplant slices; cover with some sauce. Continue to fill pan with alternating layers, ending with layer of sauce. Sprinkle the top with remaining 1/2 cup of bread crumbs and a little more nutmeg. Bake at 350 degrees for one hour. Serves 6 - 8.

Ida Liberman

Turkey Patties (Meat)

Another delicious way to serve leftover turkey.

2	cups cut-up, cooked turkey, boneless and skinned
1-2	cloves garlic
1	cup coarsely chopped celery
1/2	cup coarsely chopped zucchini
1	medium onion, cut into chunks
1/4	teaspoon pepper
	Salt to taste
3	large eggs
1/2	cup matzo meal
	Oil for frying

Place turkey, garlic, celery, zucchini, onion and seasonings into food processor in this order so that the turkey gets the finest chopping. Add eggs to the food processor. Remove to a bowl and mix in matzo meal.

Heat 1/4 inch of oil in a nonstick frying pan. Form 3-inch patties; place in pan. Fry until well browned on one side, then turn and fry other side. These are good either hot or cold. Yields 12 patties.

Suggestion: *Chicken may be used in this recipe.*

Rose Engel

Turkey Chili (Meat)

For the cholesterol conscious.
This delicious recipe is only 175 calories per serving.

1   **small turkey breast, skinned (approximately 2 pounds) celery tops**

1   **onion, sliced Poultry seasoning, to taste**

1   **cup chopped onion**

1/2   **cup chopped celery**

1/3   **cup chopped green bell pepper**

3   **cloves garlic, minced**

1 1/2   **cups broth from cooking turkey breast (add water to equal 1 1/2 cups)**

1   **28-ounce can crushed tomatoes, pureed**

1   **15-ounce can tomato sauce**

1   **tablespoon onion powder**

1   **tablespoon chili powder, or more to taste**

2   **teaspoons cumin**

1   **teaspoon garlic powder**

1   **teaspoon oregano**

1   **teaspoon soy sauce or tamari Dash cayenne pepper**

1   **cup cooked kidney beans (or canned may be used as well)**

Place the turkey breast in a nonstick baking dish with the 1 1/2 cups of water. Add the celery tops and sliced onion and sprinkle with poultry seasoning. Cover and bake at 350 degrees until tender, about 1 1/2 hours.

Remove the turkey breast. Defat the broth by chilling it in the freezer until the fat rises to the top. Discard the fat, then pour the broth through cheese cloth.

Sauté the chopped onion, celery, bell pepper and garlic in 1/2 cup of turkey broth. Add the remaining ingredients except the turkey breasts and beans. Simmer sauce for 45 minutes, uncovered, stirring occasionally.

Meanwhile, dice the turkey breast and grind in a meat grinder or in a food processor. Add the ground turkey and the beans to the chili. Cook and stir about 5 minutes. Serves 6.

Suggestions: *Ground turkey may be substituted for turkey breast, adjusting directions accordingly. This is also a good way to utilize leftover turkey and leftover chicken broth (freeze to store and thaw as needed). Dark meat turkey can be used as well, but it is higher in calories and fat.*

Ida Liberman

Hy's "North-of-the-Border" Turkey Chili (Meat)

A hearty meal that tastes better the second day—if there is any left.

2	pounds ground turkey meat (approximately)
1/2	pound green bell pepper, chopped
1	large onion, chopped
3-4	ribs celery, chopped
1	clove garlic, minced
1	teaspoon cooking oil
1-2	teaspoons chili powder or to taste
1/2	teaspoon Tabasco sauce or to taste
1	4-ounce can diced green chiles
2	pounds canned stewed tomatoes, drained
1	8-ounce can tomato sauce
	Salt and pepper to taste
1	teaspoon sugar
2	pounds cooked or canned pinto and/or kidney beans
1/2	teaspoon cumin seed
	Beer, optional
	Fresh chopped tomatoes, optional

In a large stew pot, brown meat and crumble into small pieces; set aside. In a large skillet, cook bell pepper, onion, celery and garlic for 5-10 minutes. Combine meat and veggies in stew pot. Cook over medium flame while adding all other ingredients. When mixed together, lower heat to *very low* to prevent scorching. Cover and cook for 1 hour, stirring occasionally.

Simmer on low heat, uncovered, for about 1 more hour or until veggies are cooked. Beer may be added to keep chili from drying out. Cannot be over-cooked—be sure to keep it moist. Serve with soda crackers or plain taco chips. Serves 8 - 10.

Hy Freedman

Mexican Marinade for Chicken or Beef (Meat)

A delicious, salt-free marinade with a Southwestern pedigree.

1	large lime, juiced
1-2	large cloves of garlic

Mix juice and garlic together. Marinate 1 fryer or 2 pounds skirt or chuck steak for one hour. Barbecue, broil or rotisserie until done. Needs NO SALT! Yields enough to marinate chicken or beef for 4.

Eve Marcus

Pineapple Duckling (Meat)

An unusual combination of flavors makes this a memorable dish.

5-7	pounds duck
3/4	teaspoon salt
2	tablespoons oil
1	13 1/2-ounce can pine-apple tidbits, drained (reserve syrup)
1	cup sliced celery
1/4	cup chopped onion
4	cups bread cubes
1/3	cup macadamia nuts
1	teaspoon curry powder
1	tablespoon grated orange peel
1/4	cup corn syrup
1	tablespoon arrowroot or cornstarch

Wash, drain and dry duck. Sprinkle 1/2 teaspoon salt over body and neck.

Heat oil in large saucepan. Add celery and onion; sauté until tender. Add bread cubes, pineapple, nuts, curry powder, 1 teaspoon orange peel, 1/4 teaspoon salt and 2 tablespoons syrup. Mix together. Fill neck and body cavities loosely with stuffing. Skewer neck to back. Cover opening of body with foil and tie legs together loosely. Place duck on rack in shallow roasting pan and pierce skin lightly with a fork at 1-inch intervals.

Bake at 325 degrees for 2 1/2-3 hours or until drumstick meat is fork-tender.

Glaze: In a saucepan, combine 1/2 cup pineapple syrup, corn syrup and arrowroot or cornstarch. Cook, stirring constantly, until thick and clear. Stir in remaining 2 teaspoons orange peel.

About 1/2 hour before duck is done, remove from oven and pour off fat. Pour glaze over entire duck and return to oven. Baste a few times during the last 30 minutes. Serves 3 - 4.

Rosalie Weiner

Chicken Chow Mein (Meat)

This version made famous at Grossingers in the Catskill Mountains.

2	tablespoons oil
1	cup sliced onions
1 1/2	cups sliced celery
1	cup sliced mushrooms
2	cups chicken stock
3	tablespoons soy sauce
3	cups cooked chicken, cut in strips
1 1/2	tablespoons cornstarch or arrowroot powder
1/2	cup minced scallions Chow mein noodles, crisped in oven Steamed rice

Heat oil in wok or 12 inch skillet, stir in the onions, celery and mushrooms. Cook for 3 minutes. Add 1 cup of the stock plus the soy sauce and chicken. Cook 5 minutes.

Mix the cornstarch or arrowroot powder with the remaining stock and stir into the chicken mixture until thickened. Add the scallions. Arrange mixture over the crisped noodles. Serve with rice as a side dish. Makes 6 cups or serves 6.

Variation: Bean sprouts added to the last 3 minutes of cooking time make a crunchy addition.

Muriel Kaplan

Chinese Orange Chicken (Meat)

A delicious one-dish recipe that is best prepared a day ahead.

2	chickens, cut up, or 6-8 chicken breasts or thighs
1/2	cup orange marmalade
3/4	cup soy sauce
1/2	teaspoon ground ginger
1/2	teaspoon garlic powder

In a glass baking dish, mix marmalade, soy sauce, ginger and garlic powder together. Add chicken and marinate several hours or overnight. Bake 60-75 minutes at 350 degrees.

Serve with steamed rice. Serves 6 - 8.

Pearl Roseman

Sweet-and-Sour Sauce (Pareve)

May be used with wontons or to bake chicken or duck, etc.

1/2	cup water
1/4	cup ketchup
1/2	cup sugar
1	teaspoon cider vinegar
2	tablespoons cornstarch
3/4	cup pineapple juice

Combine all ingredients. Bring to a boil, stir constantly until sauce is thick and clear. Yields 2 cups.

Min Leonard

Chicken Beijing (Meat)

For a taste of the Orient, try this one!
May be made a day or two ahead.

8	chicken breast halves (may be skinned and boned)
4	teaspoons lemon juice
2	tablespoons pareve margarine, melted
	Salt and pepper

Marinade:

3/4	cup peanut oil
8	scallions, chopped
12	thin slices ginger root
2	teaspoons crushed garlic

Sauce:

12	tablespoons soy sauce (4 tablespoons dark and 8 tablespoons light soy sauce)
8	tablespoons honey
1	teaspoon Szechuan peppercorns, crushed
1 1/2	cups hot chicken stock
3/4	teaspoon red pepper, crushed
1	tablespoon brandy or cognac
3	tablespoons cornstarch
6	drops orange extract
1 1/2	tablespoons lemon juice

Garnish:

1	head Boston lettuce leaves
	Grated rind of 1 orange
1	bunch watercress
	Crisp rice noodles (maifun)

Early in the day, rub chicken breasts with lemon juice and brush with melted margarine. Sprinkle with salt and pepper. Place in one layer in a large glass baking pan.

Cover with greased wax paper. Cover tightly with foil and bake 8-10 minutes in a preheated 425 degree oven. Uncover, set aside and cool.

Mix ingredients for marinade (ginger may be minced or grated) and pour over chicken. Marinate 20 minutes.

Place chicken and marinade in a large skillet and gently sauté for 5 minutes over low flame. Remove chicken and slice breasts. Add sauce ingredients to liquid in pan. Cook over low heat until it thickens. Pour sauce over chicken and allow to marinate for several hours or overnight in refrigerator.

Drain chicken and arrange on a bed of lettuce leaves. Garnish with orange rind, watercress and maifun (rice noodles).

Serve sauce on side.

Serves 6 - 8.

Note: You may want to puree sauce in blender or food processor.

Greta Grunwald

Cantonese Chicken with Black Beans (Meat)

Green grapes add an unusual touch.

1	pound chicken breasts
1	egg white, lightly beaten
1	tablespoon cornstarch
1/2	teaspoon salt
2	tablespoons cooked Chinese black beans (available in Oriental section)
2	cloves garlic, minced
2	tablespoons water
4	tablespoons peanut oil, for frying
1	red or green bell pepper, cut in chunks
2	tablespoons minced ginger root
10	scallions or 1 Spanish onion, cut in chunks
1	tablespoon dark soy sauce
1	teaspoon sugar
1	tablespoon dry sherry
1	8-ounce can green grapes or fresh grapes

Cut chicken into 1-inch pieces. In a separate bowl, mix egg white, cornstarch and salt. Add chicken and mix well.

Heat 1 tablespoon oil in a skillet; stir-fry the chicken only until light brown. Drain and remove from skillet.

Mash 2 tablespoons cooked black beans with minced garlic and water. Stir-fry in 1 tablespoon oil for 1 minute. Remove to a dish.

In 2 tablespoons oil, stir-fry the scallions or onion for 2 minutes, add the ginger and green pepper and stir-fry just until peppers get bright in color.

Combine black bean mixture with soy sauce, sugar and sherry. Combine the chicken with green pepper mixture. Add the black bean mixture and stir-fry over high heat one minute to heat thoroughly. Add the drained grapes and serve hot. Serves 2 - 3 as part of a Chinese meal or 2 main courses.

Min Leonard

Plum Sauce (Pareve)

Ideal for use with Oriental foods or for roasting poultry. An easy sauce that keeps well in the refrigerator for 3-4 months.

6	ounces applesauce
6	ounces orange marmalade
6	ounces crushed pineapple
6	ounces apricot jam
6	ounces plum jam
1	inch piece fresh ginger root, minced
1	clove garlic, minced
1	teaspoon Mexican chili pepper, crushed

Mix all ingredients in blender. Yields approximately 3 cups.

Rosalie Weiner

171

Lichi Chicken (Meat)

A mildly flavored Cantonese-style chicken.

2   chicken breasts, boned, cut diagonally in 1-inch pieces (approximately 1 pound)
1   egg
1   teaspoon salt
4   tablespoons cornstarch
    Oil for deep frying
4   tablespoons ketchup
4   tablespoons sugar
4   tablespoons vinegar
1   cup water
2   tablespoons cornstarch, dissolved in 4 tablespoons water
2   tablespoons Chinese sweet cucumber, optional
1/2   cup onion, cut in 1/2-inch chunks
1   bell pepper, half green, half red, cut in 1/2-inch chunks
1/2-1   cup lichi nuts (2 per person)
    Sesame seeds, optional

Beat together egg, salt and 4 tablespoons cornstarch. Coat chicken. Fry in deep oil until crispy (put in oil one piece at a time). Add ketchup, sugar, vinegar and water to pan and heat. Thicken with remaining cornstarch; simmer for 1-2 minutes. Add sweet cucumber, onion, pepper and lichi nuts, including liquid, at last minute.

Pour sauce over chicken. If desired, sprinkle with sesame seeds. Serves 3 - 4.

Variation: May add 6- to 8-ounce can of pineapple chunks or tidbits instead of lichi nuts.

Min Leonard

Plum Sauce (Pareve)

Good for dipping chicken, duck or other Oriental appetizers.

1   12-ounce jar plum jelly
6   tablespoons seasoned rice vinegar
6   ounces chutney
4   tablespoons sugar

Combine and simmer all ingredients in a saucepan until melted and well mixed. Cool. Yields approximately 2 cups.

Suggestions: May be used for roasting chicken. Keeps indefinitely in covered jar in refrigerator.

Min Leonard

Meat

"Whatsoever parteth the hoof, and is wholly cloven-footed, and cheweth the cud…that may ye eat" (Leviticus 11:3).

The kinds of meats that may be eaten in kosher homes are prescribed by Judaic dietary laws. Those include beef, lamb and veal as well as goat, deer, oxen, mountain sheep, roebuck and antelope. Not permitted are pork, of course, as well as camel, rabbit and horse meat.

Animals appropriate for kosher meat must be carefully selected, humanely killed by a *shochet* (ritual slaughterer) and thoroughly inspected at several points during the process. Animals killed during a hunt are not permissible. Only meats from the front quarters of the animal are acceptable. Kosher meats are soaked, sprinkled with kosher salt and drained of blood prior to use.

"Thou shalt not seethe a kid in its mother's milk" (Deuteronomy 14:20). The commandment is the basis for the complete separation of meat and dairy dishes — their preparation and their serving — in observant kosher homes. The way meat may be prepared is also prescribed by dietary laws. Meat dishes may never be used with dairy products.

"Ye shall kindle no fire throughout your habitat upon the Sabbath day" (Exodus 35:3) dictates the way meat — or any other warm or hot food — may be prepared on *Shabbat*. The observance of *kashrut* (kosher laws) further requires that cooking be done prior to sundown on Friday evening. This has resulted in a wealth of tender, succulent meat dishes that may be prepared well ahead of planned serving times, making them ideal for entertaining! Leftovers are usually delicious served hot or cold, and most freeze well.

Brisket (Meat)

A classic, especially for Passover.

7-8 pounds brisket
Salt, optional
1/2 teaspoon pepper
1 tablespon onion powder
1 tablespoon garlic powder
1 1/2 cups Passover ketchup
4-5 cups water (to cover top edges of the meat)

Season brisket with pepper, onion and garlic powder; place in a roasting pan. Mix ketchup with enough water to cover top edges of brisket; cover with tightly fitting lid or foil. Bake brisket at 350 degrees approximately 2 1/2 hours. Remove brisket from pan; reserve juices in pan. Cool and slice brisket. (An electric knife works well.) Return to juices in pan. Refrigerate or freeze. Before reheating, remove fat. Bake, covered, another 1 1/2 hours or until tender. Serves 12 - 16.

Beverly Barak

Brisket in Foil (Meat)

My mother, Lillian Kaluzna, gave this to me.
I've just modified it slightly.

2 chopped onions
1 chopped green bell pepper
1 4-ounce can mushroom stems and pieces, drained
3-4 pounds beef brisket, trimmed of excess fat
1/2 envelope onion soup mix
1 teaspoon pepper
3/4 cup red wine
8 peeled and quartered carrots, optional
4 peeled potatoes, cut into eighths, optional

In a medium skillet, sauté onions until lightly browned. Add bell pepper and mushrooms; sauté until soft and set aside.

Place 1/3 of the sauteed mixture on a large sheet of heavy foil in a shallow roasting pan. Place meat on top; add remaining sauteed mixture. Sprinkle with onion soup mix and pepper. Pour wine around meat. If desired, arrange carrots and potatoes around the meat. Wrap airtight in foil, allowing space for gravy to form. Bake in a preheated 325 degree oven for 3-4 hours.

Slice meat across grain and serve with pan juices and vegetables. Serves 6 - 8.

Elinor Einy

Barbecue Brisket (Meat)

A different version of a perennial favorite.

1	cup ginger ale
1	cup barbecue sauce
2	teaspoons brown sugar
2-3	medium onions, sliced
4-5	pounds brisket
1-2	16-ounce cans of butter beans, drained (see variation, below)

Variation: Butter beans are a good combination with this brisket. If desired, place them in the roasting pan with the meat and gravy. Heat covered.

In a medium bowl, mix ginger ale, barbecue sauce and brown sugar together.

Arrange onions in the bottom of a large baking pan. Place brisket on top of the onions. Pour sauce over beef and bake, covered, at 350 degrees for about 2 1/2-3 hours, or until tender. Serves 8 - 10.

Note: Brisket is best when prepared ahead of time, as it is easier to slice the meat when it is cold and to remove the fat from the gravy. To achieve a smooth, thick gravy, process onions with gravy.

Ingrid Blumenstein

Oven Beef Burgundy (Meat)

A delicious classic.

2	tablespoons soy sauce
2	tablespoons flour
2	pounds stew meat, cut into 1 1/2-inch cubes
4	carrots, cut up
2	large onions, cut up
1	cup celery, sliced
1/4	teaspoon pepper
1/4	teaspoon marjoram
1/4	teaspoon thyme
1	cup red wine
1	cup sliced mushrooms

In a large covered casserole, blend soy sauce with flour. Add meat and coat with the mixture. Add remaining ingredients except mushrooms. Stir gently. Cover tightly and bake at 325 degrees for one hour.

Add mushrooms and stir into mixture. Continue baking another 1 1/2-2 1/2 hours or until meat is tender. Serves 6 - 8.

Minerva Arthur

Luscious and Easy Meatballs (Meat)

A favorite for several generations in my family.

1	onion, diced
3	celery ribs, diced
1	large egg
1	pound ground meat
2/3	cup water
1/4	cup matzo meal
1/4	cup ketchup
3	potatoes, sliced, optional
	Boiling water

Variations: For spicier meatballs, add more ketchup. For fluffier meatballs, add more water and matzo meal.

Place diced onion and celery on bottom of 9-inch baking dish or medium roasting pan. Mix egg into ground meat and add water, matzo meal and ketchup; mix well. Form into 10 meatballs, placing them on top of the bed of onions and celery. Pour about 1 1/2-inches of boiling water into pan.

If desired, arrange sliced potatoes around the edge of the pan. Bake, uncovered, in a 375 degree oven for 1 hour, or at 400 degrees for 45 minutes. Serves 3 - 4.

Suggestion: Freezes well. Recipe may be doubled. Any surplus fat may be skimmed off after refrigeration.

Lucille Weisel

Sweet-and-Sour Meatballs (Meat)

An easy, special dish that works equally well as an appetizer or main course.

Sauce:

1	16-ounce can cranberry sauce
1	10 3/4-ounce can tomato soup
1/2	soup can cold water

Meatballs:

2	pounds ground beef
1	package onion soup mix
3	cloves minced garlic, optional
2-3	tablespoons ice water

Mix cranberry sauce, tomato soup and water in a 3-quart sauce pot; bring to a boil, then simmer.

Mix together the ground beef, soup mix and ice water and form into 1-inch balls, dropping each into the simmering sauce. Simmer 1 hour and carefully stir occasionally to prevent sticking. Serves 6 - 8.

Freda Balsham

Sweet-and-Sour Beef (Meat)

A very easy dish with a rich and flavorful gravy.

3	pounds beef stew meat
2	tablespoons oil
2	8-ounce cans tomato sauce
2	teaspoons chili powder
2	teaspoons paprika
1	teaspoon salt
1/2	cup cider vinegar
1/2	cup light molasses
2	cups carrots, cut in 1/4-inch rounds
2	cups small white onions
1	large green bell pepper, cut in 1-inch squares, optional

In a heavy stew pot, brown meat in oil. Add all ingredients except vegetables. Simmer approximately 2 1/2 hours or until meat is tender. Add vegetables and cook until tender-crisp. Serves 6 - 8.

Marcia Abelson

Rose's No-Salt Shoulder Veal Roast (Meat)

A good choice for those on sodium-free diets.

4-5	pounds veal roast
	fresh or powdered garlic
1 1/2	teaspoons paprika
3-4	large onions, cut into small pieces
1	teaspoon fresh rosemary
1	tablespoon lemon herb seasoning
1	teaspoon pepper
1/2	cup orange juice
1/2	cup Cream Concord wine
1	cup water
1/4	cup lemon juice, optional

Wash veal thoroughly and dry well. Rub lots of garlic all over the meat. Mix together paprika, pepper and lemon herb seasoning; rub over meat. Place in a medium-size roasting pan. Put onions and crumbled rosemary around veal and add approximately 1 cup of water. Cover and bake at 325 degrees for 1 1/2 hours.

Mix together orange juice, lemon juice and wine; set aside. Pour juice and wine over roast for the last 1 1/2 hours of roasting time; uncover and baste frequently.

Place in the refrigerator overnight. Slice about 1/8 inch thick. May be frozen at this point. To reheat, place in pan with gravy and heat, covered, in a 250-300 degree oven for 1 hour. Serves 6 - 8.

Rose Sonenklar

Marvelous Meat Sauce (Meat)

Make ahead of time and keep on hand.
Terrific with chicken, beef ribs, etc.

1/2	cup onion, finely chopped
3	garlic cloves, finely chopped
2	tablespoons pareve margarine
3/4	cup mixture of ketchup and chili sauce
3/4	cup tomato juice
1	8-ounce can crushed pineapple
2	tablespoons Dijon mustard
1	4-ounce can diced green chilies
1/2	teaspoon ground cumin

Sauté onion and garlic in margarine until tender. Add remaining ingredients and simmer 20 minutes. Yields approximately 3 cups.

Rosalie Weiner

Stuffed Veal Breast (Meat)

An unusual version of a traditional dish.

8-10	pounds veal breast (or a bit larger)
2	pounds chopped veal
2-3	onions (1 chopped, 1-2 sliced)
2	eggs
	Pepper, salt and garlic, to taste
4-6	tablespoons matzo meal or cracker crumbs
1	cup water

Have butcher cut a pocket in the veal breast. In a large mixing bowl, combine chopped veal, chopped onion, salt, pepper, garlic, eggs, matzo meal or cracker crumbs. Stuff mix into the veal pocket; close with a few skewers. Place sliced onions on the bottom of the roasting pan; put veal breast on top, placing some garlic on top or into the pocket.

Add about 1 cup of water, cover and bake at 350 degrees for 2 1/2-3 hours. If more liquid is needed, add a little more water.

Uncover during the last 15 minutes to brown meat. Test to see if tender. If smoother sauce is desired, put liquid and onions in blender. Serves 10-12.

Suggestion: *If breast is very large, have the butcher cut off 2 pounds and grind it.*

Ingrid Blumenstein

Boneless Stuffed Veal Breast (Meat)

An impressive dish for a special occasion.

5	pounds boneless veal breast
1-1 1/2	teaspoons each: pepper, salt, paprika, garlic powder, onion powder
	Ground ginger, to taste

In Bottom of Roaster:

6	potatoes, sliced thickly
3-4	cloves garlic, chopped
3	carrots, sliced
2	onions, sliced
3-4	whole allspice
2	bay leaves

Sauce for Top of Roast:

1/2	cup chicken broth
1/2	cup white wine

Stuffing:

1	cup cooked white rice
1	cup cooked wild rice
1	large egg, beaten
1	large onion, chopped
3-4	ribs celery, chopped
1	tablespoon dried or fresh parsley
	Salt and pepper, to taste

Have the butcher remove all bones and make pocket in the veal breast. Mix the seasonings; rub inside and outside of veal with the mixture. Mix together the stuffing ingredients and fill the pocket with the mixture.

Line the bottom of a roasting pan with potatoes, garlic, carrots, onions, allspice, and bay leaves. Place stuffed roast on top and add chicken broth and wine.

Bake, partially covered, at 300 degrees to 325 degrees for 1 hour, and uncovered for another 1 1/2 hours or until done and brown. Baste occasionally and add more liquid if necessary.

Remove roast to a serving platter; slice across the grain and cover to keep warm. Serves 5 - 6.

Eleanor Botney

Spanish Tongue (Meat)

A guaranteed crowd pleaser.

2	pounds pickled tongue
1/3	green bell pepper, diced
1	large onion, diced
2	ribs celery, diced
1	10 3/4-ounce can tomato-mushroom soup
1	8-ounce can tomato sauce
3	tablespoons brown sugar
1/4	cup water
2	tablespoons pareve margarine

Tongue: Early in the day, boil the pickled tongue until tender, approximately 3 hours. Peel, cool thoroughly and refrigerate. When cool, cut into thin slices.

Sauté green pepper, onion and celery in 2 tablespoons oil or margarine for approximately 10 minutes. Add tomato-mushroom soup, tomato sauce, brown sugar and water.

Pour half of the sauce in a 3-quart casserole dish, add tongue and cover with remaining sauce. Bake in a 300 degree oven for at least 1 hour. Serve hot. Serves 4 - 5.

Variation: Instead of slicing tongue, cube and serve as hors d'oeuvres.

Phyllis Sarto

Spicy Lamb Shanks (Meat)

Dried fruits and spices flavor this rich dish.

4	lamb shanks
	Salt and pepper, to taste
	Flour
	Oil for browning
1	10 3/4-ounce can chicken broth
1	cup prunes, pitted
1	cup dried apricots
1/2	cup sugar
1/2	teaspoon cinnamon
1/2	teaspoon ground allspice
3	tablespoons vinegar
2-3	tablespoons oil
1/2	cup water

In a paper bag, dust lamb shanks with flour, salt and pepper. In a large Dutch oven, brown shanks with oil; when well browned, add soup. Cover tightly and cook 45 minutes on low heat. Remove to 8-inch square baking dish and drain off fat. Cover and bake in a 350 degree oven for about 1 hour.

Combine fruit, sugar, salt, water and spices in a saucepan and simmer 5 minutes. Add to baking dish; cover and bake 1/2 hour or until done, when lamb is soft. Serves 3 - 4.

Eleanor Botney

Sephardic Tongue (Meat)

My children would never eat tongue, but this recipe won them over!

3 medium onions, diced
2 pounds calf or beef tongue
2 cloves garlic, sliced
1 cup water (for gravy only)
1 tablespoon cornstarch
1 teaspoon fresh cilantro (or 1/2 teaspoon dry)
2 teaspoons fresh parsley (or 1 teaspoon dry)
   Salt, pepper
1 4-ounce can drained mushrooms (stems and pieces)

Place onions in a Dutch oven. Wash tongue and place directly on top of onions; add garlic on top of tongue. Do *not* add any water. Cover and simmer slowly for at least 3 hours.

Remove tongue from Dutch oven and let stand about 5 minutes. Discard onions and garlic. Save the liquid for making the gravy. Cool, peel and trim the tongue and discard the peelings. Refrigerate the tongue for at least 5 hours or overnight.

When the tongue is firm, thinly slice on the diagonal. Make sauce using the reserved cooking liquid as a base. Add about 1 cup of water. Thicken with cornstarch; add cilantro, parsley, salt and pepper to taste. Place sliced tongue in gravy and bake covered at 350 degrees for about 1 hour. Add the mushrooms and bake 1/2 hour longer. Serve with noodles or rice. Serves 6.

Phyllis Sarto

Oven Barbecued Short Ribs

This simple to prepare recipe is a family favorite.

6 meaty short ribs
1/2 cup Burgundy or other red wine
1 8-ounce can tomato sauce
2 tablespoons chopped onion
1 1/2 teaspoons salt
2 tablespoons vinegar
1 tablespoon prepared mustard
3 - 4 drops Tabasco sauce

Brown short ribs. Combine remaining ingredients and pour over browned ribs. Bake, tightly covered, at 300 degrees for 2 hours.

Alice Barnett

Chinese Pancakes
or Peking Doilies (Pareve)

Serve with teriyaki steak, roast duck, chicken or vegetarian filling.

1	**cup flour**
1/2	**cup boiling water**
2	**tablespoons oil**

Put flour in bowl; make a well and add boiling water. Stir until all water is absorbed and all the flour comes away from side of bowl. Knead for 10 minutes and let stand for 10 minutes, covered with dry towel.

Make into long roll. Divide into eight pieces and flatten them into circles. Brush a little oil over two circles of flattened dough and place oiled sides together. Roll out until the circle is 7 inches in diameter. Repeat with balance of circles.

Heat griddle over low flame and heat the pancake. When it bubbles up, turn and heat the other side. Remove and separate pancakes. Stack pancakes on a platter and steam over boiling water for 10 minutes before serving (it is not necessary to steam if serving immediately). Yields approximately 8 pancakes.

Suggestion: *May be frozen if wrapped in plastic wrap and foil.*

Min Leonard

Ground Lamb Kebab (Meat)

*These individual mini meat loaves turn
ground lamb into a Middle Eastern treat.*

1	pound ground lamb
1	tablespoon onion, minced
1/2	teaspoon ground allspice
	Pinch ground cumin
1/2	teaspoon fresh grated ginger or pinch of ground ginger
1	egg
1	teaspoon minced parsley
	Few grinds of black pepper
1/2	teaspoon salt
3	tablespoons bread crumbs
2	medium cloves garlic, crushed
	Pinch red chili pepper

Combine all ingredients in a bowl. Shape into 8 or 9 finger-shaped pieces. Place in a 9-inch baking dish. Bake at 375 degrees for about 20 minutes or until browned. Serve with rice pilaf and a green salad. Serves 3 - 4.

Eve Marcus

Beef Noodle Casserole (Meat)

A quick dinner for an informal get-together.

2	pounds lean ground beef
1	8-ounce package wide noodles
1	medium onion, chopped
1	green bell pepper, chopped
1	10 3/4-ounce can mushroom soup
2	10 3/4-ounce cans tomato soup
	Salt and pepper, optional

Sauté onion and bell pepper. Add meat, stirring until brown. Season with salt and pepper as desired.

Cook noodles according to package directions. Add noodles, mushroom and tomato soup to meat mixture. Pour entire mixture into a glass 9x15-inch pan. Bake in a 300 degree oven, covered, for 1/2 hour and uncovered for an additional 1/2 hour. Serves 10 - 12.

Variation: *Ground turkey, chicken, lamb, etc., may be substituted for ground beef.*

Sue Ann Levine

Chili Con Carne (Meat)

A great recipe to make ahead of time — freezes well.

1/4	cup oil
1	large onion, chopped
1	green bell pepper, chopped
4	cloves garlic, minced
1	pound extra-lean ground beef
1	8-ounce can tomato sauce
1	14 1/2-ounce can stewed tomatoes
1/2	teaspoon salt
2	8-ounce cans chili beans with juice
1/8	teaspoon paprika
1	tablespoon chili powder, or to taste

In a large stew pot, sauté onions, bell pepper and garlic in oil. Remove with slotted spoon and set aside.

Brown meat slightly; add the sauteed items and the remaining ingredients. Simmer for at least 2 hours. Let cool slightly and refrigerate.

When cool, skim off any visible fat. Tastes better a day later, as flavors blend together. Serves 4.

Diane Tapper

Gayle's Beef with Peppers (Meat)

This Cantonese recipe wins rave reviews.

1	pound skirt steak, slightly frozen
1	tablespoon dry sherry
3	tablespoons soy sauce
1	teaspoon sugar
2	teaspoons cornstarch
2	green peppers, cut into 1/2-inch squares
4	tablespoons peanut oil
2	scallions, cut into 1/2-inch pieces
3	slices ginger root, cut 1/8 inch thick into very fine julienne

Cut steak diagonally into strips 1/8 inch thick. Cut each strip into small pieces, approximately 1x1 1/2 inches.

In a bowl, mix sherry, soy sauce, sugar and cornstarch. Add steak slices and mix to coat well. Let marinate for 20 minutes, if desired.

Heat 2 tablespoons oil in wok or skillet. Quickly stir fry the beef until brown; remove.

Add 2 tablespoons oil to wok or skillet, stir fry ginger and scallions, then add green peppers and meat. Blend thoroughly. Serve piping hot. Serves 2 - 4 as a main course, 4 - 6 as part of a Chinese meal.

Min Leonard

Stuffed Cabbage or Holishkes (Meat)

Can be a complete meal. Ideal for entertaining in the sukkah.

1	pound chopped beef
1/4	cup rice, uncooked
1	egg
1	onion, grated
1	carrot, grated
1/4	teaspoon salt
2	tablespoons water
10-12	cabbage leaves
1/4	cup lemon juice or vinegar
1/2	cup brown sugar
1	cup canned tomato sauce
1/2	cup raisins, optional
	Water to cover

In a large mixing bowl, combine chopped meat, rice, egg, onion, carrot and salt; add 2 tablespoons water. Blanch cabbage leaves by covering them with boiling water for 2-3 minutes. (If cabbage head is cored first, leaves will break away easily.)

Place ball of meat mixture in the center of each cabbage leaf and roll up, tucking in the ends securely. Place close together in a heavy frying pan or Dutch oven; add the other ingredients and enough water to cover. Cover tightly with lid and cook over moderate heat for 30 minutes. Reduce heat and simmer 20 minutes. Remove to oven and bake at 350 degrees for 20 minutes to brown on top, turning once with large spoon to brown underside. Hot water may be added in small quantities, if necessary, during the baking period. Serves 4 - 6.

Lela Jacoby

Stuffed Cabbage (Meat)

A special favorite of Pearl Roseman.

Cabbage:

1	**large head cabbage**
2	**pounds ground beef or turkey**
1/2	**cup raw rice**
1/2	**cup raisins**
	Salt and pepper, to taste

Sauce:

1 1/2	**cups sugar**
2	**large onions**
1	**16-ounce can tomato sauce**
1	**tablespoon lemon juice**

Cut approximately 2 inches around the core of the cabbage and steam for approximately 5-10 minutes to soften leaves enough to shape into rolls. Set aside to cool. Reserve water from steamed cabbage.

Mix meat with raw rice, raisins, salt and pepper to taste.

Place approximately 1/4-1/3 cup of filling in a whole cabbage leaf, folding in edges as you loosely roll them. Place the rolls on a bed of one sliced onion in a large, Dutch oven-type pot. Layer the rolls in the pot until all the filling is used up.

Sauce mixture: Brown sugar in heavy skillet on a low flame. Add the balance of onion, tomato sauce and lemon juice;stir together. Pour sauce mixture over all.

Cook 12-15 minutes in a 6-quart pressure cooker or bake 1 1/2 hours at 350 degrees. Serves 6 - 8.

Note: If you have extra meat filling, shape into small meat balls and drop in pan between rolls. Extra cabbage can be sliced up and added to the pot. This recipe also cooks well in a microwave. Sugar may be reduced or use a substitute. To ensure more juice, add enough water from the steamed cabbage to cover the entire contents.

Variation: Raisins may be placed in the sauce instead of the meat mixture.

Eve Wechsberg

Chinese Tomato Beef (Meat)

Delicious and attractive stir fry.

Meat:

1/2	pound skirt steak, partially frozen
3-4	tomatoes, skinned and quartered
1	large green bell pepper, cut into triangles
1	medium onion, cubed
2	ribs celery, sliced
3	tablespoons oil

Marinade:

1	tablespoon cornstarch
1	tablespoon soy sauce
1	clove garlic, peeled and crushed
1	piece ginger root, size of a quarter, crushed
1	tablespoon oil
	Salt, to taste

Gravy:

1/2	cup water
1	tablespoon cornstarch
1	teaspoon sugar
1	tablespoon soy sauce
1	teaspoon sherry wine
1	teaspoon curry powder
1	tablespoon Worcestershire sauce

Slice meat very thin across the grain. Peel tomatoes by dropping into boiling water for 20 seconds. Run under cold water and slip off skins. Cut into quarters.

To make the marinade, crush garlic and ginger; mix with other marinade ingredients. Put meat slices into marinade and mix to coat them thoroughly. Let stand for 20 minutes. Mix all gravy ingredients together while meat is marinating.

Heat an empty wok or frying pan very hot. Lightly coat bottom of pan with 1-2 tablespoons oil and a dash of salt. Sauté green pepper, onion and celery for 1-2 minutes. Add tomatoes and cook for another 1/2 minute, covered.

Remove from heat and pour into serving bowl. Wipe pan dry with paper towels. Add another 2 tablespoons oil and reheat pan until hot. Add meat and marinade mixture. Toss meat in pan. Cook until browned, about 2 minutes. Pour gravy over meat; stir until bubbly and slightly thickened. Remove from heat and pour over vegetables. Mix carefully to coat all with gravy. Serve over rice or noodles. Serves 2 - 3.

Claire Gering

Kung Pao Beef or Chicken (Meat)

Red chili peppers pack a punch in this Szechuan or Hunan dish.

1   **pound boneless chicken or beef**
1   **tablespoon soy sauce**
1 1/2 **teaspoons cornstarch**
1   **egg white**
4   **dried Colorado chili peppers**
3   **or more cups peanut oil for deep frying**
1   **cup raw peanuts or unsalted roasted, skinless peanuts**
1   **teaspoon minced fresh ginger root**
1/2   **cup leek or scallions, minced**

Sauce:
1   **clove garlic, mashed**
2   **tablespoons soy sauce**
1   **tablespoon dry sherry**
1/2   **tablespoon red wine vinegar**
1   **tablespoon sugar**
1   **teaspoon cornstarch**
1   **teaspoon dark sesame oil (use Chinese dark oil only, available in Chinese section of market); need not double oil even if doubling recipe**

Cut chicken or beef into 1-inch cubes. Mix together egg white, cornstarch and soy sauce. Coat meat; set aside for 30 minutes.

Clean, wipe dry and cut chili peppers in half. Remove stems and seeds. Heat 3 cups of oil in large frying pan or wok and fry peanuts until golden; be careful not to burn. Remove from heat and let cool. (If using roasted peanuts, don't fry.)

Reheat oil to 375 degrees or until haze forms over it. Fry the chicken or beef, a small amount at a time, for about 30 seconds. Remove and drain.

Remove all but 2 tablespoons oil from pan or wok and fry the dried peppers until almost black. Add ginger and leek or scallions and stir fry quickly.

Mix all ingredients together for sauce and add to pan or wok. Stir until thick and hot. Add chicken or beef to sauce and heat through. Remove from heat; add peanuts, mixing thoroughly. Serve hot. Serves 3 - 4.

Note: *Chili peppers must be handled with rubber gloves only or hands will burn. May cut down on pepper, if desired.*

Min Leonard

Vegetables

◆

In our vegetable collection you will find dishes representative of the many different cultures in which Jews have lived and continue to live. From all over the world, these recipes have made their way to California to become the family favorites of our contributors. No doubt the abundance and ever-burgeoning variety of California produce has played a part in shaping some of the contemporary recipes found here. Perhaps at some future date our grandchildren will think of these dishes as traditional, and the cooks of tomorrow will extol the merits of their favorite layered vegetable terrine that's "just like grandma used to make."

Our members, their friends and relatives submitted many vegetable recipes. The ones you see here, blind- and triple-tested by our panel, were the very best of the lot.

Frequently we heard comments like, "My family never liked spinach until I served it this way!" We recommend that you try all the recipes — the familiar as well as the unfamiliar, and discover why Californians are eating more vegetables all the time.

Potato Latkes (Pareve)

A Classic. Traditional at Hanukkah.

2   large White Rose
    potatoes
1/2 onion
2   eggs
1/4 cup flour
1   teaspoon salt
    Oil for frying

Wash, scrub and cut potatoes into proper size for food processor or blender. DO NOT PEEL. Add all ingredients to processor or blender using stop and start until well blended, but not too fine. Pour into bowl. Heat oil in skillet.

Drop by tablespoon into hot skillet and fry on both sides until brown.

To freeze: Spread latkes singly on a cookie sheet. When frozen, place in a plastic bag and return to freezer. To serve: place frozen latkes on cookie sheet and heat at 450 degrees for approximately 7-10 minutes. Yields 14 - 16 latkes.

Dotty Simmons

Zucchini Latkes (Pareve)

A nice alternative to potato latkes for Hanukkah, or any time.

4   cups zucchini, grated
    (2 large ones)
1   cup parsley, chopped
1   teaspoon lemon pepper
1/4 teaspoon salt
2   eggs, lightly beaten
3-4 tablespoons matzo meal
    Oil for frying

In a large bowl, mix together all ingredients, except oil. Drop by tablespoon to form 3-inch latkes and fry in hot oil until golden brown on each side. Freezes well. Yields approximately 12 - 15.

Pearl Roseman

Potato Kugel (Pareve)

Delicious traditional recipe from a Chicago restaurateur.

8	medium Idaho potatoes
2	onions
2	carrots
6	eggs
2 1/2	teaspoons salt
1/4	teaspoon white pepper
1/2	teaspoon paprika
7 - 8	tablespoons matzo meal

Grate potatoes. Drain liquid. Grate onions and carrots and add to potatoes. Beat eggs and add to potato mixture. Add salt and pepper. Add matzo meal and mix well. In a 8x11-inch baking dish, sprayed with a nonstick vegetable spray, bake 30 minutes at 400 degrees, then reduce temperature to 350 degrees, sprinkle paprika on top, and bake 30 to 45 minutes longer. Serves 6 - 8.

Sam Wigoda

Zucchini Kugel (Pareve)

From my Israeli mother-in-law, Florence Weber Alexander.

1	tablespoon oil
1	pound zucchini, unpeeled and grated
3	carrots, grated
1	potato, grated
1/2	onion, grated
3	eggs (4 if you want it fluffier), beaten
2-4	tablespoons matzo meal
1/4	teaspoon salt
1/8	teaspoon pepper or to taste
1/4	teaspoon basil and/or
1/4	teaspoon oregano

Preheat oven to 350 degrees. Place oil in bottom of 9x13-inch baking dish and place in oven to heat. Mix remaining ingredients, adding enough matzo meal to give the mixture a pudding-like consistency. Pour into baking dish. Brush lightly with more oil. Bake for 1 hour, until golden brown on top. Serves 6 - 8.

Note: This recipe can be doubled, tripled or quadrupled. It also freezes well.

Sally Weber

Layered Vegetable Terrine (Dairy)

Excellent served hot or cold; looks wonderful.

Spinach Layer:

20	ounces cooked spinach (thawed if frozen)
1/2	small onion, minced
3	tablespoons half and half
1	egg
1	teaspoon salt
1/3	teaspoon garlic powder
1/4	teaspoon pepper

Cauliflower Layer:

1	medium cauliflower, cut up, cooked
1	egg
1-2	tablespoons half and half
1	tablespoon minced parsley
1	teaspoon salt
1/2	teaspoon lemon pepper seasoning

Carrot Layer:

1	pound carrots, cooked
1	egg
1-2	tablespoons half and half
1	teaspoon dried dill weed
3/4	teaspoon salt
1/2	teaspoon ground ginger
	Sugar to taste
	Carrot flowers (for garnish)

Press moisture out of spinach. In food processor or blender, combine spinach layer ingredients, adding as much half and half as necessary to make smooth puree. Mixture should be moist but not runny. Pack evenly and firmly into bottom of greased 9x5-inch loaf pan.

For cauliflower layer, follow directions for spinach layer, adding half and half as necessary. Puree and layer evenly in pan over spinach.

For carrot layer, proceed as before, pureeing all ingredients. Layer evenly in pan over cauliflower. Cover top with buttered wax paper and place in larger pan. Add water to reach 1-2 inches up side of loaf pan.

Bake 1 to 1 1/2 hours in a preheated 300 degree oven. Test for doneness by lifting wax paper and shaking loaf pan; terrine is baked when firm. Remove from oven and let stand 15 minutes. Remove paper and run knife around edges. Invert onto serving plate. Garnish with carrot flowers.

Slice and serve hot or cold. If served hot, accompany with hot melted butter flavored with lemon juice. If served cold, accompany with mayonnaise. Serves 8.

Janis Weiss

Vegetable Chabotte (Pareve)

A traditional dish I learned from my Italian mother, Teresa Mandino, who got it from her mother, who got it from her mother. Delizioso!!!

1	tablespoon oil
1	tablespoon green onion, chopped
1/2	medium onion, cut in chunks
3	medium cloves garlic, chopped fine
1/2	cup sliced leeks, white portion only (optional)
4	stalks celery, cut diagonally in 1-inch pieces
1	14-ounce can stewed tomatoes
1	8-ounce can tomato sauce
1/2	cup water
	Salt and pepper to taste
1/2	teaspoon sugar (optional)
1/2-1	teaspoon parsley flakes
1/2	teaspoon oregano
1	green bell pepper, cut in chunks
2	small zucchini, cut in 3/4-inch slices

Heat oil in 2-quart saucepan. Add green onion, onion, garlic, leeks and celery; mix well. Cover and cook, stirring occasionally, over low flame until onions are transparent and celery is tender. In a medium bowl mix together stewed tomatoes, tomato sauce, water, salt, pepper, sugar, parsley and oregano. Add mixture to saucepan and bring to a boil. Reduce heat, cover, and simmer for approximately 15 minutes.

Remove cover. Add bell peppers and zucchini to saucepan and continue to simmer, covered, another 15 minutes.

Recipe can be prepared 2-3 days in advance and stored in covered glass bowl in refrigerator until ready to heat and serve. Reheat over low flame. Serves 6.

Variations: *Substitute 3 sprigs of fresh parsley for parsley flakes, or use eggplant instead of zucchini and/or also add mushrooms. Can be served with chicken, turkey, fish, veal, meat and omelettes.*

Mary Kovshoff

Crustless Veggie Pie (Dairy)

An unusual side dish or main course.

1	medium eggplant, peeled and finely cubed
1	green bell pepper, chopped
1	onion, diced
2	stalks celery, diced
4	ounces mushrooms
4	medium tomatoes, chopped
4	eggs
4	ounces mozzarella cheese, grated
4	ounces Parmesan cheese, grated
1/4	teaspoon garlic powder
1/2	teaspoon parsley
1/4	teaspoon oregano
	Salt and pepper to taste

Preheat oven to 350 degrees. In a skillet, sauté eggplant, bell pepper, onion and celery for 10 minutes. Add mushrooms and tomatoes. Simmer an additional 20 minutes. Cool.

In a large bowl, beat eggs and seasonings. Mix together with sauteed vegetables and place in a lightly greased 9-inch pie plate. Top with cheeses.

Bake for 35 minutes or until a nice crust has formed. Serves 4 - 6.

Joan Kramer

Cold Vegetable Platter with Sauce Verte (Dairy)

A lovely buffet salad that won't wilt.

Sauce:

3	sprigs parsley
2	whole green onions
1	cup mayonnaise
1/2	cup sour cream
2	tablespoons lemon juice
1	teaspoon seasoned salt
1/2	teaspoon tarragon
1/2	cup frozen, drained spinach

Vegetables:

1	16-ounce can baby beets
6	tomatoes, cut into wedges
1	cauliflower, cooked and chilled
1	pound carrots, cooked and chilled
1	pound fresh string beans, cooked and chilled

In a blender blend together sauce ingredients until smooth. Refrigerate until ready. Place vegetables in mounds on platter, sauce in bowl in center. Serves 12.

Note: *Other vegetables, such as asparagus, may be used.*

Ruth Nebron

Casserole on the Green (Dairy)

Delicious and suitable for company.

2 10-ounce packages frozen asparagus cuts, cooked and drained (may use 2 10-ounce packages frozen broccoli spears, cooked, drained and cut into 1-inch pieces)
2 10 3/4-ounce cans mushroom soup
1/2 cup cornmeal
1/4 cup butter or margarine, melted
1/4 cup grated Parmesan cheese
1 1/2 tablespoons chopped parsley
1/4 teaspoon garlic salt

Combine asparagus (or broccoli) and soup in a 1 1/2-quart casserole; mix well. Combine cornmeal, butter, cheese, parsley and garlic salt; sprinkle over asparagus. Bake at 375 degrees about 25 minutes or until topping is golden brown. Serves 6 - 8.

Trana Labowe

Shirley's Mushrooms (Dairy)

Great with French bread.

1 1/2 pounds medium-size mushrooms, cut in half
3/4 cup Italian seasoned bread crumbs
1/2 teaspoon oregano
2 tablespoons chopped parsley
2 cloves garlic, chopped
4 tablespoons grated Parmesan cheese
1/2 cup butter, melted
Salt and pepper to taste

In a large bowl, mix together all ingredients. Pour mixture into a greased 12x15-inch baking dish. Bake covered for 30 minutes at 325 degrees. Serves 12.

Shirley Moore

Cabbage Strudel (Pareve)

An Old World favorite adapted to today's cuisine.

2	cabbage heads, shredded (approximately 6 cups)
1	large onion
1	1-pound package filo dough
1/2	cup oil (approximately)
1	teaspoon salt, or to taste
1/4	teaspoon pepper, or to taste
1/2	teaspoon caraway seeds
1/3	cup sugar, or to taste Juice of 2 lemons

In a frying pan, sauté onions, then add cabbage, a little water, salt, pepper, caraway seeds, sugar and lemon juice. Cook for about 1 hour over medium heat. Taste and correct seasonings if necessary. When cabbage is done, allow to cool. In the meantime preheat oven to 350 degrees and prepare filo dough according to directions. For each strudel use 8 sheets of filo dough. Brush each one with oil, then put one third of the cabbage mixture on one end and roll up (jelly roll fashion), folding ends in securely. Place 3 strudels (rolls) on greased baking pan. Bake 50-60 minutes or until golden brown. Serves 8 - 12.

Ingrid Blumenstein

Hot Sauerkraut (Pareve)

My adaptation of a dish served at the Austrian restaurant at the '87 Expo in Canada.

1	medium onion, chopped
1	27-ounce can sauerkraut
1	teaspoon caraway seeds
1/2	teaspoon celery seeds
1/8	cup sherry wine
1/8	cup water
1/2	teaspoon pareve chicken soup mix
2	tablespoons brown sugar
1	small shredded potato or 1 small shredded tart apple, or both

In a 4-quart pot, sauté onions until slightly browned. Add remaining ingredients and boil on top of stove approximately 1/2 hour or until liquid is boiled down. Serves 8.

Phyllis Sarto

Eggplant Parmesan (Dairy)

Delicious version of the Italian classic.

1 1/2 pounds eggplant
1/4 cup flour
1/8 teaspoon garlic powder
Dash of pepper
Oil for browning
1 clove garlic, minced
2 cups tomato sauce or spaghetti sauce
1/2 pound mushrooms, sliced
3/4 cup grated Swiss or Cheddar cheese
8 ounces mozzarella cheese, sliced

Peel, slice and cube eggplant. Season flour with garlic powder and pepper; put into a plastic bag. Add eggplant and shake well. Let stand for 30 minutes.

Heat small amount of oil in a no-stick frying pan. Spread eggplant on paper towel to remove extra flour. Brown eggplant and garlic lightly in oil.

Spread 1/4 cup of tomato sauce (or spaghetti sauce) in a 10-inch round casserole. Spread half the eggplant, all the sliced mushrooms, half the grated cheese and half the sliced mozzarella. Sprinkle with oregano. Top with 1 cup tomato sauce and repeat another layer of eggplant, grated cheese and balance of sauce. Top with mozzarella; cover loosely with foil. Bake 20 minutes in a preheated 375 degree oven; remove foil and bake an additional 10 minutes. Serves 6 - 8.

Sylvia Price

Carrots and Potatoes with Caraway Seeds (Dairy)

Good for a cold night.

4 carrots, (about 1/2 pound), peeled
4 red potatoes (about 3/4 pound), peeled
1 tablespoon butter
1/4 cup chopped onion
1/2 cup water
1/2 teaspoon caraway seeds
Salt and pepper to taste

Cut carrots into 1-inch lengths and lengthwise into quarters. Cut potatoes into quarters. In a skillet, heat butter and sauté onions briefly. Add potatoes, carrots, water, caraway seeds, salt and pepper. Bring to a boil and cook, covered, 12-15 minutes. Serves 4.

Ruth Nebron

Marinated Carrots (Pareve)

Unusual and versatile recipe.
Delicious with salads or hot and cold dishes.

2	pounds carrots, cut in 1 1/2-inch pieces
1	10 3/4-ounce can tomato soup
1/2	cup salad oil
1	cup sugar
3/4	cup cider vinegar
1	teaspoon salt
1/2	teaspoon pepper
1/2	teaspoon dill weed
1	large green bell pepper, cut in chunks
1	large onion, sliced and ringed

Cook carrots until barely tender (not soft); drain and cool. In a saucepan, combine soup, oil, sugar, vinegar, salt, pepper and dill. Bring to a boil only to dissolve sugar and mix well. In a 2-quart container place carrots, sliced onions and bell pepper. Add the soup mixture, cover and place in refrigerator. Will keep in refrigerator for three weeks. Serves 8 - 12.

Hint: If the carrots disappear too quickly, add more to leftover sauce.

Gussie Cutter

Miriam's Carrot Tzimmis (Pareve)

A traditional family favorite for Rosh Hashanah and Passover.

3	cups parboiled sliced carrots
1 1/2	cups sliced yams
8-10	large pitted prunes
1/2	cup crushed pineapple with juice
1/3	cup honey or brown sugar
1/3	cup orange juice concentrate
1/4	cup sherry wine
1/4	teaspoon salt

In a large bowl, mix all ingredients together and pour into a well-greased 2-quart casserole. Cover and bake in a 300 degree oven for 3-4 hours. Quantities of all ingredients can be varied according to taste. Recipe freezes and reheats well. Reheat covered. Serves 6 - 8.

Miriam Wise

Carrots (Pareve)

erent way to serve carrots.

Using a vegetable peeler, thinly peel carrots and slice into thin coins or shave into thin strips. Toast walnuts. (To toast walnuts in a microwave, place walnut pieces in a small casserole and microwave on high 3-4 minutes, stirring at the end of each minute).

Combine carrot strips with margarine, water and salt in a 1-quart, microwave-safe casserole with a lid. Cover and microwave on high 4-5 minutes, stirring once with a fork, until tender-crisp. Stir in honey, pepper and lemon juice. Cover and let stand 3 minutes. Stir in toasted walnut pieces and serve immediately. Serves 2-3.

Variation: Honey-minted carrots: Stir in 2 teaspoons honey and lemon juice before standing time. Omit walnuts. Just before serving stir in 1 tablespoon finely chopped mint.

Marcia Abelson

Cauliflower Fritada (Pareve)

An unusual way to serve cauliflower as a vegetarian main dish at lunch or brunch.

2	**10-ounce boxes frozen cauliflower**
3	**eggs**
1/2	**envelope onion soup mix**
1/2	**cup mayonnaise**
	Matzo meal

Defrost cauliflower. Drain, mash and mix well beaten eggs, onion soup mix and mayonnaise. Grease 9x13-inch pan and line with matzo meal. Pour in cauliflower mixture. Top with additional matzo meal. Bake at 350 degrees for 45 minutes. Serves 8 - 10.

Variation: For an interesting contrast, substitute one box spinach or one box broccoli.

Joan Kramer

Hot Fruit and Sweet Potato (Pareve)

A low-sodium dish that's lovely with sliced cold turkey.

4	**medium sweet potatoes, baked**
1	**16-ounce can peaches (2 1/2 cups)**
1	**16-ounce can pears (2 1/2 cups)**
1	**16-ounce can pineapple (2 1/2 cups)**
1	**16-ounce can apricots (2 1/2 cups)**
1/2	**cup unsalted margarine, melted**
3/4	**cup brown sugar**
4	**teaspoons curry powder**

Peel and cut baked potatoes in 1/2-inch slices. Drain peaches, pears, pineapple and apricots. Layer potatoes and fruit in a 9x13-inch ovenproof dish. Drizzle melted margarine over all. Sprinkle with sugar and curry. Bake at 350 degrees for 1 hour. Serves 10.

Fay Auerbach

Potluck Corn Pudding (Dairy)

This is a very nice dish for Sukkot.

1	**cup unsalted butter or margarine, melted and cooled slightly**
1	**8 1/2-ounce box cornbread mix**
1	**16-ounce can corn kernels, drained**
1	**16-ounce can cream-style corn**
1	**cup sour cream**

Brush a 3-quart shallow baking dish or pan (that can be used for serving) generously with some of the melted butter. In a mixing bowl combine cornbread mix, corns, sour cream and butter; mix with spoon until all ingredients are well blended. Pour mixture into prepared baking dish and spread evenly on top. Bake on center shelf at 350 degrees until top is golden and crusty and inserted knife comes out clean, approximately 50 minutes. Remove from oven and let cool 5-10 minutes before serving. Serves 10-12.

Stan Herzoff

Creamed Parsnips (Dairy)

*Served to us when we were dinner guests of
Vera and Bill Rhodes in Grassington Village, Yorkshire, England.*

1	**pound fresh parsnips**
1 1/2	**cup hot water**
2/3	**cup half and half**
	Salt to taste
	Freshly milled black pepper to taste
1/2	**teaspoon freshly grated nutmeg**

Peel parsnips and cut into small cubes. In a saucepan, bring water to a boil; add parsnips and simmer, covered, for approximately 10 minutes or until tender. Drain parsnips, reserving the liquid. Puree parsnips in a food processor or blender, adding half and half gradually. Add nutmeg, salt and pepper. Serves 4 - 5.

Note: If mixture is too dry, add some of reserved liquid. This can be made in advance and heated when ready to serve.

Marcia Abelson

Broccoli with Ginger (Pareve)

A beautiful-looking side dish for an Oriental meal.

1	**bunch broccoli**
2	**cloves garlic**
2	**slices fresh ginger root**
1	**tablespoon oil**
2	**teaspoons water**
1/4	**teaspoon salt**

Clean broccoli, cut flowers off. Peel tough outer layer from stems and grate stems. Peel garlic and ginger. Heat a wok or frying pan until very hot. Add 1/2 tablespoon oil, then add garlic and ginger, and toss in oil to flavor. Remove garlic and ginger and add grated broccoli stems. Toss to coat with oil. Add 1 teaspoon water; cover and steam 2 minutes on high heat.

Remove from pan, drain and arrange in a circle around a serving platter.

Dry wok and reheat. Add balance of oil and salt, add broccoli flowers and toss. Add water, cover and cook on high heat 1-2 minutes. Remove from heat and put inside circle of broccoli stems. Serves 4 - 8, depending on how much broccoli you use.

Claire Gering

Broccoli and Spinach Soufflé (Dairy)

A quick and easy soufflé with a different touch.

2	packages chopped broccoli
3	12-ounce packages spinach soufflé
1/4	pound fresh mushrooms, sliced
1	tablespoon onion flakes Garlic powder

Thaw broccoli and spinach; mix together. Slice mushrooms and mix with broccoli and spinach. Add chopped onions to mixture. Add garlic powder, as desired. Pour into 9 x13-inch baking dish. Bake 45 minutes at 350 degrees. Serves 8 - 10.

Joy Lipman

Cauliflower Broccoli Beehive (Dairy)

This recipe "dresses" up regular vegetables with a flair!

Broccoli and Cauliflower to fill (tightly packed) a 4-quart glass measuring cup

Wash both vegetables and cut into small florets. Arrange a layer of cauliflower (floret side down) in measuring cup, then a layer of broccoli and repeat until it is filled to the top, packing down firmly with your hands each layer as it is put in. Add 3 tablespoons water (may be salted or seasoned with chicken soup mix). Cover with a vented, plastic wrap and microwave on high 6-8 minutes (depending on how soft-cooked you like the vegetables). Let rest a couple of minutes and then carefully invert on a serving platter. Serve with melted cheese, butter, margarine or desired sauce. Serves 8 - 12.

Variation: Steamed carrots or any combination of vegetables can be arranged in a ring, surrounding beehive.

Hint: Spray measuring cup with vegetable cooking spray. In order not to smell up the house when cooking broccoli, put a stalk of celery in it.

Bernice Glickfeld

Broccoli with Pine Nuts and Raisins (Pareve)

An unusual and elegant presentation that works well with veal chops.

4-6 cups broccoli, cut up
1 hot dried red pepper
2 cloves garlic, slivered
1/4 cup olive oil
1/2 cup pine nuts
1/2 cup raisins
1-1 1/2 cups (2 large) tomatoes, chopped
Salt and pepper to taste

Cut broccoli top into florets. Trim and peel stalks and cut them on the diagonal into thin slices. In a frying pan, sauté red pepper and garlic in hot oil. Add pine nuts and raisins and sauté just until pine nuts begin to color, about 2 minutes. Add all pieces of broccoli and sauté about 5 minutes more. Add tomatoes and cook just until heated through, about 1 minute. Season with salt and pepper. Serves 6 - 8.

Greta Grunwald

Ruth's Best Broccoli Casserole (Dairy)

Serves equally well as a side dish or main dish.

2 pounds chopped frozen broccoli, well drained and thawed
1 cup mayonnaise
2 cups shredded sharp Cheddar cheese
2 eggs
1 10 3/4-ounce can cream of mushroom soup
1 1/2 cup crushed round buttery crackers
4 ounces butter or margarine
2-3 cloves garlic, chopped finely
Pepper to taste

Spread broccoli in 9x13-inch glass baking dish. Mix all ingredients, except crackers, butter and garlic. Pour mixture over broccoli. Sauté crackers in butter and garlic. Sprinkle over broccoli mixture. Bake, uncovered, in a 350 degree oven for 30-40 minutes or until top browns. Serves 6 - 8 as a main dish, or 12 as a side dish.

Hint: *Best prepared ahead and refrigerated, then baked. Can be put into oven cold.*

Ruth Giden

Spinach/Pear Puree (Dairy/Pareve)

A most elegant way to serve spinach.

3	10-ounce packages frozen chopped spinach, thawed and drained
1	8-ounce can sliced pears in heavy syrup, drained; reserve liquid
2	teaspoons salt (or to taste)
4-6	tablespoons butter or margarine
	Pinch of nutmeg

In a food processor or blender, puree spinach and pear together, using pear juice as needed to moisten. In a large skillet melt butter until golden brown. Add puree and stir until heated through. Adjust seasoning and serve immediately. Serves 8 - 10.

Suggestion: May be made earlier and heated in microwave.

Sandra Donner

Spinach Casserole (Pareve)

A lovely, different way to serve spinach.

3	10- to 12-ounce frozen packages chopped spinach, cooked and drained well
4	tablespoons margarine
4	tablespoons flour
1 3/4	cups liquid nondairy creamer
1/2	teaspoon garlic powder
1/4	teaspoon nutmeg
3	eggs

In a large saucepot, melt margarine; stir in flour and add nondairy creamer. Bring to a slow boil until thickened. Let cool 5 minutes. Add beaten eggs. Add spinach and mix well. Pour into a 12x13-inch ovenproof pan. Bake at 350 degrees for 45 minutes. Serve at once. Serves 8 - 10.

Shirley Moore

Spinach Broccoli Soufflé (Dairy)

A lovely side dish.

1	10-ounce package frozen spinach, thawed and drained well
1	10-ounce package frozen broccoli, thawed
2	eggs, beaten
1	10 3/4 ounce can cream of mushroom soup
1	2.8 ounce can french-fried onions

In a mixing bowl, combine spinach, broccoli and soup. Place 1/2 of the vegetable mixture in a greased casserole. Cover with 1/2 of the onions. Layer balance of vegetables and top with remaining onions. Cover lightly with foil. Bake for 45-60 minutes at 350 degrees. Uncover for last 15 minutes. Serves 8.

Variation: Chopped pimiento or red pepper may be added for color.

Muriel Becker

Spinach Soufflé (Pareve)

My cousin Sara Huss created this tasty and rich soufflé.

3	10-ounce packages frozen chopped spinach, thawed and drained
3	tablespoons flour (or matzo meal, corn starch, potato starch, etc.).
3/4	cup liquid nondairy creamer
1	medium onion, chopped (or 3 tablespoons dry chopped onions)
2	tablespoons melted margarine
3/4	cup mayonnaise
3	eggs, beaten
3	tablespoons oil

Preheat oven to 350 degrees. Pour oil into a 9x13-inch pan and heat it in the oven. In a large bowl mix ingredients together and pour into the hot oiled pan. Bake 35-45 minutes. Serves 8 - 10.

*Variation:*The recipe can be varied by adding sliced mushrooms or water chestnuts.

Pearl Roseman

Spinach Fritada (Dairy)

This basic fritada recipe lends itself to endless variations.

2	10-ounce packages frozen chopped spinach
3	eggs
3	ounces (3/4 cups) grated cheese (Parmesan, Romano or mixed)
3	tablespoons oil
3	tablespoons matzo meal or bread crumbs
8	ounces small curd cottage cheese, optional

Place the spinach in a large mixing bowl and let stand until thawed. DO NOT DRAIN. Add all ingredients. Pour into a greased 9-inch square pan. Bake at 350 degrees about 1 hour or until golden brown. Allow to cool 10 minutes and cut into serving portions. Serves 8.

Pearl Roseman

Stuffed Zucchini (Pareve)

This Lebanese dish makes the cook look very accomplished.

2   **cloves garlic, minced or crushed**
1   **onion, finely chopped olive oil**
1/2 **cup rice**
1   **cup water**
1/2 **cup dried currants or raisins**
1/2 **cup pine nuts or sesame seeds**
2   **tablespoons chopped parsley**
1/2 **teaspoon cinnamon**
1/4 **teaspoon allspice**
    Salt
    Pepper
    Pinch of fresh mint
1   **pound fresh apricots, halved and pitted**
2   **medium-size zucchini, sliced lengthwise and scooped out**

Sauté garlic and onion in olive oil. Add rice, water and currants and simmer until rice is almost done. Add pine nuts, herbs and spices and fill zucchini "boats."

Oil an 8-inch square baking dish; layer bottom with apricots. Set stuffed zucchinis on apricots; cover with remaining apricots. Sprinkle olive oil and add a little water. Bake at 350 degrees 45-60 minutes or until tender. Check from time to time and add water if necessary. Don't let apricots dry out. Serves 4.

Pearl Roseman

Brussels Sprouts Puree (Pareve)

An elegant and different way to serve this underrated vegetable.

2	10-ounce packages frozen Brussels sprouts
1	tablespoon chopped onion
3	tablespoons pareve margarine
1/2	cup pareve chicken broth
	Seasonings to taste
	Parsley sprigs

Cook Brussels sprouts following package directions. Drain if necessary. Using an electric blender puree all ingredients until smooth or force Brussels sprouts through a food mill into a bowl and mix with remaining ingredients. Reheat if necessary and spoon into a serving bowl. Serves 6.

Niki Schwartz

Spaghetti Squasherole (Dairy)

A newer variety of squash prepared in an unusual way.

1	spaghetti squash (small)
1	cup Cheddar cheese, grated
1	cup (approximately 1 large) zucchini, grated
8	ounces tomato sauce
2	tablespoons grated Parmesan cheese
1/4	teaspoon salt
1/4	teaspoon pepper
1/8	teaspoon crumbled basil
	Dash garlic powder

Cut squash in half and place cut side up in 1/4 cup water. Cover and cook 7-8 minutes in microwave oven at full power or parboil.

Discard seeds; scoop out strands of squash from shell into a bowl. Add Cheddar cheese, zucchini, tomato sauce, salt, pepper, basil and garlic powder. Mix well. Spoon back into shell or casserole. Sprinkle with Parmesan cheese. Bake in oven at 350 degrees for 20 minutes. Serves 6 - 8.

Doris Goodman

Italian Vegetables (Pareve)

Can use any green vegetable.

1	bunch fresh spinach or 1 pound green beans or 1 bunch chard
2-3	garlic cloves, chopped finely
1-2	tablespoons olive oil
	Salt and pepper to taste

In a frying pan, sauté garlic in olive oil; do not brown. Set aside. Steam vegetables until done; drain. Toss with garlic/oil mixture and mix well. Salt and pepper to taste. Serve hot or at room temperature. Serves 3 - 4.

Claire Gering

Egg Fu Yung (Pareve)

A classic and easy Oriental dish.

1   **cup bean sprouts (extra-long ones may be cut up)**
1/2   **cup celery, sliced thin**
1/2   **cup onion, sliced thin**
1/4   **cup mushrooms, chopped**
6   **eggs, slightly stirred**
2   **tablespoons cornstarch**
    Salt and pepper, to taste

Sauce:
1   **cup water**
1   **tablespoon cornstarch**
2   **tablespoons soy sauce**
1   **teaspoon of either sugar, molasses or honey**

Combine above ingredients well. Grease a skillet and add about 1/4 cup of mixture. When top is almost set, turn over carefully and cook the other side. You may need to add a little oil each time. Keep pancakes warm in 300 degree oven.

Sauce: In saucepan over medium heat, make paste from cornstarch and water. Add soy sauce and either sugar, molasses or honey, stir constantly till thick. Do not boil or cornstarch will thin. Serves 4 as a side dish.

Min Leonard

Curried Rice (Pareve)

Rice gets special treatment in this dish.

3   **tablespoons pareve margarine**
1   **small onion, finely chopped**
1   **large stalk celery, thinly sliced**
2   **teaspoons curry powder**
1   **cup rice, uncooked**
2   **heaping teaspoons pareve instant chicken soup powder**
2   **cups hot water**
1/2   **cup currants or golden raisins**
    Slivered almonds or parsley (optional)

Melt margarine in skillet; add onion and celery. Sauté until tender. Stir in curry powder and rice; stir for about 5 minutes. Dissolve soup powder in hot water; add currants or raisins. Add to rice. Cook, covered, about 20 minutes. Garnish with slivered almonds or parsley. Serves 4 - 5.

Beverly Barak

Brown Rice with Peas (Pareve)

A vegetarian delight.

1 1/2   tablespoons oil (or part margarine)
1   cup brown rice
3   cups hot water
1   10-ounce package frozen small green peas
1   tablespoon water
         Seasoning to taste

Place oil in a 1-quart pot; add rice and hot water. Stir lightly. Boil for 5 minutes on a high flame, uncovered. Turn the flame down, cover pot with a heavy lid and simmer slowly for 30 minutes. Keep the cover on and let the rice stand on the burner until the water is absorbed. Add green peas, water and seasonings. Place in a buttered casserole and heat in the oven or microwave. Serves 4.

Dorothy Wolff

Bourbon Baked Beans (Pareve)

Strong coffee is the secret ingredient.

4   16-ounce cans baked beans
1   teaspoon dry mustard
1/2   cup chili sauce
1   tablespoon molasses
1/2   cup bourbon
1/2   cup strong coffee
1   8-ounce can crushed pineapple
         Brown sugar to sprinkle on top

Grease a large round casserole. Add all ingredients to casserole, except pineapple and brown sugar; mix. Cover and let stand overnight in the refrigerator.

The next day preheat oven to 375 degrees and heat 30 minutes, covered. Sprinkle crushed pineapple on top; sprinkle brown sugar over all. Bake, uncovered, for 30 more minutes. Serves 10 - 12.

Sam Wigoda

Mock Kishka (Pareve)

A modern interpretation of an old favorite; the original version was stuffed in the skin of a goose or chicken neck.

3/4   cup oil
2-3   large carrots, grated
2-3   stalks celery, finely chopped
1   medium onion, chopped
1   teaspoon paprika
1-2   teaspoons salt
     Dash of pepper
1 1/2   cups flour

In a medium bowl mix all ingredients. Place mixture on a piece of aluminum foil and form into a roll 1 1/2-inches in diameter. Tightly seal edges of foil around roll and bake for 1 hour in a preheated 350 degree oven. Cut in 1-inch slices to serve as an appetizer. Serves 20 -24.

Ingrid Blumenstein

Kasha Varnishkes (Pareve)
(Kasha with Bowtie Noodles)

A traditional eastern European holiday favorite.

1   pound medium kasha (buckwheat groats)
1   egg
6 1/2   cups boiling water
2-3   packages onion soup mix
1   8-ounce package bowtie noodles

Put the kasha in a frying pan. Add egg and mix until all grains are coated. Cook over low heat to brown, stirring frequently, and breaking up lumps until all grains are separated. Transfer kasha to a large pot. Add water and onion soup mix and let simmer, covered, over low heat for about 30 minutes or until tender. Stir occasionally during cooking.

Cook bowties according to package directions. After draining, mix with the kasha. May be served with gravy. Serves 12 - 14.

Sarah Kordish

Stuffed Vegetables (Meat)

An updated version of the classic Sephardic dish.
Choose an attractive combination; the flavors will mingle as they
cook, to the benefit of all. It is especially appropriate as a one-dish
meal for Sukkot or for do-ahead entertaining at any time.
Although it takes a bit more time to assemble,
it tastes better a day or two later, and it freezes well.

Stuffing:

2	pounds ground beef, turkey or chicken
1	cup rice, partially cooked
3/4-1	cup finely chopped onion
1/2-3/4	cup finely chopped parsley
1/2	teaspoon pepper
1	teaspoon salt (optional)
1	egg, lightly beaten
1/2	cup tomato sauce
1	tablespoon lemon juice

Vegetables (any combination of the following):

2-3	bell peppers (green, red or yellow)
3-4	thick zucchini
3-4	summer squash
3-4	medium-size tomatoes
2-3	Japanese eggplants
3-4	small red potatoes
1	large onion
1 1/2	cups tomato sauce
1	tablespoon lemon juice
2	tablespoons vegetable oil for baking pan
	Seasoned salt

Mix stuffing ingredients together and adjust seasonings to taste.

Prepare vegetables for stuffing by halving and seeding bell peppers. Cut zucchini and eggplants in half lengthwise and scoop out centers to form boats. Reserve all scooped-out portions. (If zucchini are too long, cut in desired lengths and then scoop into boats.) Scoop out centers of stemmed summer squash, tomatoes and/or potatoes. Sprinkle seasoned salt lightly on all the vegetables and stuff with filling.

Chop onion and mix well with all the reserved scooped-out portions of vegetables and spread on the bottoms of one or two large glass baking dishes that have been oiled generously. Arrange stuffed vegetables on the bed of vegetables. Spoon 1 1/2-2 teaspoons tomato sauce over each.

Cover tightly with foil. Bake for 1 hour at 350 degrees, then uncover and bake 30-40 minutes longer or until nicely browned. Baking may be done in two sections. The vegetables reheat and freeze well. Yields 16 - 24 pieces.

Pearl Roseman

Brussels Sprouts with Mushrooms (Pareve)

My friend Pauline Gershanov gave me this easy recipe that made my family learn to love Brussels sprouts.

2   10-ounce packages frozen Brussels sprouts or 1 1/2 pounds fresh, quartered (approximately 2 cups)
1/2   pound mushrooms, quartered (approximately 2 cups)
1 1/2   cups diced onions
1/2   teaspoon salt
1/2-1   teaspoon lemon pepper (to taste)
2   tablespoons vegetable oil

Heat oil slightly. Add vegetables and seasoning. Cover and sauté 5 minutes. Uncover and sauté until tender, stirring frequently. Adjust seasoning. Serves 8.

Pearl Roseman

Glazed Yams with Duchess Potatoes (Pareve)

A two-potato dish for choices at Thanksgiving.

2   24-ounce cans yam halves in syrup
1/4   cup brown sugar, packed
1/4   cup margarine
1 1/2   cups seasoned mashed potatoes
1   egg, beaten

Drain yams, reserving 1/4 cup syrup. Combine syrup, sugar and margarine. Bring to a boil, stirring often. Add yam halves and sauté quickly until glazed.

Beat together mashed potatoes and egg until blended. Grease an oven-proof, shallow casserole. Place glazed yams in center. Put potatoes through a pastry tube to form a border around yams. Bake in preheated 425 degree oven 5-10 minutes or until lightly browned. Serves 6.

Marilyn Smith

Desserts

Because Jews lived for generations in many different parts of the world, when they came to California, they brought with them the varied cuisines of the "old country." Of all the recipes they have brought, desserts are perhaps the most treasured because of their association with joyous occasions large and small.

A traditional *Rosh Hashanah*, for example, would not seem complete without a honey or apple cake for Ashkenazic Jews and *baklava* for Sephardic Jews. The Passover *Seder* frequently ends with a fruit compote. Sweets are traditionally passed out at baby-namings, *bar* and *bat mitzvahs*, and weddings.

The simplest and healthiest dessert is, of course, a serving of fresh fruit. But when a very rich dessert is called for, such as those laden with chocolate, nuts, whipped cream or rich frostings, one had best abandon all thoughts of dieting and just enjoy! Whether lean or rich, whether for special occasions, holidays, *simchas* (life cycle celebrations) or just anytime, desserts are an important part of Jewish cuisine — as you can see by the length of this section.

HINTS

- In consideration of *kashrut*, some desserts made with dairy ingredients can be made *"pareve"* (neutral) by substituting a nondairy liquid creamer for milk or cream, pareve margarine for butter and nondairy whipped topping for whipped cream. When you want a pareve dessert or when you are converting a cake recipe to a pareve version, be sure that all ingredients, such as chocolate chips or cake mix, are also pareve.

- Please note that desserts don't have to be off limits to the health-conscious. Calories and fat can be reduced by using egg whites (instead of the whole egg), yogurt, light sour cream or cream cheese; sugar substitutes and nonfat cottage cheese or milk. These will make a significant reduction in a dessert's fat and sugar content. Be aware that there will be some change in flavor and texture as well, but the result will be more healthful.

Cakes

The versatility of cakes seems limitless. Frequently they are the wonderful "final act" to a lovely dinner or a special luncheon, or they may be the centerpiece of the occasion, as in a dessert party. They can also be served at breakfast or brunch, at the mid-morning coffee break, or formed into cupcakes (decorated or not) and tucked into a box lunch. They can be as light and fat free as an un-iced angel food cake or as rich and heavy as a "to-die-for" triple-chocolate mousse cake. Several quick breads can do double duty as cakes, too [see **pp. 119-120**]. With frostings, the variations of cakes increase even more. Cheesecakes and those cakes combined with fruits seem to be almost as popular as chocolate cakes, and we include many from which to choose.

HINTS

- Have all cake ingredients at room temperature. Grease only bottoms of cake pans. Use shortening, not margarine, to grease pans (vegetable spray acceptable).

- Please review the hints in the general introduction to the "Desserts" **[p. 213]** section for dietary information.

Dark Chocolate Cheesecake (Dairy)

Artist's receptions always involve food.
When I host a reception, this cake always goes first.

Cheesecake:

5	ounces dark semisweet chocolate
1 1/2	pounds cream cheese, softened
3/4	cup sugar
3	large eggs
1	teaspoon vanilla extract
1	cup sour cream

Crust:

1 1/2	cups graham cracker crumbs
6	tablespoons butter, melted
1/4	cup sugar
1/2	teaspoon nutmeg
1/2	teaspoon ginger
3/4	cup crushed walnuts

To make crust preheat oven to 350 degrees. Mix all crust ingredients together and press the mixture onto the bottom and partly up the sides of a greased 9-inch baking dish, pie plate or springform pan. Smooth mixture along the bottom to even the thickness. Bake for 10 minutes. Cool before pouring in the filling.

To make cheesecake filling, reduce oven temperature to 275 degrees.

Melt chocolate in top of double boiler. Meanwhile, in a large mixing bowl, beat cream cheese with sugar until smooth and light. Beat in eggs and vanilla. Stir in melted chocolate, sour cream and blend well. Pour the mixture into the baked and cooled pie crust and bake for one hour and 15 minutes. Turn off heat and allow cake to cool completely in the oven. When cooled, refrigerate or may be frozen. Serves 12 - 14.

Jerry Caplan

Chocolate Cheesecake (Dairy)

*Created for my son's Bar Mitzvah, this utterly scrumptious
cake takes a long time to bake and cool down,
so start it early in the day. Well worth the wait.*

Crust:

25	chocolate sandwich cookies (approximately 2 1/2 cups crumbs)
4	tablespoons butter, melted
	Vegetable spray

Chocolate Layer:

6	1-ounce squares semisweet chocolate, chopped
3	tablespoons whipping cream

Cheese Filling:

12	1-ounce squares semisweet chocolate
3	8-ounce packages cream cheese, softened
1 1/4	cups sugar
5	large eggs (room temperature)
1	cup whipping cream
2	teaspoons vanilla extract

Finely crush cookies with a rolling pin or make crumbs in food processor. In a medium bowl, mix crumbs and melted butter until well blended. Lightly spray a 9 or 10-inch springform pan with vegetable spray. Press crumb mixture into bottom and 3/4 inch up sides. Set aside.

Melt 6 squares of chocolate in top of double boiler or micro-wave. Slowly add 3 tablespoons cream. Stir until smooth and chocolate is melted.

Pour over crumb crust and spread to within 1/2 inch of sides of pan. Set aside or cool in refrig-erator.

Preheat oven to 425 degrees. In same double boiler or micro-wave melt 12 squares chocolate. Set aside to cool slightly. Mean-while, beat cream cheese and sugar in large mixing bowl with electric mixer or food processor on medium speed until light and fluffy. Add eggs one at a time, beating constantly, stopping to scrape down sides of bowl and beaters as needed. Mix in 1 cup cream, vanilla and melted choco-late. Carefully pour into crust. Place pan on baking sheet and bake for 10 minutes. Reduce oven temperature to 225 de-grees. Bake 45 minutes longer or until center jiggles slightly. Turn off heat and allow cake to stand in oven for at least 2 hours with oven door closed.

Remove from oven to a draft-free place until it is room tem-perature. Cover and refrigerate until chilled. May be frozen, cov-ered with plastic wrap and foil. Defrost wrapped cake in refrig-erator overnight. Serves 12 - 16.

Lynda Gentilcore

Maple/Almond Cheesecake or Torte (Dairy)

Maple and almond flavorings give this cheesecake a unique flavor.

Cheesecake Mixture:

1/4	cup butter or margarine
8	ounces cream cheese, softened
1/4	cup milk
1	cup sugar
2	eggs
1	teaspoon vanilla extract
2 1/4	cups flour
1	teaspoon baking powder
1/2	teaspoon baking soda
1	cup semisweet chocolate pieces

Maple/Almond Layer:

3/4	cup maple syrup
1/4	cup unsalted butter or margarine
1/4	cup firmly packed brown sugar
1 3/4	cups coarsely chopped almonds or pecans

To make cream cheese mixture: In a large mixing bowl, cream the butter and cream cheese. Add milk and sugar; blend well. Beat in eggs one at a time, then beat mixture for two minutes. Add vanilla and mix.

Sift together flour, baking powder and baking soda; blend into cream cheese mixture. Fold in chocolate pieces. Set mixture aside.

To make maple/almond layer: Preheat oven to 350 degrees. Generously grease bottom and sides of a 10 to 12-inch fluted quiche pan. In a saucepan, heat syrup, margarine and sugar over low heat, stirring constantly, until sugar is dissolved. Bring to a boil; pour into prepared baking pan. Sprinkle with nuts to cover entire bottom of pan.

Carefully pour the cream cheese mixture over the maple/almond mixture in the pan. Bake for about 50 minutes, then check to see if done by inserting a toothpick. Invert onto a serving dish at once. This cake is at its best when served warm. Serves 8 - 10.

Shirley Azaren

Cheesecake (Dairy)

A delicious, not-too-rich version of the classic dessert.

Cheesecake:

8	ounces cream cheese, softened
1	cup cottage cheese
2	eggs, separated
1/2	cup milk
1	teaspoon vanilla extract
3/4	cup sugar
2	tablespoons flour
1/4	teaspoon salt

Crust:

1 1/2	cups graham cracker crumbs
1/4	cup sugar
1/2	cup butter or sweet margarine, melted

Preheat oven to 350 degrees. To prepare crust: Combine crumbs, sugar and butter in bowl. Mix until crumbs are moistened. Place crumb mixture in a 10-inch springform pan and press in bottom and 2 inches up sides of pan. Bake about 15-20 minutes. Let cool.

To prepare cheesecake: In a large mixing bowl, cream together cream cheese and cottage cheese. Add egg yolks and vanilla; mix well. Add sugar, flour and salt; mix well. Beat egg whites and fold into batter. Pour batter into cooled crust and bake 1 hour. Serves 12 - 14.

Ingrid Blumenstein

Chocolate Cream Cheese Swirl Cake (Dairy)

*Start with a prepared mix and swirl in
extra ingredients for a beautiful cake.*

1	package devil's food cake mix with pudding
8	ounces cream cheese, softened
2	eggs
1/2	cup sugar
1	cup semisweet chocolate pieces

Preheat oven to 350 degrees. Prepare devil's food cake batter according to package directions. Grease (or spray) a bundt pan or 9x13-inch glass baking dish. In a medium mixing bowl, cream together cream cheese, eggs and sugar. Add chocolate pieces. Pour cake batter into prepared pan. Swirl cream cheese mixture into the batter. Bake for 5 minutes less than package instructions. Serves 10 - 12.

Trana Labowe

Cream Cheesecake (Dairy)

People's eyes roll when they taste their first bite!

Crust:

2   cups graham cracker crumbs
1/4   pound butter or margarine, melted
2   heaping teaspoons brown sugar

First Layer:

2   8-ounce packages cream cheese, softened
1   egg
1   teaspoon vanilla extract
1/2   teaspoon lemon juice
2/3   cup sugar

Second Layer:

2   cups sour cream
1   egg
1/2   cup sugar (scant)
1   teaspoon vanilla extract

To make crust preheat oven to 325 degrees. Mix graham cracker crumbs with melted margarine or butter and brown sugar. Press on bottom and sides of a 9-inch springform pan. Bake 10 minutes. Remove from oven and cool.

First layer: Increase oven temperature to 350 degrees. Into small electric mixer bowl, place cream cheese, egg, vanilla, lemon juice and sugar. Beat at high speed for 15 minutes. Pour into cooled shell. Bake for 20 minutes. Remove from oven but retain oven temperature. Cool cake for 5 minutes.

Second layer: In small bowl, mix sour cream, egg, sugar and vanilla. Gently pour over first layer. Bake another 10 minutes at 350 degrees. Remove from oven and cool. Refrigerate overnight. Serves 6 - 8.

Rena Snyder

Chocolate Cake Deluxe (Dairy)

Brown sugar and coffee add a distinctive flavor to an old favorite.

1   package chocolate cake mix (darkest)
1/3   cup brown sugar, packed
4   eggs
1   cup sour cream
1/2   cup warm water
1   teaspoon instant coffee crystals
1/2   cup oil
1   cup chocolate chips, melted
1   cup chocolate mini chips, not melted

Preheat oven to 350 degrees. Combine all the ingredients except the mini chips in large mixing bowl and mix 4 minutes at medium speed. Fold in mini chocolate chips and spoon into a greased and floured bundt pan. Bake for 45-50 minutes (don't over bake!). Serves 12 - 14.

Stan Herzoff

Texas Chocolate Sheet Cake (Dairy)

*A crowd-sized cake to carry right in the pan to a
picnic or tailgate party.*

Cake:

1	cup boiling water
1/2	pound butter or margarine (sweet)
4	tablespoons (heaping) cocoa powder
2	cups sugar
2	cups sifted flour
1/2	teaspoon salt
1	teaspoon baking soda
2	eggs
1/2	cup sour cream or buttermilk
1	teaspoon vanilla extract

Frosting:

1/4	pound margarine
6	tablespoons milk
1/4	cup cocoa powder
1	box powdered sugar
1	teaspoon vanilla extract
1	cup chopped nuts

Preheat oven to 350 degrees. Mix together until boiling the water, margarine and cocoa. Set aside to cool. Sift together sugar, flour, salt and baking soda. Gradually add cocoa mixture to flour mixture. Add eggs one at a time. Beat well. Add sour cream and vanilla and beat well.

Pour into greased 10x15-inch jelly roll pan. Bake for 30 minutes. Start frosting; cook together margarine, milk and cocoa. Slowly add powdered sugar and beat until creamy and thick. Add vanilla and nuts.

Frost while hot. This is a very rich fudge cake and can be served as brownies. If you want to serve it as a torte, cut it evenly in half lengthwise. Allow to cool. Spread raspberry jam between the two layers and then frost cake with frosting. Cut into slices. Serves 15 - 20.

Ruth King

Chocolate Halo Cake (Pareve)

A rich pareve and glamorous dessert that starts with a ready-made angel food cake.

Cake:
1	large angel food cake
24	ounces semisweet chocolate bits
6	eggs
2	teaspoons vanilla extract
2	cups liquid pareve dessert topping
6	tablespoons sugar
4	tablespoons rum

Frosting:
1	cup liquid pareve dessert topping
2	tablespoons sugar
2	ounces sliced almonds, toasted in oven

Brush brown crumbs off angel cake (save crumbs for making rum balls, p. 263). Tear cake into bite-size pieces; pour rum over cake pieces and set aside. Melt chocolate bits in double boiler or microwave; remove from heat. Add eggs to chocolate, one at a time, beating with electric mixer on #5 speed. Add vanilla.

In a separate bowl, whip dessert topping until stiff, then add sugar until thoroughly incorporated. Fold dessert topping mixture into chocolate mixture. Spread 1/3 of chocolate/topping mixture over bottom of 10-inch springform pan; cover with 1/2 of cake pieces. End with remaining chocolate mixture.

Freeze dessert overnight. The next day, prepare frosting by whipping dessert topping with sugar. Remove outer band of springform pan and frost cake. Return to freezer and transfer to refrigerator 20 minutes before serving. Serves 20.

Fay Auerbach

"Turtle Cake" (Dairy)

An elegant, rich cake. A little goes a long way.

Cake:

1	package German chocolate cake mix
1/2	cup butter or margarine, softened
1 1/2	cups water
1/2	cup oil
1	14-ounce can sweetened condensed milk
1	cup chopped pecans, approximately
1	pound caramels

Frosting:

6	tablespoons butter or margarine, softened
2 2/3	cups powdered sugar
1/3	cup cocoa
1/3	cup evaporated milk
1	teaspoon vanilla extract

Preheat oven to 350 degrees. In a large mixing bowl, combine chocolate cake mix, butter, water, oil and half the condensed milk; mix well. Pour half of the batter into a greased and floured 13x9-inch baking dish. Bake for 20-25 minutes.

Melt caramels (you can use the microwave, but watch closely as they can burn easily) and mix together with remaining condensed milk; heat until smooth. Spread over baked cake layer.

Sprinkle generously with chopped pecans. Cover with remaining cake batter. Return to oven and bake 25-35 minutes longer or until cake tests done with a toothpick. Cool, then spread with frosting.

To make the frosting, combine butter, cocoa and evaporated milk in a small saucepan. Melt over low heat; remove from heat and beat in powdered sugar and vanilla until smooth. Spread immediately on cooled cake. Serves 18 - 20.

Trana Labowe

Rich Chocolate Cherry Cake (Pareve)

This "made from scratch" version of a favorite classic includes nuts.

2	cups flour
3/4	cup sugar
3/4	cup oil
2	eggs
2	teaspoons vanilla extract
1	teaspoon baking soda
1	teaspoon cinnamon
21	ounce can cherry pie filling
6	ounces semisweet chocolate chips
1	cup chopped walnuts
	Powdered sugar

Preheat oven to 350 degrees. In a large bowl, combine first 7 ingredients and mix well. Stir in pie filling, chocolate chips and chopped walnuts.

Pour into greased and floured 9-cup bundt pan. Bake 1 hour. Cool completely; remove from pan when cooled.

May be lightly sprinkled with powdered sugar, if desired. Serves 10 - 12.

Marla Gitig

Chocolate Cherry Cake (Pareve or Dairy)

A simple, rich cake that is pareve without frosting; dairy with frosting.

Cake:
1   package chocolate cake mix
1   20-ounce can cherry pie filling
1   teaspoon almond extract
3   eggs, beaten

Frosting (optional):
1   cup sugar
1/3   cup milk
5   tablespoons softened margarine or butter
6   ounces semisweet chocolate pieces

Preheat oven to 350 degrees. In a large bowl, mix all cake ingredients by hand (do not use mixer) until well blended. Grease and flour a bundt cake pan or a 9x13-inch glass baking dish. Pour in batter and bake until cake tests done with a toothpick inserted into the center (45-55 minutes for bundt pan; 25-30 minutes for baking dish). Remove from pan to cool.

While cooling, prepare frosting (if desired): Mix together sugar, milk and butter in a saucepan. Bring to a boil and remove from heat. Add chocolate pieces; stir until they are melted. Prick top of partially cooled cake with cake tester or toothpick. Pour over partially cooled cake. Freezes well. Serves 10 - 12.

Muriel Becker

Chocolate Cointreau Cake (Dairy)

Cointreau adds an elegant touch to a very rich cake.

Cake:
1   package chocolate fudge cake mix
1   4-ounce package instant chocolate fudge pudding mix
1   cup sour cream
4   eggs
1/2   cup vegetable oil
3/4   cup Cointreau liqueur
1/8   cup water
4   tablespoons grated orange peel

Frosting:
1   ounce (1 square) semisweet chocolate
1   tablespoon butter
1/8   cup Cointreau liqueur
1/4   cup powdered sugar

Preheat oven to 350 degrees. In a large mixing bowl combine all ingredients and beat 5 minutes with an electric mixer. Pour into a greased bundt pan. Bake 50 minutes. Cool 5 minutes and invert on a cake plate.

Frosting: Melt chocolate with butter. Stir in Cointreau. Add powdered sugar and stir until smooth. (May have to reheat slightly to dissolve sugar). Drizzle frosting over cooled cake. Serve with whipped cream. Serves 12 - 14.

Jackie Yaacobi

Fudge Cake (Pareve)

A delicious chocolate cake that is perfect after a meat dinner.

3   cups flour
1 1/2   teaspoons baking soda
1/2   teaspoon salt
1   cup margarine
2 1/2   cups sugar
3   eggs
1 1/2   teaspoons vanilla
        extract
1   cup chopped walnuts
        (optional)
1   cup chocolate chip
        morsels (optional)
1 1/2   cups ice water
3   1-ounce squares
        unsweetened
        chocolate, melted

Preheat oven to 350 degrees. Sift dry ingredients together; set aside. In a large mixing bowl cream margarine, sugar and vanilla.

Add eggs, one at a time, beating well after each addition. Add melted chocolate, then add water and dry ingredients alternately. Fold in nuts and chocolate chips.

Bake for 1 1/4 hours in large ungreased tube pan. Cool for 10 minutes of a wire rack, then invert to cool completely. Serves 16 - 20.

Min Leonard

Chocolate Chip Coffee Cake (Dairy)

Chocolate lovers will be pleased with this variation on sour cream coffee cake.

1/4   pound butter or
        margarine, softened
1   cup sugar
2   eggs
1   cup sour cream
1 3/4   cups flour
1   teaspoon baking soda
1 1/2   teaspoons baking
        powder
1/2   cup finely chopped nuts
6   ounces chocolate chips
        Powdered sugar

Preheat oven to 350 degrees. In a large bowl cream butter with sugar. Add eggs and sour cream; beat well. Add all other ingredients except chocolate chips. Beat for five minutes. Fold in chocolate chips. Turn batter into a greased and floured 10-inch bundt pan. Bake for 1 hour. Reduce heat to 325 degrees and bake 15 minutes longer or until cake tests done when a toothpick inserted in the middle comes out clean.

Allow to cool 10 minutes in the pan, turn out on a cake rack until cool, sprinkle with powdered sugar and transfer to serving plate. Serves 10 - 12.

Janet Arzt

Chocolate Chip Date Cake (Pareve)

A rich cake with nuts and dates.

1	cup boiling water
8	ounces chopped dates
1	teaspoon baking soda
1	cup sugar
2	eggs
4	ounces margarine, melted
1 3/4	cups flour
1	tablespoon cocoa powder
1	teaspoon salt
1	cup chopped walnuts
12	ounces chocolate chips

Preheat oven to 350 degrees. Pour boiling water over dates and soda; set aside to cool. Cream sugar, eggs and margarine together. Mix flour, cocoa and salt; blend together with margarine mixture. Add cooled date mixture to flour mixture.

Add 1/2 of the chopped nuts and 1/2 of the chocolate chips. Pour into well-greased 9x13-inch baking pan. Sprinkle remaining nuts and chocolate chips on top. Bake for 35-45 minutes. Freezes well. Serves 10 - 12.

Elke Coblens

Chocolate Torte (Dairy)

A chocoholic's delight.

Torte:

6	ounces semisweet chocolate
10	eggs at room temperature
1	cup sugar
2	tablespoons Cognac
2	cups walnuts, finely chopped

Topping:

1	cup whipping cream
1	tablespoon powdered sugar
2	tablespoons cocoa powder
1	ounce sweet chocolate

Preheat oven to 350 degrees. Grease bottom and sides of a 10-inch springform pan. Melt chocolate over (not in) hot water, or in microwave, just until melted. Set aside to cool. Separate eggs. In a large mixing bowl beat egg yolks until thick and lemon colored. Gradually beat in sugar; continue beating until sugar is dissolved. Stir in melted chocolate and Cognac. Fold in nuts.

In a separate bowl beat egg whites until stiff but not dry. Gently fold beaten whites into chocolate mixture.

Pour batter into prepared pan. Bake for 1 hour, or until cake tests done. Cool in the pan (top will sink slightly).

While cake is cooling, make topping: Beat whipping cream, powdered sugar and cocoa powder in chilled mixing bowl. Whip until cream holds stiff peaks. When cake is cooled, remove springform collar and spread topping on top and sides of cake. With a vegetable peeler, shave sweet chocolate over top of cake to decorate. Refrigerate until ready to serve. Serves 10 - 12.

Elaine Schermer

Chocolate Applesauce Cake (Dairy)

This cake keeps well, freezes beautifully and is always a hit.

Cake:

1 1/2	cups sugar
2	cups flour
1	teaspoon salt
1	teaspoon baking soda
2	teaspoons cinnamon
3	eggs, beaten
1	cup vegetable oil
1	cup buttermilk
1	cup unsweetened applesauce
1	teaspoon vanilla extract
3	ounces melted unsweetened chocolate, cooled
1	cup chopped nuts (walnuts or pecans)
6	ounces chocolate chips

Sauce:

1/2	cup buttermilk
1	cup sugar
1/2	cup butter
1/2	teaspoon baking soda
1	teaspoon vanilla extract
1	ounce unsweetened chocolate

Preheat oven to 350 degrees. Combine sugar, flour, salt, baking soda and cinnamon in large mixing bowl. Beat eggs with oil, buttermilk, applesauce and vanilla. Stir into dry ingredients. Stir in cooled, melted chocolate. Add nuts and chocolate chips.

Pour batter into large (12 cup) buttered bundt pan and bake for 50-60 minutes, or until toothpick inserted in center of cake comes out clean.

Allow cake to cool for 10 minutes. Turn out onto serving platter. Combine sauce ingredients in saucepan and simmer for 7 minutes, stirring occasionally. Poke cake with toothpick while still hot and pour sauce over. Serves 12.

Julie Breitstein

Coffee Cake (Dairy)

A cake mix base is made special by adding lots of goodies.

1	package yellow cake mix
1	cup sour cream
4	eggs
1	3 3/4-ounce package instant lemon pudding mix
1/4	pound margarine, melted
1/4	cup walnuts, chopped
10-12	maraschino cherries, cut into small pieces
3/4	cup brown sugar, packed
	Cinnamon to taste

Preheat oven to 350 degrees. In a large mixing bowl, blend together cake mix, sour cream, eggs, pudding mix and margarine; beat for 10 minutes. Fold in nuts and cherries. In a small bowl, mix together brown sugar and cinnamon. Grease a bundt pan. Pour in 1/3 of the batter and sprinkle with 1/3 of the sugar mixture. Repeat layers two times. Bake for 1 hour. Serves 14 - 16.

Jill Lasker

Cranberry Swirl Cake (Dairy)

A beautiful cake for a festive occasion.

Cake:

4	ounces margarine
1	cup sugar
2	eggs
1	teaspoon baking powder
1	teaspoon baking soda
1	cup sour cream
2	cups flour
1/2	teaspoon salt
1	teaspoon almond or vanilla extract
1	7-ounce can whole cranberry sauce
1/2	cup nuts, chopped

Topping:

3/4	cup powdered sugar
1	tablespoon warm water
1/2	teaspoon almond or vanilla extract

Preheat oven to 350 degrees. Sift together dry ingredients; set aside. In a large bowl, cream margarine; add sugar gradually. Add unbeaten eggs, one at a time, with mixer at medium speed. Reduce mixer speed and alternately add dry ingredients and sour cream, ending with dry ingredients. Add flavoring.

Grease an 8-inch tube pan. Put 1/3 of batter in bottom of pan; swirl 1/3 of the whole cranberry sauce into pan. Add another layer of batter and more cranberry sauce. Add remaining batter; swirl the remaining cranberry sauce on top. Sprinkle nuts on top. Bake for 55 minutes. While cake bakes mix together topping ingredients in small bowl; set aside.

Let cake cool in pan for 10 minutes. Remove carefully from pan and drizzle topping over it. Serves 10.

Sybil Kaplan

Chocolate Cinnamon Coffee Cake (Dairy)

An easy coffee cake that starts with a prepared mix.

Cake:

1	package yellow cake mix
3	ounce package vanilla instant pudding
1	cup sour cream
1/2	cup oil
1/4	cup milk
4	eggs

Topping:

1/2	cup sugar
2	tablespoons brown sugar
2	tablespoons cocoa powder
1	teaspoon cinnamon

Preheat oven to 350 degrees. Grease and flour a bundt pan. Beat all cake ingredients in mixer. Pour half of cake batter into prepared pan. Mix topping ingredients together. Spread topping over batter in pan. Pour rest of batter on top; swirl with a knife. Bake for 55 minutes. Serves 12.

Sylvia Levine

Sour Cream Coffee Cake (Dairy)

A classic favorite.

Cake:

1	cup butter
1 1/2	cups sugar
3	eggs
1/2	teaspoon vanilla extract
1 1/2	cups sour cream
3	cups flour
1 1/2	teaspoons baking powder
1 1/2	teaspoons baking soda

Nut Mixture:

1	cup chopped nuts
1/2	cup sugar
1	teaspoon cinnamon

Preheat oven to 350 degrees. In a large mixing bowl, cream together butter, sugar, eggs, vanilla and sour cream. Sift flour, baking powder and baking soda. Add dry ingredients to creamed mixture.

In small bowl, mix nuts, sugar and cinnamon.

Spread 1/3 of batter in large ungreased tube pan. Top with 1/3 of chopped nut mixture. Repeat 2 more times, ending with nut mixture.

Bake approximately 1 1/4 hours or until toothpick inserted in cake comes out clean. Allow to cool on rack before removing from pan. Serves 16 - 20.

Min Leonard

Pound Cake (Dairy/Pareve)

A wonderful cake with a hint of lemon.

1/2	pound unsalted margarine
1 1/2	cups sugar
5	eggs, separated
3	cups flour
3	teaspoons baking powder
	Pinch of salt
1	cup milk
	Juice of 1/2 lemon
	Rind of 1 orange and 1 lemon
3/4	cup raisins (optional)

Preheat oven to 350 degrees. In a large mixing bowl, mix together flour, baking powder and salt. Cream margarine, sugar and egg yolks. Add flour mixture, alternate with milk to creamed mixture; blend. Add lemon and orange rinds and lemon juice. Beat egg whites until stiff; fold into batter. Fold in raisins.

Bake in greased and floured tube pan for about 1 hour, or until cake tests done with a toothpick. Instead of milk you can use 3/4 cup nondairy liquid creamer plus 1/4 cup water, and the cake is pareve. Serves 16 - 20.

Ingrid Blumenstein

Gateau au Citron;
French Lemon Cake (Dairy/Pareve)

A rich-tasting, moist cake that's prepared in the food processor.

1	whole lemon
1/2	cup sugar
4	ounce stick butter or margarine, unsalted
2	large eggs
1	cup, less 2 tablespoons flour
1	teaspoon baking powder
1/2	cup powdered sugar

Preheat oven to 350 degrees. Peel the lemon, taking only the yellow outer layer of the rind. Put the steel knife in the work bowl of a food processor. Add the lemon peel, and start pouring the sugar through the feed spout; process about 20 seconds, after all sugar is in. Add butter or margarine, cut in pieces.

Add the eggs one at a time, processing about 15 seconds or until smooth after each addition. Scrape down as needed.

Fill a measuring cup half full of flour and stir in the teaspoon of baking powder. Add remaining flour to the mixture in the bowl. Cover and turn machine on and off 2 or 3 times just until flour disappears. (Longer processing will produce a tough cake instead of a soft and tender one.)

Transfer the batter to a buttered and floured 8-inch cake pan. Bake in center of the oven for 25 minutes, or until light golden brown in color and springy to the touch. Let stand a few minutes and remove from cake pan and allow to cool on a rack.

Roll the peeled lemon back and forth on the counter a few times, pressing firmly with your hand. Cut it in two and extract the juice. Mix this with powdered sugar. Spoon some of the mixture over the top of the cake while it cools. Repeat this while the cake is cooling until all the lemon juice mixture is used up. This cake keeps well, covered in the refrigerator. Serves 8 - 10.

Ruth Giden

Lucille's Lemon Cake (Pareve)

Fresh lemon juice gives this cake a tart flavor;
best made a day before serving, as flavor improves with time.

Cake:

1	**3 ounce package lemon gelatin**
1	**cup boiling water**
4	**eggs**
1	**package Lemon Supreme cake mix**
2/3	**cup oil**
	Juice of 1/2 lemon

Glaze:

Approximately 1 cup powdered sugar
Juice of 1/2 lemon

Preheat oven to 350 degrees. In a small bowl, dissolve gelatin in boiling water; set aside. In a large mixing bowl, beat eggs. Reduce mixer speed; slowly add cake mix. Add oil; beat well. Slowly add gelatin mixture, using medium speed. Add lemon juice and continue beating.

Pour batter into oiled bundt pan and bake 50-60 minutes. Cake is done when it springs back to the touch. Remove cake from oven; cool 20-25 minutes.

While cake is cooling, make glaze: Mix powdered sugar with enough lemon juice to make a thin frosting. When cake has cooled 20-25 minutes, loosen the sides and center with a knife or spatula. Invert cake on a plate and drip glaze over the top and let run down sides. Serves 12.

Note: This cake freezes beautifully. Freeze glazed cake, uncovered, until the glaze hardens; then wrap cake tightly. This prevents the glaze from sticking when you unwrap cake. Defrost at room temperature.

Lucille Weisel

Ingrid's Best Pastry for Fruit Cake (Pareve)

A European recipe with several variations to spark your creativity.
Also works well for Hamantaschen or other cookies.

1/2	pound margarine, unsalted
1	cup sugar
5	egg yolks (may substitute all or part with liquid egg substitute)
1	teaspoon vanilla extract
1	teaspoon lemon rind
1	teaspoon lemon juice
2	teaspoons baking powder
3-3 1/2	cups flour

Mix all the ingredients together, except the flour. Add flour to make a soft dough. Wrap dough in foil and refrigerate at least an hour. (Can chill for several days or can be frozen.) Makes enough pastry for 2 cakes (see Apple and Plum Cake recipes, which follow).

Note: Good way to use up your egg yolks.

Ingrid Blumenstein

Fruit Cakes (Pareve)

Great way to use fresh fruit.

Plum Cake:

1/2	recipe of pastry approximately 25 Italian plums
2	tablespoons vanilla sugar (see Note)

Apple Cake:

1/2	recipe of pastry (see above)
8 - 10	apples, peeled, cored and sliced juice of 1/2 lemon
1/4	teaspoon cinnamon

Crumb Topping:

1/4	pound sweet margarine, softened
1/2	cup sugar
1	cup flour

Plum Cake: Preheat oven to 350 degrees. Press dough into a 9x13-inch glass baking dish. Butterfly and pit plums. Slit edges of plums as needed to lay flat. Place them on top of dough, close together in rows. Bake for approximately 1 hour until dough is light brown and cake is done. Let cake cool and sprinkle with vanilla sugar. If using tart or juicy plums, consider crumb topping.

Apple Cake: Preheat oven to 350 degrees. Press 1/2 of pastry in bottom and slightly up the sides of a 9x13-inch glass baking dish. Mix apples with lemon juice and cinnamon. Place apples on pastry. Cover with rest of pastry on top of apples or use crumb topping. Bake for 1 hour, until cake is golden brown.

Crumb Topping: Preheat oven to 350 degrees. Mix ingredients together until crumbly. Sprinkle over apples instead of pastry. Bake cake 1 hour until light brown. Each cake serves 10 - 12.

Note: To make vanilla sugar place several vanilla beans in a glass jar. Add 1 cup of granulated sugar. As you use the vanilla sugar, add additional granulated sugar for an indefinite supply. Vanilla sugar is lovely in many baked goods; some recipes require it.

Ingrid Blumenstein

Blueberry Shortcake (Pareve)

A quick cake that takes advantage of canned blueberry pie filling.

Shortcake:

1/2	cup margarine, softened
1	cup sugar (scant)
2	eggs, well beaten
2	cups sifted flour
3	teaspoons baking powder
1	20-ounce can blueberry pie filling

Streusel Topping:

1/4	cup flour
1/4	cup sugar
2	tablespoons margarine, melted
1/2	cup walnuts, chopped

Preheat oven to 350 degrees. In a medium mixing bowl, cream together margarine and sugar; add eggs and mix. Sift dry ingredients and blend into creamed mixture (it will be thick). Spread more than half of the dough on the bottom of a greased 10x15-inch pan; pat it down to cover entire pan.

Pour filling on top and spread to cover entire dough. Drop rest of dough by spoon to cover entire top. Combine streusel topping ingredients in a small bowl and sprinkle over entire cake. Bake for 1 hour. May serve warm with whipped cream or ice cream. Serves 12.

Shirley Azaren

Blueberry Cake (Dairy)

A simple and satisfying coffee cake with a streusel topping.

Cake:

1/4	cup butter
3/4	cup sugar
1	egg, beaten
1	cup cake flour
2	teaspoons baking powder
1/2	teaspoon salt
1/2	cup milk
2	cups blueberries (fresh or frozen)

Topping:

1/4	cup butter, melted
1/2	cup sugar
1/3	cup flour
1	teaspoon cinnamon

Preheat oven to 375 degrees. In a large mixing bowl, cream butter and continue beating while slowly adding sugar. Add egg and beat well.

Sift together dry ingredients. Add sifted dry ingredients alternately with milk to butter mixture. Beat until smooth. Gently fold in berries. Pour into 9x9-inch greased pan. Mix together topping ingredients and sprinkle over top of cake. Bake for 35 minutes. Serves 8 - 10.

Georgina Rothenberg

Banana Cake (Pareve)

The flavor of banana permeates this substantial cake.

1/2	pound pareve margarine
2 1/4	cups sugar
3	eggs, separated
1 1/2	teaspoons vanilla extract
1 1/2	cups mashed bananas (approx. 4 medium)
3/4	cup hot water
3	cups flour
1 1/2	teaspoons baking soda
1 1/2	teaspoons baking powder
1	cup chopped nuts
1	cup diced dates (optional)

Preheat oven to 350 degrees. In a large mixing bowl, cream margarine and sugar. Add egg yolks, vanilla and bananas. Sift flour and baking powder together. Add soda to hot water. Add wet and dry ingredients alternately to batter, beginning and ending with dry ingredients. Fold in nuts and dates (if desired).

Beat egg whites stiff and fold into batter. Carefully pour into large ungreased tube pan and bake for 1 1/4 hours or until cake tests done. Cool approximately 20 minutes before removing from pan. Serves 16 - 20.

Min Leonard

Apple Dessert (Dairy)

An easy, make-ahead dessert for those with a sweet tooth.

1	package yellow cake mix
2	ounces margarine
1/4	cup nuts, chopped
2	20-ounce cans sliced apples, drained
1	tablespoon lemon juice
1/2	cup sugar
1	tablespoon ground cinnamon
1	cup sour cream
1	egg yolk

Preheat oven to 350 degrees. In a large bowl mix together cake mix with melted margarine and add chopped nuts. Press pastry into bottom and 1 inch up the sides of a 9x13-inch baking pan or dish. Bake 10 minutes and remove from oven; retain oven temperature. Mix together apples, lemon juice, sugar and cinnamon. Spread on crust. Mix together sour cream and egg yolk. Drizzle on top. Bake for 25 minutes more. Serves 10 - 12.

Note: *Can be assembled a day before and baked before serving.*

Pat Gittelson

Pumpkin Chiffon Spice Cake (Pareve)

A wonderful, light cake, perfect for Thanksgiving dinner.

Cake:

2 1/4	cups flour
1 1/2	cups sugar
3	teaspoons baking powder
2 1/2	teaspoons pumpkin pie spice
1/2	teaspoon ground ginger
1/2	teaspoon cinnamon
1/2	cup oil
5	egg yolks
1	cup canned pumpkin
1/3	cup water
1	cup (7 or 8) egg whites
1/2	teaspoon cream of tartar

Glaze:

1	cup powdered sugar
1	teaspoon lemon juice

Preheat oven to 325 degrees. Sift together flour, sugar, baking powder, pumpkin pie spice, ginger and cinnamon. Turn into a large mixing bowl. Make a well in the flour mixture and add oil, egg yolks, pumpkin and water. Beat until smooth.

In a separate large bowl, beat egg whites with cream of tartar until stiff. Fold pumpkin mixture into whites. Turn batter into an ungreased 10-inch tube pan and bake at 325 degrees for 55 minutes. Increase oven temperature to 350 degrees and bake for 15 minutes. Invert pan onto a thin-necked bottle until cooled completely.

To glaze cake, mix powdered sugar and lemon juice with just enough water to make a thin glaze. Drizzle over top of cake. Serves 14 - 16.

Phyllis Sarto

Apfelkuchen (Dairy or Pareve)

This traditional German apple cake is easy to make. Ideal for Rosh Hashanah.

2	eggs
1/4	cup butter or margarine
1	cup flour
1	teaspoon baking powder
1	cup sugar
4-5	apples, peeled, cored and sliced
	Cinnamon, sugar to taste

Preheat oven to 350 degrees. Mix first five ingredients together. Pat dough into a buttered 9-inch springform pan. Shape a small edge so dough will go up over apples when baking. Arrange apples on top of dough.

Bake for 1 1/2 hours. Cool before removing band of springform pan. While cake is still hot, lightly sprinkle cinnamon and sugar on top of apples. Serves 8 - 10.

Hildegarde Hess

Apple Cake (Pareve)

Our family's traditional Rosh Hashanah cake:
bakes for 2 hours and worth it!

3	cups flour
2 1/2	cups sugar
1	cup oil
4	eggs
1/2	teaspoon salt
1/3	cup orange juice
2 1/2	teaspoons vanilla extract
3	teaspoons baking powder
6	thinly sliced peeled apples
2	teaspoons cinnamon
3	teaspoons sugar

Preheat oven to 350 degrees. In a large mixing bowl, combine first 8 ingredients in the order listed. Mix until a smooth batter is formed. In a separate bowl, combine apples, cinnamon and sugar.

Grease and flour an angel food (tube) cake pan. Pour 1 layer of batter, 1 layer of apples into pan. Alternate layers, ending with apples on top. Bake for 2 hours. Cool on a rack for 15 minutes, then invert to cool completely. (If using a food processor to slice apples, make batter in food processor by combining ingredients in the following order: oil, eggs, juice, vanilla, sugar, salt, baking powder, flour.) Serves 10 - 12.

Linda Spivack

Apple Honey Cake (Pareve)

Guaranteed to win new devotees for honey cake.
Nice for Rosh Hashanah.

1	pound honey
3	eggs
1 1/3	cups sugar
2	cups applesauce (chunky preferred)
4	cups flour
1	teaspoon baking soda
1	teaspoon ground cinnamon
1	teaspoon ginger, optional
1	teaspoon anise, optional
1	cup chopped walnuts

Preheat oven to 350 degrees. In a large mixing bowl, beat honey and eggs. Add remaining ingredients except nuts; mix well. Stir in nuts. Grease either (A) 2 bread loaf pans or (B) 7 miniature loaf tins or (C) one cake loaf pan. Bake for approximately (A) 50 minutes (B) 30 minutes or (C) 40 minutes, respectively, or until toothpick comes out clean. Yields either 2 bread loaves, 7 miniature loaves or 1 cake loaf.

Phyllis Sarto

Aunt Ethel's Russian Honey Cake (Pareve)

From Aunt Ethel, a lady of generous heart and proportions.
(Yes, that is the correct baking powder quantity. It is 2 tablespoons.)

6   eggs, beaten
1 1/2 cups sugar
1 1/2 cups oil
1/2   teaspoon baking soda
5   cups flour
2   tablespoons baking
       powder
1/2   cup strong coffee
1   jigger Bourbon whiskey
1 1/2 pounds honey (2 cups)
1/4   teaspoon salt
1   cup white raisins
1   cup chopped nuts
       Powdered sugar

Preheat oven to 350 degrees. Beat eggs and sugar together, adding oil, coffee and whisky. In a deep pot bring honey and baking soda to a boil, then cool. Add cooled honey to egg and sugar mixture. Sift dry ingredients. Add half to the mixture in the bowl and mix until well blended. Sprinkle the raisins into the other half of the dry ingredients. Thoroughly and gently mix that into the batter.

Grease 3 loaf pans or one 10x14-inch pan and line bottom of each with wax paper. Grease and flour the paper. Pour batter evenly into each of the prepared pans. Sprinkle top with nuts. Bake on upper rack for 50 minutes. Test with toothpick to be sure cakes are done. Turn out onto racks to cool, peeling paper from bottoms. Freezes well. Makes 3 loaf cakes or one large cake. Aunt Ethel never fooled around with little cakes. Serves 30 - 36.

Rose Engel

Pistachio Cake (Dairy)

A delicious finale to a dairy meal from my aunt, Nancy Segal.

Cake:
1   package white cake mix
3   eggs
1   cup oil
1   cup 7-Up
1/2   cup coconut flakes
1/2   cup chopped walnuts or
       pecans
1 1/2 teaspoons vanilla extract

Frosting:
1 1/2 cups cold whole milk
1   box pistachio instant
       pudding
2   cups frozen whipped
       topping

Preheat oven to 300 degrees. Combine cake ingredients in a mixer. Beat at medium speed for 2 minutes. Grease a 9x13-inch glass baking dish. Bake for 35-40 minutes or until light golden brown. Allow to cool. Refrigerate for at least 1 hour. Remove from pan; carefully slice into two layers.

To make frosting whip together milk and pudding until thick and refrigerate approximately 30-40 minutes. Fold in frozen whipped topping. Frost bottom half of cake lightly. Place top layer on frosting and spread remaining frosting over cake. Serves 12.

Alexandra Volk Levine

Pies

For many people, pie is the dessert of choice, and the choices are many. One crust or two? Fruit, custard, cream or gelatin filling? A standard pie, or perhaps a deep-dish cobbler or crisp in a large baking dish? Cookie crust or the traditional crust made of flour and shortening?

More than other types of desserts, pies seem to be firmly connected with certain American holidays; pumpkin pie for Thanksgiving, cherry pie for George Washington's birthday, and cherry or apple pie for Fourth of July.

HINTS

- For the dieter, making a one-crust pie, cobbler or crisp naturally reduces the fat and/or cholesterol content, helping compensate somewhat for that sinful scoop of ice cream or dollop of whipped cream on top.

- During June, July and August, when fresh fruit is abundant and relatively cheap, cooks have a wonderful chance to make pies in abundance and freeze the fillings for use later on [see **p. 239** for instructions].

- Many cooks shy away from the traditional pie crust. But with very little practice, anyone can soon become an expert. The secret of a flaky crust is to handle the dough as little as possible. Turn it out to roll when the dough barely sticks together. It is easier to roll when placed between two pieces of floured waxed paper, beginning at the center and rolling out to the edges.

- For one-crust pies, prick crust all over with the tines of a fork before baking. For one-crust fruit pies, brush a beaten egg white over the crust or dust with flour or crumbs prior to baking to prevent the crust from becoming overly soggy.

- Please review the hints in the general introduction to the "Desserts" section [**p. 213**] for dietary information.

Absolutely Perfect, Never-Fail, Drop-on-the-Floor Pie Crust (Pareve)

My mother, Edna Bliss, says, "The title says it all!"

3	cups flour
1	teaspoon salt
1 1/2	cups vegetable shortening (butter or margarine won't do)
1	egg
1	tablespoon white vinegar
5	tablespoons ice water

In a large bowl, combine flour and salt. Add vegetable shortening; mix with pastry blender. Add egg, vinegar and water; work with pastry blender until mixture resembles small peas. (Don't be afraid to mix well and handle. If it falls on the flour, pick it up and go on; you can't hurt this recipe. In fact, one of my best pies had a crust that spent part of its prebaking time on the floor; the germs cook out you know!)

Roll out on a floured board to make pie crusts or many, many tarts. Freezes well if covered with foil. Bake as usual for pie crust. Yields 4 or 5 single 9-inch pie crusts.

Juli Kinrich

Peach Cobbler (Dairy/Pareve)

A simple, satisfying dessert.

3/4	cup sugar
1	egg, beaten
2	tablespoons butter or margarine
1	cup flour
2	teaspoons baking powder
28	ounces canned peaches
1/4	cup reserved peach juice
1	teaspoon cinnamon
1	teaspoon almond extract

In a medium bowl mix sugar, egg and butter until crumbly. Mix flour and baking powder; add to butter mixture. Drain peaches, reserving 1/4 cup juice.

Place fruit on bottom of 9x9-inch baking dish. Sprinkle with cinnamon. Top with batter.

Add almond extract to reserved juice and sprinkle over batter. Bake for 1 hour in a preheated 350 degree oven, or until cobbler tests done. Serve warm with vanilla ice cream or whipped cream. Serves 6 - 8.

Linda Krasnoff

Year-Round Fresh Fruit Pies (Pareve)

*Enjoy the taste of fresh fruit by making a supply of pies
when fruit is abundant and freeze for later use.*

**For each pie filling you will
need the following
amount of <u>fresh</u> fruit:**

2   boxes blueberries, or
3   boxes raspberries or
     boysenberries, or
6 - 8   large peaches or
     nectarines, peeled
     and sliced, or
3 - 4   cups sliced apricots, or
3 - 4   cups sliced Satsuma or
     Santa Rosa plums
3/4 - 1 cup sugar
3 - 4   tablespoons dry
     pearls of tapioca
1/2   teaspoon cinnamon
     (for peach, nectarine,
     or apricot pie)

**Dough for 4 single pie crusts
(to freeze ahead):**
4 1/2   cups sifted flour
1/2-1   teaspoon salt
1 1/2   cups vegetable
     shortening
1/2   cup water

To make any pie filling: In a large bowl, combine any one of the fruit choices with sugar; let stand 10 minutes. Add tapioca; let sit 15 more minutes. (If making a peach, nectarine or apricot pie, add cinnamon at this point.)

Line a 9-inch pie tin with a piece of aluminum foil large enough to hang well over the sides of the tin. Place the filling into the foil-lined tin; tightly wrap up and secure the overhanging foil; freeze. When the filling is hard, remove the tin. Stack frozen fillings; they will keep for at least one year.

To make pie crusts: In a large mixing bowl, combine flour and salt. Remove 1/3 cup of flour-salt mixture to a small bowl; set aside. Add vegetable shortening to large bowl of flour mixture; cut into flour mixture with a pastry blender until crumbs are the size of small peas. Add water to flour mixture in a small bowl to make a paste. Add paste to mixture in large bowl; gather pastry dough together to form a ball.

Divide pastry into four parts.

Roll out each part into a 12-inch circle. Place each circle in a 9-inch pie tin. Trim and flute edges. Seal well in plastic bags; store in freezer.

To bake pie, preheat oven to 450 degrees.

Remove foil from frozen filling and place, unthawed, in preformed, unthawed 9-inch pie crust. Place a pan or cookie sheet on bottom rack in preheated oven; place pie on middle rack. Bake for 25 minutes, then lower oven temperature to 350 degrees and bake for 30-45 minutes more, or until crust is nicely browned and fruit is well cooked. Serves 6 - 8.

Eleanor Botney

Bourbon Apple Pie (Dairy)

An extraordinary pie.

3/4-1	cup sugar (or to taste)
2	tablespoons flour
1	teaspoon cinnamon
1/8	teaspoon nutmeg
1/4	teaspoon salt
6 - 7	apples; peeled, cored and sliced
2	tablespoons bourbon
1/2	cup toasted pecans or walnuts
1/2	cup raisins, plumped in bourbon
	Dough for a 2-crust 9-inch pie
2	tablespoons apricot jam, melted
1	tablespoon butter or margarine
1	tablespoon milk
1	tablespoon sugar

Fit a 9-inch pie pan with half the rolled-out dough. Combine sugar, flour, cinnamon, nutmeg and salt. In a large bowl, mix apples with bourbon. Add sugar mixture, nuts and raisins to apples. Paint bottom pie crust with apricot glaze. Put apple mixture into bottom shell. Dot with butter. Cover with top crust. Seal edges with fork, trim and pierce several times with fork to allow steam to escape. Brush with milk and sprinkle with sugar. Bake 50-60 minutes in a preheated 425 degree oven or until golden brown. Serves 8 - 10.

Pearl Roseman

Coconut Pie In a Blender (Dairy)

A crustless pie for those who count calories.

4	eggs
3/4	cup sugar
1/4	cup butter or margarine
2	cups cold milk
1/2	cup flour (no need to sift)
	Dash of salt
1 1/4	cups flaked coconut

Put all ingredients into a blender. Blend at high speed for 10-15 seconds. Pour into greased 10-inch pie pan. Bake for 40 minutes in a preheated 350 degree oven or until lightly browned on top. Serves 6 - 8.

Trana Labowe

Fresh Peach Pie (Dairy)

Fresh Freestone peaches at the peak of their season make this dessert a special treat. Pecans gently pressed into the crust add to the flavor of this summertime pie.

1	**9- or 10-inch unbaked pie shell**
1/4	**cup chopped pecans, optional**
8	**ounces whipped cream cheese**
8-10	**cups sliced fresh peaches**
1	**cup currant jelly, melted**

Line a 9- or 10-inch pie plate with pastry and sprinkle with chopped pecans. Press nuts gently into crust and bake in a preheated 375 degree oven for approximately 10 minutes or until light golden brown. Allow to cool. Just before serving (up to 1 hour ahead) spread whipped cream cheese on crust and pile peach slices on top of cream cheese. Glaze with melted currant jelly. Serves 8 - 9.

Pearl Roseman

Mock Cheese Pie (Dairy)

Applesauce makes a pleasant addition to this light pie.

16	**ounces applesauce**
1	**14-ounce can sweetened condensed milk**
	juice of 1 lemon
1 1/2	**cups graham cracker crumbs (28 squares)**
4	**ounces butter, melted**
4	**eggs, separated**

In a large bowl, combine applesauce, condensed milk and lemon juice; mix well. Beat egg yolks; add to applesauce mixture; mix well. Beat egg whites until stiff but not dry. Fold egg whites into applesauce-egg yolk mixture. Mix melted butter with graham cracker crumbs. Place a layer of crumbs on bottom of glass pie plate, then alternate layers of the apple mixture and the crumbs. Save enough crumbs to sprinkle on top. Bake for 35 minutes in a preheated 350 degree oven. Serves 6 - 8.

Ann Wigoda

Key Lime or Lemon Pie (Dairy)

My cousin, who lives in Florida,
makes the best Key Lime pie we have ever tasted.

Filling:

1	**cup sugar**
1/4	**cup cornstarch**
1 1/4	**cups milk**
3	**egg yolks, slightly beaten**
1	**teaspoon lemon or lime rind**
1/3	**cup lime or lemon juice**
1/4	**cup margarine or butter**
1	**cup sour cream**
1/4	**teaspoon green food color (optional)**
	9-inch graham cracker crust or baked pie crust (recipe follows)

Crust:

1 1/2	**cups flour**
1/4	**cup sugar**
1	**scant teaspoon baking powder**
4	**ounces margarine**
1	**egg**
1	**teaspoon vanilla extract**

Pie filling: Stir sugar and cornstarch together in a saucepan. Add cold milk slowly and stir until smooth. Stir in slightly beaten egg yolks, lime rind and juice. Add margarine, stirring constantly. Bring to a boil and boil for 1 minute at medium heat. Pour into a large bowl. Cover with plastic wrap. Refrigerate 40-50 minutes.

Prepare crust: Mix dry ingredients together at low speed in mixer. Cut margarine into small pieces into dry ingredients and mix at low speed. Add egg and mix. Add vanilla and mix. Remove bowl from mixer. Form dough into 2 balls and roll 1 ball between 2 pieces of plastic wrap. Reserve remaining ball for future use.

Fit into pie pan. Prick bottom with a fork.

Bake crust in a preheated 350 degree oven for about 20 minutes or until lightly browned. Remove filling from refrigerator and fold in sour cream. Put filling into crust. Refrigerate 2 hours or until firm. Garnish with frozen whipped topping. Serves 6 - 8.

Lucille Weisel

Pumpkin Pie (Pareve)

*This pareve version goes perfectly with
the traditional Thanksgiving turkey dinner.*

3	cups canned pumpkin
1	cup brown sugar
1	cup granulated sugar
1	teaspoon salt
1	teaspoon nutmeg
1	teaspoon cinnamon
1	teaspoon ginger
1/4	teaspoon cloves
1/4	teaspoon allspice
4	eggs, beaten
1/4	cup melted margarine
1	10-inch unbaked pie shell

In a large bowl mix together pumpkin, sugar, salt and spices. In a small bowl mix together eggs and margarine. Add to pumpkin mixture; mix well. Pour mixture into pie shell. Bake for 10 minutes in a preheated 450 degree oven. Reduce heat to 350 degrees and bake 40 minutes longer or until a knife inserted into center comes out clean. Serves 8 - 10.

Lela Jacoby

Pumpkin-Pecan Pie (Pareve)

Two traditional Thanksgiving flavors in one pie to please everyone.

1	9-inch unbaked pie shell
3	eggs, slightly beaten
1	cup dark corn syrup
1/2	cup sugar
1/2	cup canned pumpkin
1	teaspoon vanilla extract
1	cup pecan halves
1	tablespoon margarine, melted
	Pareve whipped topping

In a large bowl, gently combine eggs, corn syrup, sugar, pumpkin and vanilla. Stir in pecan halves and margarine. Pour into pie shell. Bake in a preheated 400 degree oven for 15 minutes. Reduce heat to 350 degrees and bake about 25 minutes more or until filling is set. Cool. Serve with whipped (pareve) topping. Serves 8.

Marilyn Smith

243

Plum Crunch (Dairy/Pareve)

Delicious; best when served warm.

3   cups pitted blue plums,
    cut in quarters
    (available in August
    and September only;
    a.k.a. Italian/Prune
    plums)
3   tablespoons brown sugar
5   tablespoons granulated
    sugar
1/4 teaspoon nutmeg

Topping:
1   egg, well beaten
1   cup flour
1   cup sugar
1   teaspoon baking powder
1/4 teaspoon salt
1/2 cup butter or
    margarine, melted

Place plums on bottom of a 7x10x2-inch pan. Mix sugars and nutmeg; sprinkle over fruit.

Sift dry ingredients together. Add egg to sifted dry ingredients.

Mix with pastry blender or fingers (finger method is best) until crumbly. Sprinkle over plum mixture. Pour butter or margarine over all. Bake immediately for 45 minutes in a preheated 375 degree oven or until crust is golden brown. Serve warm with ice cream or sherbet. Serves 10 - 12.

Suggestions: If you want to make this during the year when plums are not available, pit and quarter the 3 cups of plums, place in an airtight bag and freeze for later use. Use less butter or margarine for a crunchier crust.

Variation: Recipe also works well with blueberries (used whole). When freezing berries, do not wash; just wrap in airtight container and place in freezer until ready to use.

J. D. Weiss

Lemon Mousse Pie (Pareve)

This incredibly easy-to-make pie tastes most refreshing on a warm, balmy day!

24 ounces nondairy dessert
    whip
1   12-ounce can frozen
    lemonade
1   10-inch graham cracker
    crust
    Frozen nondairy
    whipped topping
    Berries, optional

Defrost lemonade; mix with dessert whip. Pour into pie crust; set in freezer. Remove 10 minutes before serving. Top with frozen whipped topping and berries. Serves 6.

Mickey Freedman

Peachy Plum Squares (Dairy/Pareve)

Mix or match fresh fruit when it is plentiful for a summer treat.
Serve hot or cold.

1/2	cup shortening
1	cup brown sugar, packed
1 1/4	cups sifted flour
1/2	teaspoon baking soda
1/2	teaspoon cinnamon
1 1/2	cups quick oats
2 1/2	cups thinly sliced peaches
2	cups thinly sliced plums
3/4	cup sugar
	Whipped cream (optional)

In a large bowl, cream shortening and brown sugar. Sift together only 1 cup flour, baking soda and cinnamon. Cut the dry ingredients into shortening with oats, blending thoroughly. Press 1/2 of the mixture into a well-greased 9x13-inch pan.

In a large bowl combine plums and peaches. Add remaining 1/4 cup flour and sugar. Arrange fruit mixture over oat mixture in pan, then top with other 1/2 of the crumbs. Bake for 30-35 minutes in a preheated 350 degree oven or until lightly browned. Cool slightly and serve with topping of whipped cream. Serves 10.

Note: Substitute nondairy whipped topping for whipped cream to make this recipe pareve.

Ivy Liebross

Strawberry Yogurt Pie (Dairy)

A low-calorie, make-ahead pie for the freezer.
Take one slice or the whole pie out as needed.

2	pints fresh strawberries
1	9-inch graham cracker pie crust
1	small container frozen whipped topping
2	8-ounce containers strawberry yogurt

Clean and slice 1 box of berries. Place sliced berries on bottom of pie crust. Mix together yogurt and frozen whipped topping and pour into pie shell. Clean remaining berries and decorate top of pie with them. Cover and freeze overnight.

To use, take out of freezer and place in refrigerator for 2 hours before serving. Serves 8.

Note: Dry, frozen, unsweetened berries may be used in place of fresh. Use them frozen.

Elinor Einy

Cookies

Cookies are everyone's favorite and are a great alternative to cakes as a dessert. They can be very simple and plain, or rich and fancy enough to enhance any party. In fact, an assortment of cookies makes a beautiful dessert selection. Add some finger-size portions of sliced cake, and you have a perfect dessert buffet for a wedding or baby shower, a "wine-and-cheese" party, or a coffee or tea reception.

Some cookies are associated with holidays — *rugelach* for Hanukkah and *hamantaschen* for Purim. *Kamish brot* is a frequent Sabbath treat, and *mandelbrot* is an anytime treat. Each of these desserts is associated with a part of the world in which Jews once lived, or still live.

Because most cookies can be made ahead in quantity, they are a good dessert choice when you are serving a crowd.

HINTS

- Adding ingredients such as rolled oats, dried fruits, peanut butter, wheat bran or nuts will enhance the fiber and nutritional value of cookies.

- With the exception of those made with meringue, cookies freeze well, so they can be made in advance and taken out whenever needed.

- Grease cookie sheets unless otherwise directed in a recipe. Bake cookies one pan at a time. When greasing cookie sheets, vegetable sprays are more healthful and simpler to use than butter or margarine. For easier storage and cleanup, line baking pans with foil, especially when baking bar cookies.

- Please review the hints in the general introduction to the "Desserts" [p. 213] section for dietary information.

Strudel (Dairy)

Goodies in the filling make a delightful strudel.

Pastry:

8	**ounces butter or margarine (at room temperature)**
1	**cup sour cream**
2	**cups all-purpose flour**

Filling:

1	**cup apricot-pineapple jam, combined with**
1/2	**cup orange marmalade**
1	**cup golden raisins**
1	**cup chopped walnuts**
1	**large apple, peeled, cored and grated**
1	**cup graham cracker or cookie crumbs**
	Powdered sugar

In a large bowl, blend margarine and sour cream. Mix in flour to make a soft dough. Wrap in wax paper and refrigerate for at least 1 hour.

Divide pastry into 4 parts. Roll each part of the dough into a rectangle approximately 8x14x1/4 inches thick. Spread fillings, beginning with jam mixture. Roll up, jelly roll fashion. Place on ungreased cookie sheet.

Bake for 40 minutes in a 350 degree oven or until light brown. Cut and sprinkle with powdered sugar. Yields approximately 40 pieces.

Dotty Simmons

Edy's Strudel (Dairy)

An elegant dessert; the pastry dough has other uses as well.

Pastry:

8	**ounces margarine**
1	**cup cottage cheese**
2	**cups flour**

Filling:

1	**cup apricot/pineapple jam**
1/2	**cup shredded coconut**
1/2	**cup raisins**
1/2	**cup chopped walnuts or pecans**
1/2	**teaspoon cinnamon**
	Graham cracker crumbs
1	**egg white, beaten**
	Cinnamon and sugar

In a large mixing bowl, beat together margarine, cottage cheese and flour. Divide into 4 balls. Wrap in wax paper and refrigerate overnight.

Combine filling ingredients.

To assemble: on a lightly floured board, roll out each ball to approximately 10x12 inches. Spread filling mixture on pastry. Sprinkle with graham cracker crumbs and roll up like a jelly roll. Place on cookie sheet, allowing a couple of inches between each roll. Baste top of each roll with beaten egg white and sprinkle with cinnamon and sugar.

Bake for approximately 35 minutes at 350 degrees. Cut into serving-size portions. Yields approximately 40 pieces.

Edythe Merkow

Rugelach (Dairy)

A traditional Jewish cookie, a real treat!

2	cups flour
8	ounces butter
1	egg yolk
3/4	cup sour cream
3/4	cup sugar
1	tablespoon cinnamon
1/2	cup chopped nuts
1/4	cup mini-chocolate chips

In a large mixing bowl, cream butter with flour. Add egg yolk and sour cream. Mix well and shape into a ball. Wrap in plastic wrap and refrigerate several hours or overnight.

Combine sugar, cinnamon, nuts and chocolate chips. Sprinkle board with flour. Remove dough from refrigerator and divide into 4 parts. Roll out dough on board into circle.

Take 1/4 sugar-nut mixture and sprinkle over circle. Cut circle into 12 wedge-shaped sections. Roll up each section, starting with widest portion, towards center. Place on an ungreased cookie sheet. Repeat with remaining dough. Bake for 25-30 minutes at 350 degrees. Yields 48 pieces.

Cirel Blitz

Kamishbroit (Pareve)

This traditional Ukrainian cookie was handed down through the ages and passed on to me by a good friend.

3	eggs
1	cup sugar
1	cup oil
1	teaspoon vanilla extract
3	cups all-purpose flour (unsifted)
1	cup sliced almonds

In a large mixing bowl, beat eggs at high speed until light and fluffy. Add sugar and vanilla; continue beating to a creamy consistency. Slowly add oil and blend well. Stop mixer. Add flour all at once and blend well. Add nuts. Dough will be soft. Turn dough into warm 13x9-inch pan and flatten with spoon or spatula. Bake for 15-20 minutes in a 350 degree oven. Remove from oven and cut into bars approximately 2 1/2x1/2 inches. Place on ungreased cookie sheet (separating the bars). Bake another 15-20 minutes or until golden brown. Cool and store in covered container. Yields approximately 80 bars.

Mary Kovshoff

Taiglach (Pareve)

My mother, Anna Kaplan's, recipe. An absolute must at Rosh Hashanah and important simchas.

6	**eggs**
	Dash salt
1/4	**cup oil**
3	**cups flour plus 1 cup**
1 1/2	**teaspoons baking powder**
1 1/4	**cups honey**
1	**cup chopped nuts**
1 1/2	**teaspoons ground Ginger**
	Poppy seeds

Mix together eggs, salt, oil, flour and baking powder. Turn dough out on floured brown paper. Use 1/2 to 1 cup additional flour as needed because dough is very sticky. Divide dough into small portions, approximately 1/2 cup each. Roll each portion into a 10- to 12-inch-long rope. Cut each rope into 1/2-inch pieces.

Bake on ungreased cookie sheet lined with brown paper at 450 degrees. Shake pan after 5 minutes, separating little pieces if they are stuck together. Bake 10 minutes more until golden brown. Cool.

Heat honey to boiling point in 3-quart saucepan. Add ginger. Reduce heat and add baked pieces.

With a wooden spoon stir constantly for approximately 15 minutes. Add nuts and mix thoroughly. When honey becomes stringy and color is golden brown, turn out on a wet board. Flatten to approximately 3/4-inch thick, using hands wet with cold water or use a wet rolling pin. Use **great caution**, as honey is very hot. Sprinkle top with poppy seeds.

When the taiglach have hardened cut into approximately 1 1/2-inch diamond-shaped pieces. Yields about 35 pieces.

Note: *Recipe doubles well.*

Idele Deutsch

Mandelbrot (Pareve)

A favorite in my family for more than 40 years.

1/2	cup oil
1	cup sugar
3	eggs
1	teaspoon vanilla extract
1/2	teaspoon almond extract
3	cups flour
3	teaspoons baking powder
1/2	teaspoon salt
1-1 1/2	cup nuts (preferably almonds)
	Cinnamon
	Sugar

In a mixing bowl combine oil, sugar, eggs, vanilla and almond extracts. Mix flour, baking powder and salt; slowly add to mixture. Fold in nuts. Turn out dough on floured board. Shape into 2 or 3 long rolls. Bake on greased cookie sheet for 40 minutes at 350 degrees. Remove from oven (maintain oven temperature). Slice into 1/2-inch thick pieces while still hot. Lay slices flat on cookie sheet; sprinkle with cinnamon and sugar to taste. Return to oven for 10 minutes, turn to other side and sprinkle with cinnamon and sugar mixture. Bake another 10 minutes. Yields approximately 40 pieces.

Dotty Simmons

Judith's Deluxe Mandelbrot (Pareve)

This recipe made my mother, Judith Kamerman, the "mandelbrot queen" of Hallandale, Florida.

1	cup sugar
1	cup oil
4	large or 3 extra-large eggs
3	cups flour
2	teaspoons baking powder
1	teaspoon salt
2	teaspoons vanilla extract or any other flavoring
1	cup finely chopped walnuts or pecans

In a large bowl, mix together sugar, oil and eggs. Add dry ingredients and vanilla. Mix well; batter will be very stiff. Add nuts. Dust hands with flour.

On two lightly greased cookie sheets form batter into three or four loaves approximately 1/2 inch high and 2 1/2 inches wide. (The loaves will rise and expand.) Bake 20-30 minutes at 350 degrees or until light brown. Remove loaves from oven and cut in 3/4-inch slices; replace on cookie sheet and return to oven to brown. Turn slices after approximately 10-12 minutes and brown other side for another 10-12 minutes. Approximately 50 pieces.

Ruth Giden

Macadamia Mandelbrot (Pareve)

Macadamia nuts add new richness to this classic.

3	large eggs
3/4	cup vegetable oil
1	cup sugar
1/4	cup orange juice
1 1/2 - 2	tablespoons grated orange peel
1	teaspoon almond extract
3 3/4	cups all-purpose flour
1	tablespoon baking powder
1/4	teaspoon salt
1	cup coarsely chopped Macadamia nuts Additional flour, as needed

In a large bowl, with electric mixer at medium speed, beat eggs and oil for 5 minutes until fluffy. Gradually beat in sugar, orange juice, orange peel and almond extract. At low speed beat in flour, baking powder and salt. Beat in additional flour if dough appears too sticky. Stir in chopped nuts. Wrap dough in plastic and refrigerate 1 hour.

Grease large cookie sheet. Divide dough in half. Shape each half into 14x2-inch log. Place logs on cookie sheet, spacing well apart; bake 25 minutes in a preheated 350 degree oven until lightly browned. Remove cookie sheet from oven (maintain oven temperature). Remove logs to cutting board and cut into 1/2-inch diagonal slices. Place slices, cut side up, on cookie sheet and return to oven. Bake approximately 15 minutes more until crisp and golden. Cool on racks. Yields 30 slices.

Marcia Abelson

Eastern European Hamantaschen (Dairy)

Yeast makes the difference in this version.

1	**package yeast**
3/4	**cup milk**
2	**ounces butter**
1/4	**cup sugar**
3	**eggs**
2	**cups flour**
1/4	**teaspoon salt**

In a small bowl, dissolve yeast in 1/4 cup of the lukewarm milk with 1 teaspoon of the sugar. Set aside.

In a large bowl, combine remaining lukewarm milk, remaining sugar, butter and 2 eggs; blend well. Mix in yeast mixture, flour and salt, blending thoroughly to make a soft dough. Place on floured surface and knead for 2-3 minutes until dough is not sticky, adding more flour if necessary.

Put dough in an oiled bowl, turning over once to oil all around. Cover with plastic wrap or towel and set in a warm place until doubled in bulk, about 45 minutes.

Punch dough down. On a floured board, roll out 1/2 of the dough to 1/4-inch thickness. Cut into 3-inch circles. Spoon 1 teaspoon filling (see page 255) in center of each circle and bring edges up to form a triangle. Pinch edges to hold triangle shape.

Place on a greased cookie sheet. Brush with remaining beaten egg and bake in a preheated 350 degree oven for 25 minutes or until golden. This recipe can be doubled. Yields 24 pieces.

Rosalie Weiner

Low-Cholesterol Hamantaschen (Pareve)

Rave reviews for this healthier version.

6	egg whites
1	cup sugar
3/4	cup oil
1	teaspoon vanilla extract
4 1/3	cups flour
1	tablespoon baking powder
1/2	teaspoon salt
1/4	cup poppy seeds
1	egg white, beaten, (for brushing)

In a large bowl, beat egg whites, sugar, oil and vanilla together. In a second bowl, mix flour, baking powder, salt and poppy seeds together. Blend flour mixture into egg mixture; mix well.

Roll out a portion on a floured board and cut into 3 1/2-inch circles. Place a teaspoon of filling (see page 255) in the center of each circle of dough. Bring up dough to cover filling and pinch together to form a triangle. Place on lightly greased cookie sheet. Brush with egg white and bake at 350 degrees for 20 minutes or until golden. Yields 5 dozen.

Note: Can be frozen before baking by placing on a rack. When frozen, transfer to a sealed container and bake when desired.

Rosalie Weiner

Easy Hamantaschen (Pareve)

For cookie dough lovers, this one is a treat!

1/2	pound margarine
1/2	cup sugar
2	eggs, slightly beaten
2	cups flour
2	teaspoons baking powder
1	teaspoon vanilla extract
1	tablespoon orange juice
1	tablespoon grated orange rind

Cream together softened margarine and sugar. Add eggs and flavorings and beat well. Add sifted flour and baking powder to the creamed mixture. Knead into a ball and use a little extra flour if needed as dough is very soft. Chill in refrigerator at least 2 hours.

Divide dough into 3 portions. Roll each portion on a floured board until 1/8- to 1/4-inch thickness. Cut dough into 3- or 4-inch rounds with a floured glass or cookie cutter.

Place desired filling by teaspoonfuls in each round. Pinch together sides of circle to form triangle. Place on lightly greased cookie sheet. Bake about 25-30 minutes in a 350 degree oven or until golden. Yields approximately 2 1/2 - 3 dozen.

Ruth King

Classic Hamantaschen (Pareve)

A favorite at Purim.

4	eggs
1	cup oil
1 1/4	cups sugar
1	teaspoon vanilla extract
1	tablespoon baking powder
1/2	teaspoon salt
4 1/2 -5	cups flour

In a large bowl, beat eggs. Beat in oil, sugar, vanilla, baking powder and salt. Add flour gradually; mix thoroughly. Knead until smooth enough to roll on floured board or pastry cloth. Roll dough out in 4 portions about 1/4-inch thick.

Cut into 3- or 4-inch rounds with glass edge. Place desired filling by teaspoonfuls in each round. Pinch together sides of circle to form triangle. Place on lightly greased cookie sheet. Bake about 20-25 minutes in a 375 degree oven or until done. Yields approximately 6 dozen.

Rose Engel

Hamantaschen Fillings

*Prepared fillings such as prune, poppy seed, cherry, apricot,
blueberry, etc. may be purchased in large supermarkets
or gourmet food stores. However, our homemade versions
are less expensive and often more delicious.
They also work well as filling for other cookies or pastries.*

Applesauce Hamantaschen Filling (Pareve):

1	cup applesauce (homemade, if possible)
1/2	cup raisins
1/2	cup chopped nuts
1/2	teaspoon cinnamon

Mix together. Yields 2 cups.

Apricot Hamantaschen Filling (Pareve):

8	ounces dried apricots
3/4	cup sugar
1/2	cup raisins
1	cup apple juice
1	tablespoon grated lemon peel
1/2	cup coarsely chopped nuts

In a small saucepan, cook apricots with sugar, raisins, apple juice and lemon peel. Boil 15-20 minutes, uncovered, until almost all liquid is evaporated. Cool. Add nuts. Yields 2 cups.

Poppy Seed Hamantaschen Filling (Dairy):

1	cup poppy seeds
1/2	cup milk
1/4	cup honey
1/3	cup chopped dates
1/3	cup raisins
1/4	cup chopped nuts
1/2	teaspoon cinnamon
1/2	teaspoon nutmeg

Cook all ingredients over low heat and stir occasionally until almost all liquid is evaporated. Yields 2 1/2 cups.

Date Hamantaschen Filling (Pareve):

1	pound chopped pitted dates
2	cups sugar
1	cup water
2-3	tablespoons lemon juice
1	tablespoon grated lemon peel
1/2	cup ground nuts

Cook dates, sugar and water over medium heat, stirring often. Cool. Add lemon juice, peel and nuts. Yields 4 cups.

Honey Walnut Hamantaschen Filling (Pareve):

3/4	cup honey
1	cup chopped walnuts
1/3	cup pareve bread crumbs
1	teaspoon orange peel

Cook all ingredients over low heat, stirring constantly. Cool. Yields 2 cups.

Chocolate Hamantaschen Filling (Dairy/Pareve):

1/2	cup unsweetened cocoa
1/3	cup sugar
1/4	cup milk or coffee
1	cup chopped nuts

Combine all ingredients. Yields 2 cups.

(continued)

(Hamantaschen Fillings continued from page 255)

Prune-Apricot Hamantaschen Filling (Pareve):

1	pound pitted prunes
1/2	cup chopped nuts
1/2	cup raisins
1/2	cup sugar
1/4	cup dried apricots
2	teaspoons cinnamon
1	teaspoon lemon juice

Grind or chop all ingredients. Mix together. Yields 4 cups.

Any Preserves Hamantaschen Filling (Pareve):

1 1/2	cup preserves
1	tablespoon grated lemon peel
2-3	tablespoons lemon juice
1/2	cup chopped nuts
1/2	cup pareve cake or bread crumbs

Combine all ingredients. Yields 2 1/2 cups.

Prune-Nut Hamantaschen Filling (Pareve):

1	pound pitted prunes
1/2	cup orange juice
1	cup water
1/4	cup orange liqueur
3/4	cup honey
1/2	cup ground nuts
1/8	teaspoon cloves
1/2	teaspoon cinnamon
1/2	teaspoon grated lemon peel

Cook prunes slowly with orange juice and water until almost all liquid evaporates. Add orange liqueur. Bring to quick boil and remove from heat at once. Combine remaining ingredients. Yields 2 1/2 - 3 cups.

Rosalie Weiner

Prune Jam (Pareve)

An ideal sugar-free spread or filling.

12	ounces pitted prunes
1 1/2	cup unsweetened prune juice

Puree prunes and juice in food processor or blender until smooth. Cook in a saucepan over medium heat; stir until thick and darkened. Approximately 2 1/2 cups.

Variation: *Sugar and nuts may be added to prune mixture for Hamantaschen or coffee cake filling.*

Gussie Cutter

Pecan Squares (Dairy/Pareve)

This festive cookie is much richer when made dairy.

Crust:

2/3	cup powdered sugar
2	cups flour
8	ounces butter or margarine

Topping:

2/3	cup melted butter or margarine
1/2	cup honey
3	tablespoons whipping cream or liquid nondairy creamer
1/2	cup firmly packed brown sugar
3 1/2	cups coarsely chopped pecans

Line a 9x13-inch pan with greased foil or parchment paper. Sift together sugar and flour. Cut in butter until butter is in pea-sized bits. Press mixture into pan. Bake for 20 minutes at 325 degrees.

While crust is baking, mix together melted butter, honey, whipping cream, brown sugar and pecans. Pour mixture over baked crust. Spread evenly and return to oven; bake for 25 minutes longer.

When top looks set, remove from oven. Cool 5-10 minutes. Loosen parchment or foil immediately. Cool before cutting. Yields 48 pieces.

Ruth King

Carrot Bars (Dairy)

For carrot cake fans.

Cookies:

4	eggs
2	cups sugar
1 1/2	cups salad oil
2	cups sifted flour
2	teaspoons baking soda
2	teaspoons cinnamon
1	teaspoon salt
3	cups finely grated carrots
1 1/2	cups flaked coconut
1 1/2	cups chopped walnuts

Frosting:

8	ounces cream cheese, softened
2	tablespoons milk
5	cups powdered sugar
2	teaspoons vanilla extract
1/4	teaspoon salt

In a large bowl, beat eggs until light and fluffy. Gradually beat in sugar. Sift flour with salt, soda and cinnamon; add alternately with oil to eggs. Mix well. Fold in carrots, coconut and walnuts. Spread evenly in two 9x13-inch greased pans. Bake for 25-30 minutes at 350 degrees. Cool, uncut, on rack.

Blend all frosting ingredients in large bowl. When cookies are completely cool, spread with cream cheese frosting. Cut in 1x3-inch bars. Store in freezer. Yields 6 1/2 dozen.

Pearl Roseman

Preposterous Pecan Chocolate Bars (Dairy)

The title says it all!

1 1/2 cups roasted pecans
(or other nut)
8 ounces butter, softened
1/2 cup brown sugar, packed
1/2 cup sugar
1 egg yolk
1 teaspoon vanilla extract
1/2 teaspoon almond extract
1 3/4 cups flour
12 ounces semisweet
chocolate bits,
chopped

Preheat oven to 300 degrees. Line a baking pan with foil and roast pecans for 8-10 minutes. Shake several times; set aside to cool. Increase oven temperature to 350 degrees. In a large bowl beat butter, brown sugar and sugar until light and fluffy. Add egg yolk, vanilla and almond extract. Blend ingredients thoroughly. Slowly blend in flour.

Spread mixture in a greased 9x13-inch baking pan. Bake for 20 minutes. Remove from oven and cover immediately with chocolate chips. Spread chocolate evenly as it melts (may be put into oven for a few minutes to melt any unmelted bits). Sprinkle pecans over chocolate mixture and press lightly into chocolate with fingers. Cool completely. Cut into any size bars. Yields 24 2-inch square bars.

Ruth King

Apricot Cheese Pastry Hearts (Dairy)

*This rich Austrian pastry was my daughter's
favorite when she was little.*

Pastry:

1	cup all-purpose sifted flour
1/8	teaspoon salt
4	ounces butter or margarine, softened
4	ounces cream cheese, softened

Filling:

1/2	cup apricot preserves
1	egg, beaten

Topping:

Sugar to sprinkle

In a large bowl, mix flour and salt. With a pastry blender or two knives, cut butter and cheese into flour mixture until well blended. Lightly shape dough into a ball; wrap in waxed paper. Refrigerate until well chilled.

Preheat oven to 400 degrees. Grease 2 cookie sheets. On floured surface, roll out dough to 1/8 inch. Cut out hearts, approximately 3 1/4x2 1/2 inches. Save trimmings, re-roll and cut more hearts. In center of each heart, place 1 teaspoon of preserves. Brush edges with beaten egg, cover with another heart and flute edges with a fork. Sprinkle with sugar and bake 10-12 minutes or until golden brown. Approximately 24 cookies.

Note: *Pastry may be prepared 1 or 2 days ahead and stored in refrigerator.*

Janet Arzt

Aunt Sophie's Almond Bars (Pareve)

Our family loves these.

Dough:

2	cups flour
1	teaspoon baking powder
1/2	cup sugar
1/4	teaspoon salt
1/2	cup corn oil
2	eggs, lightly beaten
1	teaspoon almond extract

Filling:

1/2	cup any jam

Sift together flour, baking powder, sugar and salt. Make a well in the flour mixture and add oil, eggs and almond extract. Mix until dough holds together (very oily). Let it rest 5 minutes. Cut into 2 parts. Pat each part into an approximate 12x4-inch strip in a jelly roll pan.

Put filling down the center of each strip. Fold long sides toward the middle and seal. Bake 35 minutes at 350 degrees or until golden brown. While hot, cut each strip into approximately 10 pieces. Cool on rack. Best fresh, but can be frozen. Yields 20 pieces.

Variations: *Any flavor extract can be used. With jam, combinations of any desired fillings can be used, i.e., nuts, cinnamon and sugar, or chocolate chips, etc.*
Hint: *Must use hand to pat out dough; it is soft and oily.*

Eve Marcus

Almond Coconut Chews (Dairy/Pareve)

This recipe requires a candy thermometer.

Crust:

2	cups flour
2	tablespoons sugar
3/4	teaspoon baking powder
	Pinch of salt
4	ounces margarine
1	egg, beaten
3	tablespoons whipping cream or liquid nondairy creamer

Coconut Layer:

1	tablespoon margarine
1	cup sugar
1/4	cup whipping cream or liquid nondairy creamer
1	14-ounce bag flaked coconut

Almond Topping:

1 1/2	cups sugar
4	ounces margarine
1/2	cup corn syrup or honey
1/2	cup whipping cream or nondairy creamer
1 1/2	cup sliced or slivered almonds
1/2	teaspoon vanilla extract

Crust: Sift flour, sugar, baking powder and salt together into a bowl. Cut in margarine until mixture is crumbly. Fold in egg and cream, 1 tablespoon at a time, until mixture is moistened. Pat mixture into a greased 12x15-inch jelly roll pan. Bake for 10 minutes at 375 degrees or until lightly brown. Maintain oven temperature; remove from oven and cool.

Coconut layer: Combine margarine, sugar and whipping cream in a saucepan. Stir over low heat until margarine melts. Stir in coconut until moistened. Spread over crust with moistened fingers.

Almond topping: Combine sugar, margarine, syrup and whipping cream in a saucepan. Heat over low heat, stirring constantly, until mixture boils. Add almonds and cook until temperature reaches 240 degrees on a candy thermometer. Remove from heat and add vanilla. Stir until mixture of nuts and sugar is blended. Pour over coconut layer. Smooth out in pan. Return to oven and bake 15-20 minutes longer or until top is caramelized. Cut into 2-inch squares while still warm. Yields 42 2-inch square bars.

Ruth King

Crunchy Brownies (Dairy)

All the world loves brownies, and these are yummy!

8	ounces margarine
2	cups sugar
6	tablespoons unsweetened cocoa
2	teaspoons vanilla extract
4	eggs
1	cup flour
1/2	teaspoon salt
1	7-ounce jar marshmallow cream
1	cup peanut butter (chunky or smooth)
1	12-ounce package chocolate chips
3	cups crispy rice cereal

In a large bowl, cream margarine, sugar, cocoa and vanilla very well. Add eggs, one at a time, and beat well. Fold in flour and salt. Spread mixture in a greased 15x10-inch pan. Bake at 350 degrees for 25 minutes. Remove from oven and cool.

When cool, spread marshmallow cream on top. Using heavy pot over low heat (or in microwave), melt peanut butter and chocolate chips together. Remove from heat and add crispy rice cereal. Spread mixture over marshmallow topping. Refrigerate to harden and cut into 2-inch squares. Freezes very well. Yields approximately 35 2-inch brownies.

Edythe Merkow

Magic Cookie Bars (Dairy)

It's easy, foolproof, delicious and a sure hit every time. Not low-calorie; it's low-nothing.

4	ounces butter, melted
1 1/2	cups Graham cracker crumbs
1	cup walnuts, coarsely chopped
1	cup (6 ounces) chocolate chips
1	cup (6 ounces) butterscotch morsels
1 1/3	cups (3 1/2 ounces) flaked coconut
1 1/3	cups (15-ounce can) sweetened condensed milk

Pour melted butter into 9x13-inch baking pan. Layer each ingredient evenly in order given. Bake for 25 minutes at 350 degrees or until lightly browned. Cut into desired size bars or squares. Yields 30 bars or 36 squares.

Note: *Quantities of ingredients may be varied as desired.*

Bea Reynolds

Chocolate Mint Brownies (Dairy/Pareve)

A showstopper!

Brownies:

3	1-ounce squares unsweetened chocolate
3/4	cup butter or margarine
3	eggs
1 1/2	cups granulated sugar
3/4	cup flour
	Pinch salt
3/4	cup chopped nuts

Icing:

1/4	cup butter or margarine
2 1/4	cups powdered sugar
3	tablespoons milk or nondairy liquid creamer
1 1/4	teaspoons peppermint extract
1/2	cup semisweet chocolate chips
3	tablespoons butter or margarine

Brownies: Melt unsweetened chocolate and 3/4 cup butter or margarine in top of a double boiler over hot water or in microwave. Beat eggs and granulated sugar until light and fluffy. Stir in flour, salt and nuts. Add to chocolate mixture. Pour into a greased 13x9-inch pan and bake in a 350 degree oven 20-25 minutes. Cool.

Icing: Cream 1/4 cup butter or margarine until light and fluffy. Add powdered sugar, milk or nondairy liquid creamer, and peppermint extract; beat well. Spread over the cooled brownies and let stand until firm, approximately 1-1 1/2 hours.

Melt chocolate chips with 3 tablespoons butter or margarine. Drizzle over the white icing. Allow chocolate to set and cut into squares or bars. Yields 48 squares approximately 1 1/2-inches in size.

Idele Deutsch

Chocolate Rum Balls (Dairy)

*An elegant no-bake cookie that can use
leftover cake and/or cookie crumbs.*

1 1/4	cups chocolate chips
3	tablespoons light corn syrup
1/2	cup rum
1/4	cup orange juice
2 1/2	cups crushed vanilla wafers, or any leftover cookie or cake crumbs
1	cup chopped nuts
1/2	cup sifted powdered sugar
	Granulated sugar for decorating

Melt chocolate chips over hot water; remove from heat. Stir in corn syrup, rum and orange juice; mix well. Mix in crushed wafers and nuts. Add powdered sugar and mix well. Add chocolate mixture, stirring well (it forms a ball-like mass). Let stand 30 minutes or more.

Roll into 1-inch balls. Roll balls in granulated sugar. Place in boxes lined with waxed paper. Flavors ripen and cookies become firm in 24-48 hours at room temperature. Refrigerate. Yields approximately 5 dozen.

Variation: *Balls may be rolled in powdered sugar or chocolate sprinkles instead of granulated sugar.*

Sylvia Price

Persimmon Cookies (Pareve)

An unusual adaptation of a spice cookie.

1	cup persimmon pulp
1	cup sugar
1/2	cup margarine, softened
1	egg
2	cups flour
1	teaspoon baking soda
1	teaspoon cinnamon
1/2	teaspoon nutmeg
1/4	teaspoon cloves
1/2	teaspoon salt
1	cup chopped walnuts
1	cup raisins

In a large bowl, beat persimmon pulp, sugar and margarine until creamy. Beat in egg. Mix together flour, baking soda, cinnamon, nutmeg, cloves and salt; add to persimmon mixture. Fold in nuts and raisins. Wrap in plastic wrap or wax paper and chill for several hours or overnight.

Preheat oven to 375 degrees. Drop by spoonfuls on greased baking sheets. Bake 12-15 minutes. Yields about 3 dozen.

Emma Schlesinger

Three-Ingredient Cookies (Pareve)

Good "rainy day" baking for young children.

1	cup brown sugar
8	ounces margarine or 1 cup safflower oil
2	cups flour
40	walnut or pecan halves

Preheat oven to 350 degrees. Mix brown sugar, margarine and flour; roll into walnut-size balls. Place balls on greased cookie sheets. Press down with fork to 1/4-inch thick. Put half pecan or walnut on top. Bake 10 minutes or until golden. Yields 3 1/2 dozen large cookies.

Variation: One teaspoon of any flavoring can be added to change the flavor — lemon rind, vanilla, almond, rum flavor. Each new flavor creates a new treat!

Loretta Allen

Forgotten Cookies (Pareve)

Put these in the oven and forget them until time to eat.

2	egg whites
1/2	cup sugar
1	teaspoon vanilla extract
1	cup chopped nuts
1	cup chocolate chips

Preheat oven to 400 degrees. Beat egg whites until stiff peaks form. Gradually add sugar and continue beating. Add vanilla. Stir in nuts and chocolate chips. Drop by teaspoons onto a foil-lined cookie sheet. Place in oven and turn it off. Forget for 1 1/2 - 3 hours. Yields 3 dozen.

Variation: One cup chopped dates, coconut or maraschino cherries may be substituted for chocolate chips.

Cirel Blitz

Raisin Cheesecake Cookies (Dairy)

A favorite from Nana Bea Lichter.

1/3	cup soft butter or margarine
1/3	cup brown sugar, packed
1	cup sifted flour
1/2	cup raisins
1/2	cup chopped walnuts
8	ounces cream cheese, room temperature
1/4	cup sugar
1	egg
2	tablespoons milk
1	tablespoon lemon juice
1/2	teaspoon vanilla extract

Preheat oven to 350 degrees. In a medium bowl, cream butter and brown sugar until fluffy; add flour, raisins and nuts. Blend with fingers until crumbly. Reserve 1 cup of mixture. Press remainder into an 8-inch lightly greased square pan. Bake for 15 minutes or until golden at edges; cool. (Retain oven temperature.)

Mix together cream cheese and sugar until smooth. Add egg, milk, lemon juice and vanilla. Beat until smooth. Spread mixture over baked crust. Sprinkle reserved crumbs over top. Bake for 25-30 minutes or until firm in center. Cool to room temperature. Cover and chill until serving time. Cut into bite-sized squares. Yields about 3 dozen.

Cirel Blitz

No-Bake Oatmeal Cookies (Dairy)

For oatmeal cookie lovers in a hurry.

1	cup sugar
1/2	cup milk
4	ounces margarine
4	tablespoons cocoa powder
1/2	cup chunky peanut butter
4	cups quick oats
1	tablespoon vanilla extract
1/2 - 3/4	cup raisins
	coconut, chocolate sprinkles or ground nuts for rolling balls

Combine first 4 ingredients in a saucepan and heat until well blended. Remove from heat and add peanut butter, oats, vanilla and raisins. Mix thoroughly and form into 1-inch balls. Roll in chopped coconut, sprinkles or ground nuts. Place on ungreased cookie sheet and refrigerate. Yields about 36 balls.

Note: *May be frozen.*

Frances Hoffnung

Nel de Groot Icebox Cookies (Dairy)

My neighbor who comes from Holland gave me this recipe for very thin, crisp cookies. I often double the recipe and give loaves of cookie dough to friends.

1	**pound butter**
1 1/2	**cups sugar**
1 1/2	**cups brown sugar, packed**
2	**teaspoons cinnamon**
1 1/2	**teaspoons nutmeg**
5	**cups flour**
1	**tablespoon baking soda**
2	**pinches salt, optional**
3	**eggs**
2	**cups almonds, walnuts or pecans, chopped fine**

In a large bowl, cream butter, sugar and spices. Add eggs. Mix flour, soda and salt together; gradually add to butter mixture. Either mix all nuts in dough or reserve some for rolling. Divide dough into 3-4 equal parts and shape into loaves. (Roll in reserved nuts at this point.) Wrap in waxed paper and refrigerate until firm.

Preheat oven to 350 degrees. Slice loaves into circles 1/8 to 1/4-inch thick and place on greased cookie sheet. Bake for 10-12 minutes. Cookies bake quickly and should brown only around edges. Yields about 6 dozen.

Note: *Dough keeps 6 to 8 weeks in the refrigerator.*

Linda Krasnoff

Oatmeal Chocolate Chip Cookies (Dairy)

The favorite cookie of my granddaughters, Alisa and Jenny Schlesinger.

1 1/4	**cups light brown sugar, firmly packed**
4	**ounces margarine**
1	**egg**
1 1/2	**cups sifted all-purpose flour**
1/2	**teaspoon baking soda**
1/4	**cup milk**
1 1/2	**cups regular or quick oats**
1/2	**cup chopped nuts**
1	**6-ounce package semisweet chocolate chips**

In a large bowl, cream together sugar and margarine until fluffy. Beat in egg. Sift together flour, salt and soda. Add alternately the sifted dry ingredients and milk to creamed mixture. Stir in oats, nuts and chocolate chips; mix well. Drop by teaspoonfuls onto greased cookie sheet. Bake for 10-12 minutes in a preheated 350 degree oven or until lightly browned. Yields about 4 dozen cookies.

Emma Schlesinger

Chocolate Marble Squares (Dairy/Pareve)

Delicious, easy to make and bakes in only 12 minutes.

4	ounces butter or margarine
6	tablespoons sugar
6	tablespoons brown sugar
1/4	teaspoon water
1/2	teaspoon vanilla extract
1	egg
1	cup plus 2 tablespoons flour
1/2	teaspoon baking soda
1	6-ounce package chocolate chips

Preheat oven to 375 degrees. Cream thoroughly butter and sugars. Add water, vanilla and eggs; beat well. Add flour and soda to creamed mixture. Spread with a fork in greased 9x13-inch pan. Sprinkle chocolate chips on top. Place in oven for 2 minutes. With knife, marbleize the slightly melted chocolate into dough. Replace in oven for another 10-12 minutes. When cool, cut into desired size squares. Yields approximately 45 bars.

Grace Mitnick

Disappearing Delights (Dairy)

So delightful they disappear quickly.

Bottom Crust:

2	cups flour
1	teaspoon baking powder
1/2	teaspoon salt
1/2	cup sugar
1	egg
4	ounces melted margarine (not butter)

Topping:

2	eggs
8	ounces cream cheese, softened
1	pound powdered sugar
1/2	cup shredded coconut, plus more for sprinkling
1/2	cup chopped walnuts

In a large bowl, mix dry ingredients. Add egg and margarine to form a coarse meal. Pat into a well-greased or sprayed 10x15-inch jelly roll pan. In a large bowl, mix all ingredients for topping thoroughly and spread carefully over the bottom crust. Sprinkle a little more coconut over top and bake until light brown for about 50 minutes at 325 degrees. Cool on wire rack and score for 2-inch squares. To avoid crumbling cool thoroughly, cut into squares and remove each one carefully. Yields 36 pieces.

Gussie Cutter

Peanut Butter Balls (Dairy)

Peanut butter and chocolate lovers, this is for you!

1	cup nutty or crunchy peanut butter
2	tablespoons butter
1/2	cup powdered sugar
1 1/2	cups crispy rice cereal
12	ounces chocolate chips or semisweet baking chocolate

Mix first 4 ingredients and refrigerate or freeze for 30 minutes. Form into walnut-size balls. Melt chocolate over hot water (not over direct heat) or in microwave on medium high. Dip balls in chocolate coating and place on wax paper. Refrigerate to set. Approximately 12 balls.

Note: Recipe doubles easily. Keeps well in the refrigerator.

Susan Brandes

Lemon Poppy Seed Bowties (Pareve)

A crisp cookie with a subtle lemon flavor.

4	ounces margarine
1	cup sugar
1	large egg
1	tablespoon lemon juice
1	teaspoon grated lemon peel
1 3/4	cups all-purpose flour
1/4	teaspoon baking powder
1	beaten egg white
	Poppy seeds

In a large bowl with electric mixer at medium speed, beat margarine and sugar until fluffy. Thoroughly beat in egg, lemon juice and lemon peel. In a small bowl combine flour and baking powder. Stir into margarine mixture. Wrap dough in plastic, refrigerate 1 hour.

Preheat oven to 375 degrees. Grease 2 large cookie sheets (be sure the cookie sheets will fit in your freezer). Roll out dough to 1/8-inch thickness on lightly floured surface. Cut into 2 1/2x1-inch strips. Gently twist strips to form bowties; place on cookie sheets 1 inch apart. Brush with beaten egg white and sprinkle with poppy seeds. Freeze 5 minutes. Bake 10-12 minutes or until light golden brown. Cool on racks. Yields 5 dozen.

Note: Stay crisp and keep exceptionally well.

Eve Marcus

And Other Desserts

Fruit is frequently the first choice for dessert in California. With a dairy meal, a dish of ice cream can also satisfy. For a touch of elegance, add a sauce or some fresh berries and a spoonful of liqueur.

Some of the desserts in this section, such as compotes or gelatin molds, may also be served as a side dish. And some quick breads, such as persimmon or zucchini bread, are sweet enough to be sliced and served like a cake for dessert [see "Breads," **pp. 105-120**].

HINTS

- If you are looking for ways to "slenderize" a dessert, many of the custards and puddings used as fillings in pies stand very well on their own as a delicious dessert, and, by eliminating the crust, you reduce calories as well as fat.

- Please review the hints in the general introduction to the "Desserts" section **[p. 213]** for dietary information.

To-Die-For Hot Chocolate Sauce (Dairy)

The title says it all. Serve over ice cream, cake, etc.

1	cup heavy cream
6	tablespoons butter, cut in small pieces
1	cup dark brown sugar, packed
1/3	cup sugar
1	cup Dutch process cocoa
1	tablespoon Grand Marnier (optional) or 2 teaspoons vanilla extract

In a heavy-duty saucepan, combine the cream and butter; stir over medium-high heat until mixture reaches a slow boil. Add sugars and stir for about 4 more minutes to dissolve the sugars. Reduce heat to medium and whisk in the cocoa.

Remove from heat and let sit for 2 minutes. Then stir in Grand Marnier. Serve hot or warm. It can be stored in the refrigerator for up to 2 weeks. Reheat in the top of a double boiler. Yields 2 cups.

Paddi Bregman

Chocolate Mousse (Dairy)

I created this mousse to reward our son and daughters when they earned good grades and honors.

6	ounces semisweet chocolate
6	ounces margarine
3/4	cup sugar
4	eggs
1/3	cup Kahlua liqueur
1	pint whipping cream, whipped

Melt chocolate pieces in a double boiler. In a food processor or mixer cream margarine and sugar; slowly add melted chocolate. Add eggs, one at a time, then add Kahlua. Gently blend in the whipped cream and pour into small cups or glasses. Serves 12.

Variation: 1/2 cup of ground almonds may be added.

Ann Lauterbach

Pistachio/Pineapple Mold (Dairy)

*This quick and easy dessert has a mousse-like texture,
and a delicate flavor and color.*

1	3-ounce package pistachio instant pudding mix
2	8-ounce cans crushed pineapple, with juice
1	12-ounce carton nondairy topping

In a large mixing bowl, combine pudding mix and pineapple with its juice; mix well. Add nondairy topping; mix well.

Pour into pretty serving bowl and let stand until ready to serve. Dessert may be frozen in a mold. Remove from freezer to refrigerator at least 2 hours before serving. Keeps well in the freezer indefinitely. Serves 8 - 10.

Elinor Einy

Strawberry Bavarian Dessert (Dairy)

A dressed-up gelatin dessert.

1	10-ounce package frozen, sliced strawberries, thawed, with syrup reserved
1	cup boiling water
1	3-ounce package strawberry gelatin
1	cup chilled whipping cream

Drain strawberries, reserving syrup. In a a large bowl, pour boiling water over gelatin, stirring until dissolved. Add enough cold water to syrup to measure 1 cup. Stir into gelatin. Chill until almost set.

In a chilled bowl, whip cream until stiff. Beat almost-set gelatin until foamy. Fold gelatin and strawberries into whipped cream. Pour into a 4- to 6-cup mold. Chill until firm. Serves 6 - 8.

Jacqueline Wise

Frozen Fruit Delight (Pareve)

A blend of fruits flavor this light dessert.

1 1/4	cups water
2	cups sugar
	dash of salt
2	pounds strawberries (may be frozen)
2	mashed bananas
1	10-ounce or 12-ounce package frozen raspberries
1	6-ounce can frozen orange juice
3	tablespoons lemon juice
4	egg whites, beaten stiff

In a large saucepan, boil 3/4 cup water with sugar and salt for 5 minutes. Remove from heat. Add rest of water, fruit and juices. Pour into freezing tray and freeze to a mush.

Turn into a mixing bowl and beat thoroughly. Fold in egg whites and freeze. (You may freeze in bowl).

For a very smooth and creamy ice mixture, beat mixture once or twice more. Yields 12 large scoops.

Variation: Substitute any fruits you prefer.

Adelaide Suplin

Molded Cranberry-Apple Dessert (Pareve)

A perfect accompaniment at Thanksgiving.

1	6-ounce package raspberry gelatin
2	cups boiling water
1 1/2	cups cranberry-apple drink
1	8-ounce can whole berry cranberry sauce
2	cups nondairy topping
1	unpeeled apple, cored and finely diced

Dissolve gelatin in boiling water. Add cranberry-apple drink. Measure out 2 cups of the mixture and chill until slightly thickened. Add cranberry sauce to remaining gelatin, blending well. Set aside. Blend whipped topping into measured gelatin mixture; add apple and chill until thickened.

Pour into 7- or 8-cup mold and chill until set but not firm. Chill remaining gelatin mixture until thickened. Spoon over creamy layer in mold. Chill until set, about 3 hours. Serves 12.

Trana Labowe

Brandy Hot Fruit Compote (Pareve)

As a dessert or a side dish, it's yummy!

12	coconut macaroons, crumbled
4	cups canned fruit, drained well (any combination of peaches, pears, pineapple, apricots or cherries)
1/4	cup melted margarine
1/4	cup brown sugar
1/2	cup toasted, slivered almonds
1/2	cup peach brandy

Preheat oven to 350 degrees. Butter a 2 1/2-quart casserole. Cover bottom of casserole with 1/3 of crumbled macaroons, then 1/2 of fruit, alternating macaroons with fruit layers, ending with macaroons. Sprinkle top with melted margarine, brown sugar, nuts and brandy. Bake for 30 minutes. Serves 8 - 10.

Marcia Abelson

Sherry Hot Fruit Compote (Pareve)

Make a glamorous presentation with this delicious dessert or accompaniment, any time of the year.

1	pound mixed dried fruit (apricots, peaches, pears, prunes)
1	16-ounce can pineapple chunks
1	8-ounce can mandarin oranges
1	16-ounce can cherry pie filling
2	tablespoons Sherry wine (or to taste)
2 - 3	tablespoons brown sugar

Soak dried fruits in enough water to cover in a 4-quart saucepan. Add all the other ingredients and simmer 10 minutes. Let stand in the refrigerator several days or more. Heat to serve. Serves 12 - 16.

Pearl Roseman

Sugar-Free Fruit Compote (Pareve)
A light dessert with a great flavor.

1 1/2 - 2 pounds assorted dried fruit (plums, peaches, apricots, etc.)
1 12-ounce can apple juice concentrate
2 - 3 whole cloves (remove after cooking)
1 tablespoon lemon juice

For dried fruit: In a large saucepan, bring apple juice to boil. Pour over dried fruits and let stand overnight. For fresh fruit: Cook fruit in apple juice 2 or 3 minutes and let stand. A pinch of cinnamon may be added to peaches. Serves 8 - 10.

Walter Richheimer

Easy Baklava (Dairy/Pareve)
Fewer steps to assemble, but the same delicious flavor.
A great dessert for a large group.

3/4 pound sweet butter or margarine
1 pound filo dough
1 pound (4 cups) ground nuts (walnuts or almonds)
1 cup sugar
1 tablespoon cinnamon
Dash of powdered cloves
1 tablespoon rose water or orange zest (approximately)
1/2 - 3/4 cup honey

Melt 2/3 of a stick of butter in a 10x14-inch pan. Mix together nuts, sugar, cinnamon, cloves and rose water. Place 1/2 of the filo dough on butter and spread nut mixture evenly over filo. Pour 1 stick of melted butter over nut mixture. Place balance of filo over nut mixture. Melt the balance of butter (1 1/3 sticks) and pour over baklava evenly. Cut clear through into diamond-shaped pieces to desired size. Bake for 45 minutes in a 350 degree oven or until golden brown. Drizzle honey evenly over top after baking. Yield 30 - 35 pieces.

Hint: To keep filo from drying out, place damp towel over remaining filo while you work. When filo sheets are larger than the pan you are using, fold the excess over toward the center of the pan. It will make the dessert a bit higher.

Ann Lauterbach

Rice Pudding (Dairy)

A delicately flavored dairy dessert.

1/2	cup long-grain rice
2	quarts milk
1/2	cup raisins
3/4	cup sugar
6	eggs
2	tablespoons vanilla extract
	Cinnamon

Combine rice and milk in large saucepan. Bring to boil; lower heat and simmer, uncovered, for 30-40 minutes, stirring occasionally. Add raisins; simmer 5 minutes more. Add sugar and stir until dissolved.

In mixing bowl combine eggs and vanilla, beating well. Fold into rice mixture and stir over low heat until completely blended and slightly thickened. (Heat should be very low to prevent curdling.) Turn into serving dish; sprinkle with cinnamon and serve warm or chilled. Serves 8.

Helyn Friedman

Fried Won Tons (Pareve)

An easy and popular finish for an Oriental meal.

1	package large egg roll skins
	Fat for deep frying

Cut one package of large egg roll skins into strips as desired. Separate strips and cut a slit into each strip. Do entire package before you start to cook the strips.

In a wok or large frying pan, fry a few strips at a time. Drain on paper towels and sprinkle with powdered sugar. Serve in a fancy bowl. Serves 8.

Min Leonard

Glossary of Terms

Afikoman - The middle of the three ceremonial matzot served as the dessert to all at the Passover Seder.

Ashkenazi, Ashkenazim, etc. - Jews of Middle or Eastern European descent.

Bimuelos - Sephardic doughnuts served at Hanukkah.

Blintzes - Crepes made with different fillings, most often cheese.

Borscht - Cold beet or spinach soup.

Challah - Special braided egg bread (see p. 108-110) for Shabbat and holidays.

Cholent - A long-cooking bean and vegetable stew, usually made with meat.

Dreidel - A four-sided spinning top with Hebrew letters, used at Hanukkah.

Erev - The evening preceding. All Jewish holidays, as well as Shabbat, begin at sunset and conclude after sunset of the following day.

Farfel - A small round pasta. Matzo farfel is crumbled matzos.

Foulares - A Sephardic Purim pastry.

Hag Sameach - "Happy Holiday" greeting.

Haggadah - The book used to conduct the Passover Seder; relates the story of the Exodus.

Hamantaschen - "Haman's pocket." Traditional filled Purim pastry. (see p. 252-256)

Hametz - Leaven or any food unsuitable for Passover.

Havdalah - (Separation) The ceremony that concludes Shabbat.

Huppah - Wedding canopy.

Knaidlach - Matzo balls (see p. 72-73). Ashkenazim traditionally serve these in chicken soup.

Kosher, Kashrut - The system of dietary laws governing Jewish foods.

Kosher l'Pesach - Foods appropriate to be eaten during Passover.

Kreplach - A Jewish version of ravioli or won ton.

Kugel - A noodle or potato casserole.

Latkes - Potato pancakes.

Menorah - A seven-branch candelabrum - official symbol of the State of Israel.

Mishloah Manot - Purim gifts of food or money.

Mitzvah - Religious commandment popularly referred to as a "good deed."

Nyafat - A brand name for a seasoned Kosher vegetable shortening.

Pesach - Hebrew word for the Passover festival.

Seder - Literally means "order," as in the Passover Seder.

Sephardi, **Sephardim**, **Sephardic** - Jews descended from those who once lived in Spain.

Shabbat - The Jewish Sabbath, which begins at sundown Friday evening and concludes after sundown on Saturday evening.

Shalach Manot - Hebrew for Purim food or money gifts.

Shehechiyanu - A special blessing, recited to offer thanks for having lived to celebrate a joyous occasion.

Shochet - A ritual slaughterer of meat and fowl.

Shofar - A ram's horn used to call the observant to worship on Rosh Hashanah and Yom Kippur.

Simchat Torah - The Jewish holiday following Sukkot that celebrates the giving of the Torah.

Sufganiyot - Israeli jelly doughnuts served at Hanukah.

Sukkah - The temporary shelter inhabited during the festival of Sukkot.

Tavla de Dulces - "A tray of sweets," traditional in Sephardic hospitality.

The Temple - The ancient center of worship in Jerusalem, of which only the Western Wall remains.

Torah - The Hebrew Bible. Source of Jewish law.

Tzimmes - A traditional Rosh Hashanah dish that combines carrots, yams, sweet potatoes and prunes. Can be either meat or pareve. Also used colloquially to make a fuss over someone or something.

Yom Ha Zikaron - Israel's day of mourning for those who gave their lives for the State.

Yom Ha' Atzma'ut - Israel's independence day.

Yom Kippur - The Day of Atonement.

INDEX

D – Dairy   *P – Pareve*   *M – Meat*

C

D – Dairy　　　　*P – Pareve*　　　　*M – Meat*

D – Dairy   **P** – Pareve   **M** – Meat

D – *Dairy*　　　　　**P** – *Pareve*　　　　　**M** – *Meat*

D – Dairy   *P – Pareve*   *M – Meat*

D – Dairy   *P – Pareve*   *M – Meat*

D – Dairy   *P – Pareve*   *M – Meat*

D – Dairy   *P – Pareve*   *M – Meat*

D – Dairy   *P* – Pareve   *M* – Meat

Women's League of ADAT ARI EL
California Kosher
12020 Burbank Blvd.
North Hollywood, California 91607

Please send me _____ copies
    of **California Kosher** at $19.95 @ $_____
Postage and Handling (First copy)   2.50 @ $_____
Additional copies to same address   1.50 @ $_____
California Residents, please add appropriate sales tax $_____
                                         Total $_____

Please make checks payable to *Women's League, Adat Ari El.*
❐ Check Enclosed

Please charge my: ❐ VISA   Expiration Date:
              ❐ Mastercard

              ❐ Gift Wrap ($2.00 per book)   MONTH   YEAR
Card Account Number:

Card Holder's Signature _____

(Complete reverse side of order form)

— —

Women's League of ADAT ARI EL
California Kosher
12020 Burbank Blvd.
North Hollywood, California 91607

Please send me _____ copies
    of **California Kosher** at $19.95 @ $_____
Postage and Handling (First copy)   2.50 @ $_____
Additional copies to same address   1.50 @ $_____
California Residents, please add appropriate sales tax $_____
                                         Total $_____

Please make checks payable to *Women's League, Adat Ari El.*
❐ Check Enclosed

Please charge my: ❐ VISA   Expiration Date:
              ❐ Mastercard

              ❐ Gift Wrap ($2.00 per book)   MONTH   YEAR
Card Account Number:

Card Holder's Signature _____

(Complete reverse side of order form)

Sending a copy of *California Kosher* to a friend is a long lasting reminder of your thoughtfulness. Proceeds from *California Kosher* will benefit Jewish education.

Mail book to: Name _____

Address _____

City _____

State _____ Zip Code _____

All copies will be sent to your address unless otherwise specified. If you wish books sent as gifts, please note below and enclose your gift cards with this order. If you would like a brief message inscribed in the front of the book send message(s) on a separate piece of paper.

Send gift(s) to: **Address(es):**

_____   _____

_____   _____

_____   _____

_____   _____

— —

Sending a copy of *California Kosher* to a friend is a long lasting reminder of your thoughtfulness. Proceeds from *California Kosher* will benefit Jewish education.

Mail book to: Name _____

Address _____

City _____

State _____ Zip Code _____

All copies will be sent to your address unless otherwise specified. If you wish books sent as gifts, please note below and enclose your gift cards with this order. If you would like a brief message inscribed in the front of the book send message(s) on a separate piece of paper.

Send gift(s) to: **Address(es):**

_____   _____

_____   _____

_____   _____

_____   _____